The Complete Idiot's Reference Card

Ten Steps to Greater Creativity

Celebrate each individual's creative gifts and reward yourself and your child with creative things and experiences.

1. Become a kid again. Remember the things you enjoyed doing when you were young and how it felt when you exercised your imagination.
2. Play. Give yourself and your child the freedom to explore, experiment, and make a mess!
3. Believe in your creativity. Repeat affirmations that reinforce the existence of your own creative genius.
4. Take pride in your creations. Be a show-off and display what you've made.
5. Make a study of creativity. Read books, watch creative people, and spend time with very young children.
6. Exercise it. Challenge yourself often to solve puzzles, experience new people, places, and things, and do what you normally do a different way.
7. Feed it. Expose yourself to the creativity of others through music, art, books, and travel.
8. Give yourself quiet time. Let your mind wander. Close your eyes and see what you "see." Take some time for yourself every day.
9. Capture it. Find ways to preserve your creative thoughts and ideas.
10. Reward creativity.

Ten Reasons for Crafting with Kids

1. Crafts teach us how to experiment and the value of the process of trial and error.
2. Crafts teach us patience.
3. Crafts teach us how to follow directions and rules. Then they encourage us to use our creativity to see if those rules can be broken.
4. Crafts help make us self-sufficient and instill confidence.
5. Crafts give us resources to draw upon in every aspect of our lives.
6. Crafts teach frugality and ways we can make things ourselves to save money.
7. Crafts teach us how to use ordinary materials we might otherwise throw away.
8. Crafts teach us new ways of seeing.
9. Crafts are a springboard for learning about other cultures, eras, and places.
10. Crafting together can foster greater intimacy, understanding, and respect between adult and child.

alpha
books

Ten Saboteurs to Crafting Success

1. Being unprepared. Resist the temptation to "wing it." Read through project instructions and assemble all your materials ahead of time.

2. Beginning with too difficult a project. Be honest about your (and your child's) ability and choose a project you both can enjoy.

3. Not allowing enough time. Don't try to sandwich a complicated crafts project between soccer practice and dinner. You'll rob yourself of half the fun!

4. Trying to control everything. Give your child the freedom to make his own decisions and to struggle with something for a while.

5. Being too judgmental. Praise often; criticize rarely. This **isn't** a test!

6. Worrying too much about neatness. If you're fretting the whole time about your work surface, the floor, or your clothes, it's pretty hard to have a good time.

7. Trying to do too much.

8. Hovering. Walk out of the room, bite your lip, but **don't** interfere or take over.

9. Working when you're too tired. Be aware of your energy level and don't start a project when you're tuckered out or your child is obviously ready to pack it in.

10. Insisting on success. Allow room for things not to work. Give yourself and your child room to make mistakes.

Seven Tips for Happy Crafting

1. Make yourselves comfortable. Work surfaces and chairs should be at the right height.

2. Provide adequate light. What might be okay for dining or watching TV may not be good for fine craft work. Supplement your lighting as needed.

3. Learn your basic materials. There are many types of paints, glues, scissors, tapes, and papers. It's in your best interest to become familiar with the different types and what they're best used for.

4. Learn skills before attempting projects. Let your child practice hammering a nail into scrap wood before you build your first birdhouse.

5. Pick a quick and easy first project. If you start with something too difficult, you may lose interest in the project or give up on the craft altogether.

6. Allow for spontaneity. Have some basic crafting materials always ready in a box that can be taken out at a moment's notice.

7. Have a sense of humor! If you find yourself getting too intense or losing your temper, LIGHTEN UP!

Five Steps to Removing Soils and Stains

1. Identify the soil or stain.
2. Remove what you can.
3. Apply the right cleaning agent (see Chapter 5).
4. Wait for the cleaner to work.
5. Remove the dirt and cleaner using the best method (see Chapter 5).

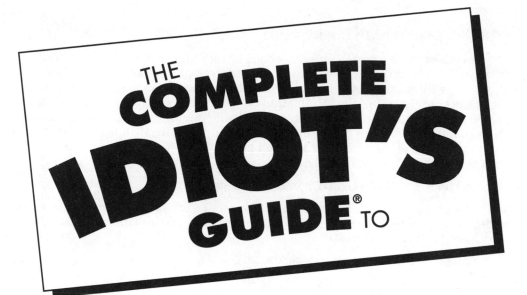

THE COMPLETE IDIOT'S GUIDE® TO

Crafts with Kids

by Georgene Lockwood

alpha books

A Division of Macmillan General Reference
A Simon & Schuster Macmillan Company
1633 Broadway, New York, NY 10019

THE COMPLETE IDIOT'S GUIDE name and design are trademarks of Macmillan, Inc.

Macmillan Publishing books may be purchased for business or sales promotional use. For information please write: Special Markets Department, Macmillan Publishing USA, 1633 Broadway, New York, NY 10019.

International Standard Book Number: 0-02-862406-8

Library of Congress Catalog Card Number: 98-85129

00 99 98   8 7 6 5 4 3 2

Interpretation of the printing code: the rightmost number of the first series of numbers is the year of the book's printing; the rightmost number of the second series of numbers is the number of the book's printing. For example, a printing code of 98-1 shows that the first printing occurred in 1998.

Printed in the United States of America

Note: This publication contains the opinions and ideas of its author. It is intended to provide helpful and informative material on the subject matter covered. It is sold with the understanding that the author and publisher are not engaged in rendering professional services in the book. If the reader requires personal assistance or advice, a competent professional should be consulted.

The author and publisher specifically disclaim any responsibility for any liability, loss or risk, personal or otherwise, which is incurred as a consequence, directly or indirectly, of the use and application of any of the contents of this book.

Alpha Development Team

Publisher
Kathy Nebenhaus

Editorial Director
Gary M. Krebs

Managing Editor
Bob Shuman

Marketing Brand Manager
Felice Primeau

Senior Editor
Nancy Mikhail

Development Editors
Phil Kitchel
Jennifer Perillo
Amy Zavatto

Editorial Assistant
Maureen Horn

Production Team

Production Editor
Robyn Burnett

Copy Editor
Lynn Northrup

Cover Designer
Mike Freeland

Photo Editor
Richard H. Fox

Illustrator
Jody P. Schaeffer

Designer
Dan Armstrong

Indexer
Nadia Ibrahim

Layout/Proofreading
Angela Calvert
Megan Wade

Contents at a Glance

Contents

Foreword

As a child, I spent many hours with an elderly neighbor who loved to watch me draw. One day, she explained to me that everything in this world that was not created by nature was created by an artist, designer, or inventor. I realized that meant there must be a great many artists in this world. If they could change the world through their creations, then maybe I could, too.

So I learned to paint, draw, and create crafts, which allowed me to express feelings I had no words for. I began to make gifts to give to family members and learned that I could express my love through my creativity, and that unique objects held special value to others. I learned the meaning of business and the value of work and money by selling the crafts I made. In short, I learned to be an artist, and that has defined my life, my joys, and my relationships with others.

I have spent nearly 20 years sharing that joy and enthusiasm for art with elementary children. I teach visual arts at Herrera School for the Fine Arts in Phoenix, Arizona. Through my job, I've learned that teaching the arts to children builds their self-confidence and communication skills.

When parents and teachers ask me how they can encourage their children's and students' art talents, I always tell them to spend time together creating art. Share the experience of trying to make something new—and share the failure and the success of that attempt. Take pride in the original ideas your child creates.

As Georgene Lockwood wonderfully expresses in this book, we need to bond with the children in our lives and create a feeling of acceptance and love. Crafting is a fun way to capture your child's attention and can build a great foundation for communication. Crafting can also open the door to a lifelong hobby or a career for the children in your life. Most of all, crafting is fun for everyone.

This book is a treasure chest of ideas that can make creating crafts easy. Keep it handy, dog-ear the pages, and write comments about your experiences in the margins. Treat it as a road map to creating a special time with your child. You'll find plenty of projects for beginners, as well as ideas that will challenge the most experienced crafters.

Throughout, Georgene also describes how to organize your crafts supplies and how to create an atmosphere that encourages creative risk-taking. She discusses many new crafting materials and offers great ideas on how you can use them at home with your children. Best of all, she has included many Internet resources. There are many sites on the Internet where Webmasters (like me) can link you to craft lessons, craft supplies, and images of art objects from museums all over the world.

If you are determined to make a difference in your child's life and have a willingness to "get messy" and explore your own creativity, this book has all the information you need to succeed. And who knows? You might be inspiring a future artist, architect, designer, decorator, inventor, engineer—or even an art teacher!

—Bettie Lake

Visual Arts Teacher, Herrera School for the Fine Arts

Founder, The Art Teacher Connection (www.primenet.com/~arted)

Introduction

The challenges of parenting healthy, happy, productive kids today seems more daunting than ever. I've already raised my kids into reasonably sane adults, and I'm beginning to know the joys of grandparenting, but I believe that it's tougher today than it was yesterday.

Strong families don't just happen, they are created. It takes purpose and hard work. It takes commitment. It takes thinking, and most of all, it takes love. But love is one of those words that defies defining. It means different things to different people. We each show our love in different ways. But quintessentially, we all know it when we see it, or should I say, when we *feel* it. As Marilyn Ferguson said in her book, *The Aquarian Conspiracy*, "Love is a context, not a behavior."

In a way, *The Complete Idiot's Guide to Crafts with Kids* is about the context of love. Yes, it's also about crafts and how to create them and teach them to your child. But spending time with your child crafting offers unlimited opportunities to create a context of love and intimacy.

This book will give you enough ideas, tools, and projects to keep you busy for this lifetime and the next. You can dive in all at once or just try individual projects one at a time. You can immerse yourselves in one craft or sample a variety. Everything's here to get you started—AND keep you going.

Learn a craft. Do some projects. Follow my suggestions for further reading or interesting side trips. Have fun and make lots of wonderful things. Just don't forget the love.

How the Book Is Organized

To make it easy for you, I've divided this book into five major parts. I suggest reading them in order, since each one builds upon the previous part. This should help you prepare for the best possible crafting experiences, understand the specific materials and tools available to work with, gain experience with a variety of crafts, incorporate crafting into your daily life, and share your handiwork with others.

Part 1, "How to Grow Crafty Kids," is about crafts in a larger context. You'll learn the ins and outs of getting in touch with and fostering creativity, and avoiding the things that might stifle or hinder it. You'll discover the secrets to nurturing the creative genius in your child and rediscovering your own. You'll also read about the importance of organization and preparation, safety, how to avoid messes, and how to clean them when they do happen. Finally, you'll understand the greater lessons crafts have to teach and ingenious ways to weave those lessons into your life.

Part 2, "The Nine Basic Crafting Materials: Creating Your Crafting Repertoire," takes you through the nine basic crafts materials (paper, fabric, beads, leather, wood, metal, clay, plastic, and glass) and introduces to you to the tools and skills you'll need to craft with each one.

Part 3, "Mixed Media," combines crafting materials according to different themes. Here, you'll learn about crafts you can make in your own kitchen, crafts that use natural materials, how to make simple and not-so-simple homemade toys, constructing real musical instruments, and making useful and attractive items from throwaways like glass jars and tin cans. In these chapters, you'll get to apply many of the skills you learned in Part 2 (and if you skipped some, you may find yourself motivated to flip back and learn some more).

Part 4, "Holidays Are for Crafty Kids of All Ages!," shows you how to incorporate crafts into all your holiday celebrations—and maybe even create some new reasons to celebrate. All of the major holidays are here—Christmas, Chanukah, Kwanzaa, Valentine's Day, Halloween, Thanksgiving, Easter, Independence Day, New Year's—plus other events you may not have thought of. You'll also find some unique ways to add crafts to your own personal celebrations, and I've provided you with some great excuses for spontaneous festivities. There are enough ideas in this part to keep you busy for the entire year!

Part 5, "Presenting 'Handmade by You!'," will help you and your child make your creations the star of any show. Whether you're giving them as presents (and want the wrappings to be as creative as the gifts themselves) or simply want to show them off in their best possible light, the chapters in this part will teach you how. There's even a guide for kids who want to sell their crafts.

Appendix A includes some special resources to help you refine your skills so you and your child can continue your crafting adventures for many years to come. Appendix B is a glossary of crafting terms you'll need to become familiar with as you read through this book.

Extras

The *Complete Idiot's Guide to Crafts with Kids* is filled with special sidebars. These are valuable additions to the text that will alert you to important safety considerations, additional background information, tips for more successful results, new words to add to your crafting vocabulary, and ways to use projects as springboards to even more enriching experiences. Look for these icons for yet more ways to enjoy crafting with your child:

Bonding Experiences

Here, you'll find many ways to turn your crafting experiences into something more. You'll find ideas for field trips, books and magazines to read, Web sites to explore, and other activities to enhance your crafting activities with your child.

Bet You Didn't Know

These boxes contain little-known facts and tidbits you can ponder while you craft.

Crafty Clues

These boxes contain tips and shortcuts to make your projects come out even better.

Safety Signals

Make sure you read each of these safety warnings and guidelines before you begin a project. A safe crafter is a happy crafter!

Handiwords

Check these boxes for definitions that will help you understand the language when reading directions, researching a craft, or shopping for supplies.

In addition to these helpful sidebars, you'll also notice that individual crafts projects have been placed in convenient boxes. Listed in each box is the project's difficulty rating, recommended age level, materials list, and step-by-step directions.

Acknowledgments

I would like to thank the many people who helped bring this book to print and who contributed their expertise, resources, and encouragement along the way. Thanks to: Nancy Mikhail, Jennifer Perillo, Robyn Burnett, Lynn Northrup, and Maureen Horn for their patience and timely input. Terri Nyman for her deft technical editing. Carole Abel, my agent, for all the things she does so well. Joan Ransom and Jan Fawson for making their extensive crafts libraries available.

Coty Fowler and Charlotte Libov just for being there.

My Mom for letting me play in the mud when I was little.

My Dad for not thinking that saws and hammers were just for boys. My daughters, Amanda Classen and Rachel Griffiths, for their great ideas and for all the happy hours they shared with me as children "making things."

My husband, Jim, for understanding the reasons why the paper airplanes in the hallway, paint in the sink, and glue in my hair had to be there; and for lending his expertise to the chapter on leatherwork (oh, and for doing the dishes).

Special Thanks to the Technical Reviewer

The Complete Idiot's Guide to Crafts with Kids was reviewed by an expert who not only checked the viability of the crafts projects in this book, but also provided valuable insight to help ensure that this book tells you everything you need to know to enjoy crafting with your kids. Our special thanks are extended to Terri Nyman.

An avid crafter for many years, Terri Nyman is the former editor of *Creative Product News*, a crafts trade magazine. She later edited *Quilt Craft* and *Lady's Circle Patchwork Quilts*, two national consumer magazines for quiltmakers and fabric crafters. A firm believer in introducing children to crafts at an early age, she is the author of numerous articles on crafting for children.

Terri is currently the Director of Development for the Metropolitan Police Boys and Girls Clubs in Washington, D.C. In that position she has implemented a number of programs for children, including a quilting program for youngsters ages 7 to 13.

Trademarks

All terms mentioned in this book that are known to be or are suspected of being trademarks or service marks have been appropriately capitalized. Alpha Books and Macmillan General Reference cannot attest to the accuracy of this information. Use of a term in this book should not be regarded as affecting the validity of any trademark or service mark.

The following trademarks and service marks have been mentioned in this book: Armour Etch cream, Astroturf, Band-Aid, Barbie doll, Biz, Cernit, Crayola, Dawn, DEKA paints, Duco cement, Fels Naptha soap, Fiebing's Leather Balm, Fiebing's Professional Oil Dye, Fiebing's Saddle-Lac, FIMO, Formica, Friendly Plastic, Jaquard's Procion, Jello, Jolly Ranchers, Lifesavers, Lucite, M&Ms, Mylar, Necco, Peel 'N Etch, Plexiglas, Polyurethane, Popsicle, Post-It Note, Promat, PVC, Pyrex, Q-Tip, Red Hots, Reddi-Etch, Rit, Rub 'N Etch, Sculpey, Sculpey III, Starlight mints, Styrofoam, Tinkertoys, Tootsie-Roll, Tupperware, Velcro, X-Acto, and Zud. E-6000, Play-Doh, Pack-O-Fun, *Painting*, *The Cross Stitcher*, *Bridal Crafts*, Dremel, Vic's Crafts Mosaic Glass Kit.

Part 1
How to Grow Crafty Kids

Crafts are a way of bringing out and nurturing creativity, self-esteem, problem-solving ability, inquisitiveness, and a whole host of other desirable qualities in your children. To make crafting the most fertile ground possible, however, it takes someone to plant the seeds and tend the growth. That's your job as a parent, and this part of the book will help you do your job better.

In addition to basic issues like safety, organizing your materials and tools, and efficiently cleaning up, in this part you'll learn how to make crafting with your child a more rewarding experience for both of you. You'll learn how to provide an environment where all kinds of important learning goes on, while you're making some pretty nifty stuff.

You'll not only be crafting some beautiful objects, but also a better relationship with the ones you care about most.

Chapter 1

How Kids Learn About Crafts

In This Chapter

➤ Creativity: The essence of crafts

➤ How to get in touch with your own creativity and nurture it in your kids

➤ Making time for crafting with your children

➤ Incorporating crafts into family rituals

➤ What crafts teach us

This book isn't really about crafts. Well, yes, it has lots of crafts in it, but what it's REALLY about is creativity—yours and your child's. You may think that creativity is something you're either born with or you're not. Or you may believe that only a select number of people, *artists*, are somehow mysteriously injected with creativity.

Well, I'm happy to tell you, you're wrong. You're creative and so am I. Everyone is. Creativity may be in the recesses of that 90 percent of your brain you don't use, but it's in there! Your task is to unlock it, nurture it, and watch it grow. The good news is that creativity can be learned. And the more in touch with your own creativity you are, the more likely you are to have happily creative children.

The fact that you've picked up this book says that you're interested in having a positive experience engaging in activities with your children (or children you care for). You've picked up this book because you want to do it *right*, or at least *better*. Well, that's what this chapter is about.

Finding Your Inner Genius—the 10 Steps to Creativity

I happen to know you're a genius. It's true. It's always been true. You just forgot. We all have some kind of genius, but for many of us, life experiences, whether at home, in school, or in the workplace may have done little to confirm that. I'll bet you don't want that for your child.

So, how do you find your hidden creative genius—and how do you ensure your child does the same? One way is through crafts. I believe there are steps you can take to make crafting a process of creative discovery, not only for your child, but also for yourself. Take these 10 steps to greater creativity. Once you get started, I guarantee you'll find more!

1. *Become a kid again.* Watch what little kids do, especially in uninstructed situations. Remember the things you enjoyed doing as a kid? Who supported you in them? Who discouraged you? What did it feel like when you were playing and feeling free to use your imagination? Pretend to be five again.

2. *Play.* What is play? In my dictionary, one part of the definition is, "freedom of movement within a space; freedom for action or scope for activity." Note the emphasis on FREEDOM. You can feel free to unleash your creative instincts, no matter what your age.

   Go to the store and get some play things—stickers, crayons, Play-Doh, bubbles, chalk, pipe cleaners—whatever appeals to your "inner child." Set aside an afternoon or evening to play with them, all by yourself. Sit on the floor with a big piece of paper. Don't worry about making a mess. Try drawing with the opposite hand than you normally do and feel what it's like to be a little kid learning to write again. Play like this often.

3. *Change your inner voices.* As you play, notice the inner voices you hear. Perhaps they sound like this: "I'm too old to be doing this." "I can't draw...I'm not artistic." "This is silly." Don't let your inner voices stop you.

   You can change your "self-talk" any time you want. Start using affirmations (positive statements you repeat often to reinforce changes you'd like to make in your thinking). Develop affirmations that feel good to you, like, "I am a talented, creative person." "I am an ARTIST." This may seem a little strange at first, but as you work at it, it becomes easier. The more you start affirming your own genius, the more you'll be able to affirm your child's.

4. *Take pride in your creations.* Have a place to display what you create. If you're not audacious enough to hang your works up for all to see, keep them in a folder, portfolio, or scrapbook. Better yet, hang or otherwise display them in a prominent place. Admire them and say, "I made this!"

5. *Make a study of creativity.* You can do this in lots of ways. Look at the people in your life you consider really creative. Study them closely. Ask them questions. Interview them. Ask if you could follow them around for a day. Once you observe the behaviors associated with creativity you can begin to model them yourself.

   Or, read about creativity. Find out what we've learned about it and how to teach it (or, as I prefer to say, find it). I list some resources later in this chapter.

   Spend some time with really young children and watch the way they create. Constantly look for new creativity tools—mindmapping, storyboarding, NLP (neuro-linguistic programming), visualization, new software, books, tapes, Web sites—whatever techniques intrigue you.

   Some other tools for developing creativity you might like to experiment with are:

   ➤ Mindmapping: a technique originally devised for taking more meaningful notes, which uses icons, images, and keywords to map ideas and relationships between them. You can learn more about this technique in the book *The Brain Book* by Peter Russell.

   ➤ Storyboarding: an adaptation of the method used by movie makers to visualize the action in a particular scene from the screenplay before shooting. This technique can also be used for problem-solving or improving recall. A good book that explains storyboarding is *Show Me: The Complete Guide to Storyboarding and Problem Solving* by Harry I. Forsha.

   ➤ Neuro-linguistic programming: NLP for short, this is a way of "re-programming the brain" using various techniques such as modeling and self-hypnosis. One of its leading proponents, who has added many of his own ideas to basic NLP theory is Anthony Robbins.

6. *Exercise your "creativity muscle."* Creativity is a lot like a muscle. It's stronger when it gets plenty of exercise. Learn more about problem-solving techniques and try them. Challenge yourself with creative problems and puzzles. Seek out people who are different from you (people from different places and people who hold different beliefs). Try to see things from their point of view. Seek out new experiences that force you to stretch your mind and emotions. Every week, try something new—a class, a lecture, an event—that's not something you'd usually do.

7. *Feed your creativity.* Along with exercise, creativity also requires good food to grow strong. Feed it with experiences, books, music, and art. Expose yourself to other people's creativity. Give yourself experiences that stimulate your imagination. Take lots of field trips. Try to take some alone, just for you. Notice what happens. Follow your nose and pursue ideas and events that intrigue you. Make sure there's space in your life to feed your curiosity.

8. *Give yourself quiet time.* If you're like me, you have a lot of demands on your time. After all, you're a responsible adult. But, no matter what, give yourself some quiet

time EVERY SINGLE DAY. Call it your "time out." Put your head down on the desk and close your eyes, just like you did when you were in elementary school. Take a long soak in the tub, *with* bubbles. Take a solitary walk. Guard your quiet time and take good care of it. Put it on your schedule and stick to it.

9. *Capture your creativity.* Find ways to preserve your creative thoughts and ideas. Keep a daily journal or a sketchbook. Or, if you tend to be technology-oriented, keep a tape recorder handy to record your thoughts. Try to do this every day for one month (it helps to do it at the same time each day). Don't read your journal until the month is up and don't show it to anyone. Write about anything that comes into your head; don't judge yourself. See what happens.

10. *Reward creativity.* Celebrate often. Develop your own rituals for celebrating, whether you are observing a traditional occasion or a special accomplishment. Give yourself creative gifts, whether they be material or experiential. Reward yourself well and often. Encourage others to reward you, too, and include them in your celebrations.

There are lots of tools to help you develop your own creativity. I could list hundreds of them here, but since we need to get on to crafting, I'll list just a few of my favorites. (For full bibliographic information, see Appendix A, "Resources").

➤ *The Creative Companion: How to Free Your Creative Spirit*, by Sark, inspires the reader to explore the artist within.

➤ *Simple Abundance* by Sarah Ban Breathnach. Not expressly about creativity, but full of exercises for developing your inner self. It's aimed at women, but I think this book can be useful for anyone.

➤ *The Artist's Way* by Julia Cameron. This is actually a 12-week course in creativity, aimed at recovering creativity from the blockages caused by various inhibiting forces.

➤ Anything on neurolinguistic programming (NLP). Anthony Robbins' books are a good start. Try *Unlimited Power* or *Awaken the Giant Within*. Concentrate on the information on changing habits and problem solving.

➤ *The Universal Traveler: A Soft-Systems Guide to Creativity, Problem-Solving, and the Process of Reaching Goals* by Don Koberg and Jim Bagnall.

➤ Shakti Gawain's books, including *Creative Visualization* and *Living in the Light*. Gawain sees us as "channels for the creative power of the universe," and gives exercises and ideas to help us tune in.

➤ The Creativity Home Page: http://www.ozemail.com.au/~caveman/Creative

➤ The Enchanted Mind: http://enchantedmind.com/

You'll find lots of other resources once you start looking. Begin this journey toward discovering your own genius: Share what you find with your child and you'll both experience enjoyment, intimacy, and growth.

Nurturing Creativity in Kids

As you get in touch with your own creative self, you'll find out that the best way to help your kids develop their creativity is to let them be. Not that you don't need to be a parent and ensure their safety or share what you know. But think about what stifled your own creative impulses in the past. Chances are you'll conjure up memories of criticism, compulsive control, and condescension, the three killers of a dynamic learning environment. If you create a non-judgmental, self-determined environment where your children have a voice and are taken seriously, you'll see results you never dreamed possible.

Children learn best by example, and as they see you nurturing, indulging, and developing your creativity, they'll do the same. Here are some ways to further share and enjoy creativity together:

➤ Play by yourself, but also play together. Do puzzles and games with kids.

➤ Re-read *The Little Prince* and *Peter Pan* together (or read them for the first time, if you never have).

➤ Introduce yourself and your kids to music, literature, and art of all kinds. You don't have to know anything about a topic to start. Approach it with curiosity and an open mind. Allow yourself to feel something about it...even if it's dislike.

➤ Create plenty of room for your child to have his or her own reactions. Encourage verbal expression by being non-judgmental and by listening and asking questions.

➤ Turn off the television occasionally. I'm not suggesting TV doesn't have value; it does. But we all can become selective about what we watch and how we use our time. Try leaving the set off for an entire week and see what happens. Get the kids to cooperate by planning other things they would like to do instead of watching TV. Plan a fun reward for the end of the week. Have everybody express their reactions after the week is over. I guarantee this will be an enlightening experience.

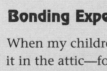

Bonding Experiences

When my children were growing up, I unplugged the TV and stored it in the attic—for almost a year! My kids balked and moaned, but this experiment changed the way we looked at TV forever after. During those months we rediscovered our own inner resources. We became far less passive about entertaining ourselves. I also provided lots of art supplies, games, and books, to keep new ideas coming.

My older daughter, who's now nearly 30, doesn't watch television. She and her husband own a TV set, but use it only for viewing rented movies. They feel TV robs them of the time they want to spend on other things, and both are involved in creative activities. I wonder if that early experiment had anything to do with it!

Make time to nurture your own creative spirit and then pass it on to your child. You'll be giving both of you a gift that will last a lifetime.

Celebrations: Crafts in Context

One of the most natural ways to begin adding crafts to your daily life is to make them part of your family celebrations. Hobbies, crafts, and pastimes make celebrations more meaningful, and add festivity and a sense of continuity. For example, every year I have an ornament-making party, usually just after Thanksgiving. I look forward every year to coming up with new ideas and making ornaments for gifts and as additions to the tree.

You can learn new skills and try new projects as you go through the year searching out opportunities to celebrate and using your hands to express your joy. This is how you create and pass on traditions.

You can choose to observe special occasions in a cursory way, purchasing all the accessories, decorations, and foods, or you can make them your own by crafting these things yourself. In Part 4 of this book you'll find several chapters on celebrating holidays through crafts. I hope you'll try some of the suggestions and begin searching out other ideas together as a family.

Bonus Points: The Hidden Value of Handicrafts

There are things you will gain by making things by hand that may not be immediately obvious. Crafts bring you back in touch with simpler ways of life. They slow you down and give you quiet time to think and breathe. Working with your hands is calming. I honestly believe that crafting can mean the difference between knowing how to relax and being treated for stress-related conditions!

Through crafts, you will come to know the rhythm of working with your hands. You'll learn the feel of new materials and tools, adjusting until, eventually, these tools and materials feel comfortable.

Being a "creator" or "maker" gives you a feeling of competence...of control over your environment.

Crafts bring you closer to history: You and your kids can learn about your ancestors by engaging in some of the same activities they did. I'm not saying you shouldn't use modern tools and appliances, but now and again, it's enlightening to try to make something "from scratch" or do a task the "old-fashioned way."

When I first started quilting, I resisted using a sewing machine. Since I spend a lot of time in front of a computer every day, I just couldn't favor the idea of sitting in front of another machine during my "off time." I made my first quilt entirely by hand—hand-pieced and hand-quilted. I still enjoy piecing and quilting this way, and it gives me pleasure to realize that that's how my ancestors made quilts.

There's a reason why certain crafts have endured: We need them. Sometimes certain crafting techniques fall out of favor, but they keep coming back. I believe the popularity of crafts will continue to grow as we become increasingly surrounded by technology.

Through traditional crafts, you begin noticing the seasons and relying on traditions to acknowledge them. Family customs, like recipes, are made to be handed down. This is the stuff memories are made of.

But When Do You Have the Time?

You may be wondering when you're going to do all these arts and crafts when you're running to soccer games, trying to get the laundry done, rushing to finish a project for your boss on time, and struggling to get a meal on the table every night.

Stop. Look. Listen. Where is your time going and are you in control? What do you REALLY want to be doing? How much of what you're doing is really necessary? What kind of outside activities are your children involved in? How many? How about yourself? Weigh the value of these things against the value of doing things together as a family.

Of course, basic household chores have to be done. But you can do them as a family; you can even turn them into celebrations and rituals. For example, pick one day a week when the kids make the dinner. You'll have to help them at first, but once they have mastered a few recipes, all of you will look forward to "kid's cook night."

The more you can organize the basic everyday chores, the more time you will have to play! My previous book, *The Complete Idiot's Guide to Organizing Your Life*, shows you lots of ways to help you get organized and create time to do the things you really want to do. Here are a few suggestions:

➤ Encourage your kids to organize themselves and pitch in with household chores. Hold a family meeting to determine together who does what.

➤ In many families, especially those with older children, everyone tends to go in different directions. That's fine up to a point, but there's real value in instituting regular family time—no excuses, no exceptions. Insist on Sunday dinner together, for instance, or daily family breakfasts. Schedule hikes and other outings. Set aside weekly time for crafts.

➤ Consider instituting a weekly Family Night and plan a whole month's activities in advance. One week it could be making a particular craft, another it could be playing board games or going out to play miniature golf. As you discover which crafts your family most enjoys, you may want to set aside even more time for those crafts.

Crafts can also be used to make your family routines more enjoyable. Here are a few ways crafts can help organize and enhance your life.

Use crafts to make convenient, attractive storage spaces. Having places to store things—hooks, cubbies, shelves, and cabinets—will encourage your kids (and you) to put things away and to stay organized.

Use crafts to make family mealtimes more special. Make or buy cloth napkins and make a napkin ring for each family member with his or her name on it. The cloth napkins add an air of importance to meals, and the napkins can be reused so you can cut down on your laundry. (If each person has their own napkin and napkin ring, a napkin can be used for more than one meal.)

Make some of your table linens and accessories, such as place mats (see Chapter 20), and use them regularly. Children enjoy seeing things they've made used by the rest of the family. Decorate the table with flowers or seasonal displays every so often. Don't forget candles (I show you how to make them in Chapter 15).

Leave enough time in the morning to have breakfast together. (A place mat made by each child at his or her place at the table makes that more likely.) Use this time to set up the day, find out what's happening, and offer words of encouragement.

The evening meal can also be a time for the family to come together. Ask your kids, "What new thing did you learn today?" "What made you wonder today?" "What goal did you have and how close did you come to achieving it?" Discuss a news item. Make dinnertime fun by finding a puzzle or riddle for your children to solve. Say "No" to all early evening meetings or classes. And make it a rule not to accept phone calls during certain hours. Maintain a "No TV" rule until after dinner.

Let Sunday dinner be another time to incorporate crafts into your daily life. Dress up the table with a centerpiece of natural materials. Dress up for dinner. It may seem silly at first, but kids (especially younger ones) usually enjoy it. Create a party atmosphere. Put out special place mats and napkins. Let the kids make a festive dessert. Try out new recipes and repeat regular favorites. Ask every family member to share the best thing that happened all week. Invite someone over.

Make Sunday your one day of leisure. Stay home. Walk. Sing. Play games. Make it a rule that all homework has to be done before Sunday, so there's no frantic Sunday night cramming. Don't do household chores, either. Refresh the spirit.

Another opportunity to make crafts a part of everyday life is to incorporate them into family bath and bedtime rituals. Make your own bubble baths and potions (see Chapter 15). Add personalized decorations to linens, toothbrushes, and cups, using techniques in Chapters 7, 13, and 14. Make hampers for each person. Kids love things with their names on them and it encourages them to take care of their own things.

Spend time before bed making up stories that kids can later write or illustrate in hand-made books or act out in plays.

Give your kids a half hour of uninterrupted attention every day. Use this time for touching, stroking, massaging tired shoulders, or holding each other. Take time to talk.

But What Do We DO?

Okay, you've got everything shipshape and you've scheduled a regular family crafts night. Now what do you do? Well, that's why you bought this book! There are hundreds of ideas, projects, and resources here. But if you're feeling overwhelmed and just want some quick ideas to get you started, here they are:

➤ In Victorian households, children (and adults) worked on scrapbooks. Scrapbooking has been revived in a big way; it's HOT and the possibilities are endless (see Chapter 6). This is an easy starter craft, incorporating rubber stamping, photographs, and all sorts of paper crafts.

➤ Start crafts for the next holiday. For example, if it's June, start thinking about 4th of July projects you can do (see Part 4).

➤ Concentrate on making music. Make your own musical instruments and have a concert (see Chapter 18).

➤ Make games or toys. Make things for dolls to wear or places for them to live (see Chapter 17).

➤ Conjure up crafts in the kitchen. You can learn about clay, for example, by making up a batch of craft clay or dough (see Chapter 15).

➤ Make crafts out of natural materials you find from hikes and days in the yard (see Chapter 16).

Obviously, a book of this length can't possibly teach you everything you need to know about each craft. Its purpose is to get you started, teach you the most basic skills, and show you how to further explore those crafts that capture your imagination. I've also shown you how to use crafts as a way of learning more about the world, the past, each other, and yourself. Think of each chapter as a springboard for intimacy and learning.

Maybe you haven't grown up working with your hands. In many ways you may feel like a child, learning crafting techniques for the first time. Although that may seem like a disadvantage, it can actually be a positive thing. Experience the humility of being new at something. Share those feelings with your child. Learn together. You'll be closer to the learning experience and better able to teach.

And if you're looking for still MORE reasons to read this book and begin doing crafts together, here they are!

➤ Crafts teach us how to experiment and the process of trial and error. They teach us that it's fun to play, and that sometimes it's more fun to color outside the lines.

➤ Crafts teach us patience.

➤ Crafts teach us how to follow directions and follow the rules. Then we can see if they can be broken. First we do it according to the directions, then we can change them and come up with variations. A life lesson learned through crafts.

➤ Crafts teach us to notice our environment.

➤ Crafts help make us self-sufficient and instill confidence.

➤ Crafts give us resources to draw upon in every aspect of our lives.

➤ Crafts teach frugality and ways we can save money by making things ourselves.

➤ Crafts teach us how we can recycle ordinary materials we might otherwise throw away.

Couple these practical reasons for engaging in crafting with the satisfaction and enjoyment that comes with creating something yourself and it's a wonder why everybody doesn't do it.

The Least You Need to Know

➤ The best way to teach creativity is to get in touch with your own creativity.

➤ Through crafts, families can bind closer together, creating their own rituals and making time for sharing.

➤ Family time doesn't just happen. It has to be designed.

➤ The values and skills learned through crafts will enrich your life and your children's lives.

Chapter 2

Setting Up for Success

In This Chapter

➤ Ten things to avoid that stifle creativity and joy

➤ Keys to successful crafting

➤ Finding the right materials and tools for the job

➤ How to supplement and enhance your crafting experiences

Success is something you plan for. Perhaps you never thought of it that way, but that's the truth. Study the lives of the most successful people, and you'll learn that most of them had a clear vision or master plan and persistently pursued it.

I want to do everything I can to ensure your success in crafting with your kids and I'm sure you do, too. There are some secrets of success that aren't really that secret, they're just common sense. Other clues are hidden in what you know best—your own child. So look, listen, and tune into the keys to making your time together fun, meaningful, and enlightening. This is the stuff memories are made of!

No Time for Toy Tools

When first setting up for a new craft there's an inherent dilemma—you don't want to spend a lot of money on tools and equipment if your child is going to lose interest, but having improper tools that are hard to manipulate (or simply inadequate) almost ensures she will. Crafts kits can be a good way to get started, but many contain inferior tools and materials.

Whenever possible, get properly-sized, high-quality tools. They should fit in your child's hand comfortably. If you need a tool you won't use for other types of projects, try to borrow it. If you end up buying specialized tools and then find a particular craft is not for you, you may be able to sell them.

Price doesn't necessarily dictate quality, but often it does. The tools that do the job may not have to be the top of the line, but should be good quality, meaning they're not going to break, they adequately perform the task they were designed for, and they're comfortable to use.

Crafty Clues

Sometimes the best kits to buy are those that are put together specifically for a particular craft by a supplier to the trade or a crafts store, rather than prepackaged kits. Ask your local crafts store or check in craft-specific catalogs.

Do a little research. Ask crafters who specialize in a particular craft what they use. When it comes to materials, buy small quantities of several different types if you can and see for yourself which one works best.

If you're considering a kit, look it over with a critical eye. What's actually there? Do you need to provide additional tools or materials or is it complete? Although you may not actually be able to hold the tools and materials included, try to evaluate them by how they look. Perhaps you can get the store owner to open the wrapping on one. If not, return the kit if the tools are inadequate and assemble your own.

Often the tools you'll need for the crafts presented in this book are simple household tools like scissors, a hammer, pliers, and maybe a glass cutter. These are things that are handy to have around the house anyway, so why not have the very best quality you can afford? It's amazing the difference a good tool makes in getting a job done.

Ten Success Saboteurs

Sometimes the best ways to ensure success is to know the pitfalls beforehand so they can be avoided. Before I tell you some sure-fire ways to make crafting with your kids a joy, let's look at the deadly dampeners—the things you need to avoid.

1. Being Unprepared

You've set aside the time to do a project with your child and both of you have been looking forward to it. You've got the picture of the finished product and can't wait to get started. Then you spend the next two hours walking from room to room, rummaging through drawers and closets looking for the things you need. You finally end up going out to the store because you forgot something.

When crafting, resist the temptation to "wing it." Read through the project instructions thoroughly before you start. Make sure you have all the materials you need in one place, that they're in good working order, and that you have enough to complete the project. Being able to simply sit down and begin will keep the enthusiasm and interest high and your nerves calm.

2. Beginning with a Project That's Too Difficult

It's easy to overestimate your own ability (and your child's) when you see something you like in a picture and want it for your own, but there's nothing more discouraging than getting part-way through a project and finding you don't have to skills to complete it. Make an honest evaluation of the skills needed (I've given you skill and age level indications for each project) and determine how much your child can actually do without your help, plus be sure you can do the steps that might be too difficult for your child. Be careful of expectations that are too high.

If you're learning a craft for the first time, start with something extra-simple to get the feel of the tools, materials, and techniques. Practice the techniques on something that doesn't count first before actually beginning a project. If the project is relatively easy, your child will gain confidence and quickly want to try something more challenging. Follow up as soon as possible with a more advanced project and explore other aspects of the craft whenever your child seems ready.

3. Not Allowing Enough Time

If you try to make a stained-glass window between soccer practice and supper, you're almost guaranteed a pile of broken glass and cut fingers.

You need time to do things right, and that's true of any activity, no matter how seemingly uncomplicated it is. Give yourself and your child time—to think, to enjoy what you're doing, to be creative, to experiment, and to enjoy each other.

Part of what makes crafting so enjoyable, and, as some doctors believe, healthy to do is that it slows us down and helps us relax. Rushing through a project is anything but relaxing and makes it more likely that we'll make mistakes or do a shoddy job. Schedule enough time to complete the project, clean up, and bask in the glow of your accomplishments.

4. Trying to Control Everything

Nothing can stifle enthusiasm and creativity faster than lack of freedom. Restrain your desires to orchestrate and control. Whenever possible, let your child make the decisions about color and design. Look for projects that allow variations and choices. Even if you're working on a structured project, give your child as much control of it as possible (while always observing safety precautions, of course).

Be patient and give your child time to struggle with something for a while. If she can't do it right away, don't take over, regardless of how tempting it is. Your unwanted "help" may actually hinder your child by sending the hidden message that you are disappointed with her or feel she's incompetent.

5. Being Too Judgmental

Crafting isn't a contest. In fact, it isn't any kind of test. This is supposed to be fun! There are plenty of situations in your child's life where he's being judged and evaluated; this doesn't need to be another one. This may actually be one of the few situations where your child can feel free to express himself without fear of judgment. No one's keeping score, there's no final exam, no grade, and no one's going to make fun of him if he doesn't do it "right."

Ask your child how *he* feels about what he's accomplished. Praise often, criticize rarely. Get into the process more, rather than concentrating completely on the results. So what if the mobile hangs a little crooked? The next one will be better. Besides, maybe it actually looks better that way.

6. Worrying Too Much About Neatness

If you can't make a mess, don't do something messy. Or perhaps it's better put this way: If you're going to do something messy, make sure you do it somewhere you can. Don't try painting in the living room or using a glue gun on the dining room table without putting newspaper down first. It's hard to have a good time if you're worried about the floor, your work surface, or your clothes. If you're doing something particularly messy, like tie dyeing or making paper, try to do it somewhere that's easy to clean up. How about outside or in the kitchen?

Crafty Clues
Consider making crafts aprons just for your child and yourself. You could embroider your names on them, or make them out of your favorite colors. Look for apron or smock patterns in your favorite pattern catalogs the next time you go to the fabric store.

Clear away things that might be damaged by an errant paintbrush or a splattering pot of wax. Make sure there's enough space to work safely and efficiently. Wear protective clothing or old clothes. Have plastic or rubber gloves in the right sizes available. Pull hair neatly out of the way. Again, take the time to prepare and everyone will have a better time.

7. Trying to Do Too Much at Once

Again, slow down. Sure you'd like to finish the project in one sitting, but it may require drying time. If you've read the instructions thoroughly, you know what the steps are and the time you'll need for each one. Break the project up into several sessions, if necessary, or plan a hot chocolate break for the time when the glue or paint is drying. Don't try to take shortcuts or rush the process. You're actually teaching a valuable lesson when you let things take their course and exercise patience.

Be realistic about the time you have and what you can accomplish in that time. Just because you only have a couple of hours to devote to a project doesn't mean you shouldn't start it. Instead, plan to break it up into more than one session and let your child know that's what you'll be doing. Be flexible: If it's bedtime but the project's not finished, agree on a time when you'll complete it together (and don't renege).

8. Hovering

Sure, you need to watch what's going on, but don't overdo it. In fact, you might consider doing the project yourself and letting your child do her own. You're working together, but on different versions of the same project.

That way you'll be involved in your own process and more likely not to meddle, watch too closely, or take over. Walk out of the room if you have to, bite your lip, but DON'T interfere. Making mistakes and struggling with new skills is part of life. Allow your child to experience those things, so she can experience the thrill of mastery.

9. Working When You're Too Tired

This one goes for both of you—adult and child. Be aware of your energy level and don't work when you're tuckered out or when it's obvious your child is ready to pack it in. It can only lead to disaster: short tempers, unnecessary mishaps, and avoidable accidents (since we're most likely to violate safety rules when we're over-tired).

Avoid this situation by scheduling time for crafts for when you're most likely to be rested. Saturday mornings or Sunday afternoons might be good. A session right after school might fit in best; or schedule a longer session on a school holiday.

The key is planning, but sometimes even the best-laid plans go awry. Acknowledge when you're just too tired to do a craft, apologize (yes, apologize), and agree on another time that's not too far away. Allow your child the out, as well.

10. Insisting on Success

I know, you want your child to be an achiever. No failures in your family! But did you know some of the greatest achievements in human history have been born out of failure? There has to be room for things not to work. Children (and adults) need to have a secure environment in which to make mistakes and learn from them. One of the best ways to ensure success is to allow room for failure or, as I like to put it,

Crafty Clues
Perhaps Friday night would make a good Family Crafts Night since kids don't have to worry about getting homework done and adults generally don't have to contemplate work in the morning. Make it special: Order supper out or make something ahead you can just pop in the oven to create more time to concentrate on crafts.

Bet You Didn't Know
The Post-It note was the result of a failure. While trying to develop a better glue, a researcher inadvertently made a batch that didn't stick at all, at least not permanently. That mistake produced a product most of us would be hard-pressed to do without!

"successes in progress." Children learn to give themselves permission to make mistakes when parents do. Give that same permission to yourself.

Keys to Crafting Success

Now that we've explored what NOT to do, what are some things you can do to ensure a positive experience for you and your child? Here are seven to get you started, but I'll bet you can easily think of more.

1. Make Yourselves Comfortable

Make sure your crafting table is at a comfortable height for you and your child. If you need to, provide two different work surfaces, one that's comfortable for each of you. A smaller, lower folding table and chair might be best for a young child, while you work alongside on a surface better suited to your own size. Put a cushion on a chair to both raise your child to the proper height and make it more comfortable to sit.

2. Provide Adequate Light

Crafty Clues
You may need to purchase some special lighting, depending on what kind of craft you're doing. My husband, who's a professional leather artist, uses a magnifying lamp to do certain tasks. I use a small adjustable desk lamp to do some beading.

This an easy one to overlook, but can make all the difference. Lighting that may be fine for family dining might not be bright enough for picking up small beads on the end of a needle. You may need to add additional lighting with a clamp-on lamp or a floor lamp you can move to the work area and put away when you're not crafting.

If you're working during the day, try to introduce some natural light, since that's the best of all, but you don't want it glaring you in the face.

As part of your project planning, analyze the lighting situation and make adjustments. Ask your child if she's comfortable with the lighting and can see adequately.

3. Understand Your Basic Materials

If you're planning on doing a lot of crafting (or even if you're not), it's worth the effort to understand the differences between paints, glues, scissors, papers, and other basic tools and materials. I've included some information about these materials throughout this book. You can also look for articles and ads in crafts magazines. Sometimes they give you a lot more information about what a material is best suited for.

Look for books on crafts materials, as well. There's a book available just on the subject of glues called *The Crafter's Guide to Glues* by Tammy Young that helps you decipher all those different chemical names and choose the right glue for the task. Usually, beginner's books for a particular craft will cover materials and tools. (I've included books on nearly every craft covered here in Appendix A.) Read these sections carefully and then talk to your local crafts supplier. There may be new and better products on the market.

I've found a wealth of information on various crafts forums (which are on CompuServe) and newsgroups online (such as the ones on America Online). There's a newsgroup or mailing list for just about any craft you can imagine. Throughout this book, I'll point you to some useful Web sites.

4. Hone Your Skills Before You Start a Project

Many times it's best to concentrate on mastering a basic skill before you try to apply it; for example, learn to hammer a nail *before* you try to build a birdhouse. Give your child an opportunity to practice on something non-threatening, like a piece of scrap wood, before tackling an actual project where it "counts."

Kids get a real kick out of practicing skills like hammering and sawing anyway. (Anything that makes noise, right?) You may also want to choose projects that are skills-oriented, developing one level at a time. In learning beading, for instance, it sometimes helps to start with simple stringing techniques first, so you can learn the basic tools and develop an eye for color and design. Then you can graduate to the more difficult techniques. Allow time just for learning, without any specific goal in mind.

5. Pick a Quick and Easy First Project

I say this with some reservations, since I can only speak from my own experience and I don't always reflect the norm. I sometimes learn best when I'm making something I really want to make, even if it's a little more difficult than a beginner's project. I may need help at various stages, but I'm more likely to stick with something I'm really excited about. I suspect some people might be like me, but others prefer the exhilaration of a first success and then move with confidence to a project they find more exciting.

If a project's too long and involved I can lose interest, so I often pick one that can be done in a day or a weekend for the satisfaction of completing something quickly. Gauge yourself and your child and determine what suits you. Choose your projects carefully, and certainly give your child as much say as possible in the choices.

6. Allow for Spontaneity

I know, I just told you to plan. That's true, but there's a more general way of planning that sparks unplanned crafting sessions that can be just as much fun. Fill up a medium to large box with crafts materials that your child can work with at any time. This means no toxic materials or dangerous tools (gear this to your child's age and ability). Check the box periodically and make sure it's well-supplied. It should contain crayons, colored pencils, glue, construction paper, rubber stamps, ink pads, stickers, scissors, paper fasteners, pipe cleaners, popsicle sticks, fabric scraps, yarn, string, scraps of ribbon and gift wrap, recyclables…whatever you feel comfortable letting your child play with when you aren't supervising closely.

Make up another box that's labeled "Adults Only." This box can contain other crafts materials that require supervision or raise safety concerns. Teach kids the difference and explain that one box is off limits without an adult and the other is theirs to play with on their own.

Provide your kids with their very own crafts apron, gloves, eye protection, crafts box, and a clean, well-lighted work area. Then watch them go!

If your child has become especially interested in a particular craft, you can put together a kit with lots of materials for that specific craft. If the hobby is rubber stamping, for example, create a rubber stamp box. If it's woodworking, have a toolbox just for her and some scrap wood to use whenever an idea strikes. Encourage your child to decorate the box and personalize it.

Keep crafts boxes, tools, and supplies in an easy-to-reach location to encourage your child to use them AND to put them away when she's done (I'll talk more about organizing in the next chapter). Teach your child to clean up carefully and return everything neatly to the box for the next crafting session.

7. Have a Sense of Humor

If you can't laugh, then what's the point? This is play, remember? So if you find yourself getting too intense or losing your temper, lighten up! Laugh at yourself and you'll be giving permission for others to laugh along with you. Everybody else thought the glitter stuck on Mommy's nose was funny, too.

It's More Than Crafts

You may think this book is about crafts, but it's really about love. Don't believe me? You'll see. Just read on. I know you want to do things with your child because you want him to enjoy new experiences, learn new things, and you want to spend time with him. I also know you want to share and teach. Sounds like love to me!

If you approach this book and the time you spend crafting with your child with love in mind, you'll find opportunities abound everywhere to express that love. Give a hug. A smile. Some praise. No, lots of praise. Make some hot chocolate together when you take a break or pop some popcorn while the glue dries. Sing a song while you work. Play word games. Pretend.

Crafting is a springboard for a whole world of experiences you can share with your child. The Bonding Experiences sidebars in the chapters ahead will give you plenty of ideas. Do as many of them as you can. Learn about the history of your craft. Read more together.

Take field trips and see what others are doing with the same tools and materials. Ask "Why?" Ask "What if?" Provide an environment where everyday life is filled with imagination and homemade objects. Use what you make and make what you use.

Celebrate…often. Any silly excuse will do. Crafts are a way of enhancing any party. Make amazing Technicolor eggs for Easter, spectacular hearts and flowers for Valentine's Day, and celebrate a snow day with the most delightful paper snowflakes you've ever seen!

Appreciate each other. Tell each family member often what you love about them and lovingly display what you've made together. Guard your time together jealously and don't allow anything to take it away. Turn off the tube. Don't answer the phone. Your family time is precious.

You can begin crafting with kids at any time, but if your child is still quite young, all the better. Start early and don't let your lives get so busy that you let your crafting time slip away. By making things together, you're instilling some of the most important values and skills your child can ever learn. You're setting your child up for success.

The Least You Need to Know

➤ Provide the best tools and materials you can and avoid toys or kits that have inferior ones.

➤ By knowing the things that can stifle creativity and tear down self-esteem, like criticizing and hovering, you can avoid them.

➤ You can help create successful crafting experiences by being aware of a few basic principles, such as understanding materials and starting with simple skills first.

➤ Crafting with your child teaches more than how to do a craft. It teaches lessons about living and life skills, plus it gives you a chance to show love and appreciation for who your child is.

Chapter 3

Getting Organized

In This Chapter

➤ Crafts supplies or clutter?

➤ Ten rules for unstuffing your life

➤ Storage 101: How to put things away so you can find them again

➤ The two basic crafts kits and their contents

➤ Organizing space for crafts

Crafts can bring an enormous amount of "stuff" in their wake, especially if you're in the exploratory phase and don't know yet what you really want to do. There's a kind of tension between space limitations and the need to have a variety of materials on hand to experiment with. Crafts can just be an excuse for the die-hard clutterer/collector to clutter and collect.

I touched on this a bit in the last chapter, but now I'm going to look at organizing crafts materials and preparation for creating crafts in all their glory. As I've mentioned, I "wrote the book" on organization, *The Complete Idiot's Guide to Organizing Your Life*, so I know a thing or two about the most effective ways to handle clutter and storage, as well as space and time. So let's dive in.

A Little Place for Your Stuff

Maybe you remember the comedy routine that George Carlin did back in the '70s called something like "All I Need is a Little Place for My Stuff." In it, he talks about how accumulated stuff can sometimes become a burden. In Carlin's terms, "a house is just a pile of stuff with a cover on it."

But, you say, you NEED all 60 colors of pencils and 150 crayons. Or you HAVE to have six boxes of fabric. Well, maybe you do. But being organized and keeping the clutter from choking out the fun requires regular and sensible choices, and you have to make many of them BEFORE the stuff ever reaches your front door.

This is the time to evaluate what space you have available and to de-clutter to create more space. This process isn't just for crafts materials, but for all aspects of your life.

As you're getting things organized, keep in mind my Ten Rules for Un-Stuffing Your Life:

1. If you don't use it, lose it.
2. Put it away.
3. Give it away.
4. Take just 15 minutes to get started organizing. Small blocks of time can accomplish big things when added together.
5. Group like things together.
6. Consolidate and compress.
7. Alphabetize whenever possible. Things like patterns, books, and some materials lend themselves to alphabetical order.
8. Label it. Why should you have to go through a box every time you need to find something? Label its contents and you can go right to it.
9. Go for quality, not quantity.
10. Think multi-purpose, not single purpose.

Here's another handy organizing tip: Take five boxes or bags and label each one *Trash, Pass On, Put Away, Mystery,* and *Fix It.* Now begin to sort through your stuff and place every item into one of these five containers. Here's how it works:

> **Crafty Clues**
> Rather than let broken items sit unmended in the Fix It box forever, set yourself a deadline by which to fix them. If you don't fix them by the set time, put the items in the Trash box, or donate them to a charitable agency. Your local Salvation Army or Goodwill, for example, might be able to repair and reuse them.

➤ If you haven't used an item in five years, or if it's broken and you don't know how (or want) to fix it, put it in the Trash or Pass On box. Then throw it away or pass it on to someone who can really use it.

➤ If the item belongs in another place, put it in the Put Away box.

➤ If you just can't decide what to do with an item, put it in the Mystery box (be real selective about this one). Put a time limit on keeping these items (a few days or a week will suffice) and then go back and make a decision to use them or lose them.

➤ If the item is broken, but with a little work could be good as new, put it in the Fix It box.

There, now you've created some breathing room. The next step is to decide what crafting materials you absolutely need to have and to designate a place for them.

Crafty Containers

As I explained in Chapter 2, you should keep at least two containers in your crafts storage space: one labeled "Kid's Crafts Kit" and another labeled something like "Crafts Supplies/ Adults Only." Later in this chapter I'll list some things you'll probably want to have in each container.

The containers don't have to be anything fancy. I like tough plastic containers because they can be washed and they take a fair amount of abuse.

Within these larger, more general containers you'll need smaller containers to sort and store various crafts items. They don't have to be anything fancy. Baby-food jars, zip-lock plastic bags, shoe boxes, cigar boxes…whatever seems to fit the bill. By reusing small containers, you'll be able to sort all your materials and recycle at the same time.

Try to sort your crafts materials together. For example, if you store all your buttons, clay, fabric, and beads together in one place, you'll know exactly where to find the item you want. You'll also be able to see what duplicate tools you may have you can pass on to another crafter. Perhaps you can trade for something you don't have.

However you store your child's craft materials, make sure that the Kids Crafts Kit is easy to reach and that the container won't come apart and spill its contents. If the kids have outgrown their toy box, you might be able to appropriate it to store their supplies.

Be sure to involve your child in this organizing process. You know that you're more likely to keep up a system that you yourself had a hand in designing. Children are no different.

Building the Basic Kids Crafts Kit

In Chapter 2, I talked briefly about what materials you should place in a basic box of crafts supplies that your kids are allowed to play with on their own. Here, I'd like to go into it in more depth.

By having certain crafts materials available that are safe and can be used pretty much without supervision, your kids are encouraged to respond to their creative impulses and turn to crafts to entertain themselves.

Crafty Clues
Use clear storage containers whenever possible so you can see what's in them, but label them, too. That way you'll be reinforcing your child's reading skills at the same time you encourage him to put things in their proper place.

Crafty Clues
You'll need to establish some rules about when and where your kids can use their crafts materials. They may be allowed to craft only after the homework's done, or only on the kitchen table with newspaper put down first, for example. You may want to post the rules directly on their crafts box.

25

Once you've found the box you're going to use for your Kid's Crafts Kit, decorate it together. Here are some ideas for things to put in it:

- Blank sketch books
- Scrapbooks
- Writing books
- Non-toxic glues (Aleene's has several different types)
- Tapes
- Scrap paper of all kinds
- Different kinds of papers (gift wrap, construction, watercolor, pastel, drawing, etc.)
- Stickers
- Fabric scraps
- Felt
- Elastic
- Buttons
- Yarns
- Stuffings, including beans
- Feathers
- Scissors
- Bells
- Beads
- String
- Empty spools
- Empty toilet paper and paper towel rolls
- Empty jars and cans
- Pipe cleaners
- Popsicle sticks
- Stiff cardboard
- Soap
- Wood pieces
- Sandpaper
- Natural materials such as shells, pebbles, and pine cones (collect these on walks and hikes)
- Wallpaper scraps
- Empty matchboxes
- Disposable pie plates
- Plastic trays
- Styrofoam trays
- Tins and containers
- Egg cartons
- Paper bags of all sizes
- Envelopes
- Small boxes
- Index cards, white and colored
- Art supplies like crayons, paints, colored pencils, and markers
- Regular pencils
- Rulers and templates
- Non-toxic clays and play doughs
- Rubber stamps and ink pads
- Non-toxic paints
- Paintbrushes

As you create projects, you'll think of other things to keep in the Kids Crafts Kit, but this list should get you started. Just have a few of each item on hand.

You may also want to keep a supply of newspapers near your crafts boxes for covering your work area.

Organizing Your Ideas

The next organization challenge is what to do with project ideas. The more you craft, the more ideas you'll see (or come up with yourselves) that you'll want to keep on file.

One idea is to keep a card file where you jot down project ideas (you can keep folders or envelopes for larger pages). I have a file drawer devoted to crafts, with separate folders for each holiday or type of occasion, plus one for each medium I like to work in. I even have a folder for each family member. When ideas pop up in magazines, on TV, or whatever, I clip them or jot them down and throw them in the folder.

I keep the ideas that turn out really well; I toss those that only produce so-so results. I try to purge these files periodically (usually when a particular holiday comes up) so they don't get too bulky.

Another way to organize projects is by the month—a kind of "calendar of crafts." Decide together what projects you want to do for the coming month, or what crafts you want to make for the celebrations in a particular month. That way you can pull out a folder and decide together what you'd like to do.

Another way to store crafts instructions and ideas is to rip articles out of magazines, make holes with a three-hole punch, and store them in a binder. Be selective and periodically throw out ideas you've lost interest in.

How you organize your ideas depends on how you approach crafting. You can take the seasonal approach, as I mentioned, or explore one particular medium, or zero in on one particular craft. Adjust your organization system accordingly. Aim to have a place for everything, so you and your child are encouraged to keep everything in its place and spend time crafting rather than searching for supplies or directions.

Crafty Clues

Paints may be okay for an older child to work with alone, but you may want to keep them out of the Kids Crafts Kit altogether if you know your child will make a mess with them. (Any craft material that causes a problem can be removed from your child's kit and placed in your Adult Kit.)

For Adults Only: Your Crafts Kit

This crafts container is filled with materials that are X-rated—for safety, that is. This kit is filled with tools and supplies that your child can only work with under careful supervision—and possibly some things he cannot work with at all.

This container should be clearly labeled—perhaps you might decorate it with a large skull and crossbones, like they used to put on bottles of poison. It's certainly an arresting symbol. Your children should be taught to recognize the symbol and the box should be stored where they can't get at it.

You may also want to store especially messy materials in this container—anything you don't want your child getting into unless you're nearby.

Here's what goes in your kit:

➤ Toxic paints

➤ Toxic clays

➤ Toxic glues

➤ Lead products for glasswork, etc.

➤ Paint thinner

➤ Alcohol

➤ Acetone

➤ Kerosene

➤ Craft knives

➤ Cutters

➤ Snips

➤ Punches

➤ Awls

➤ Resins

➤ Glues, including washable fabric glues, silicone glue, epoxies, Duco cement, and E-6000

➤ Glue guns

➤ Soldering irons

➤ Power tools

➤ Anything you feel your child might be tempted to swallow

➤ Anything you don't want your child playing with when you're not working directly with him

➤ Anything you're saving for a special project

➤ Materials that might shatter or break easily, like glass

We'll be considering safety in much more depth in Chapter 4, and after reading the material there you'll probably have more ideas about what you need to keep in your "Adults Only" box.

UFOs and Other Space-Devourers

Much as I'm an advocate of having materials for a variety of activities at your fingertips, ready to respond to spontaneous attacks of creativity or the unexpected snow or sick day, I'm also aware of how easy crafts materials can take over the house. Don't let this happen! Be rigorous about it or you'll find yourself surrounded with so much stuff you'll never get to work on any crafts.

Don't start too many crafts projects at once. That will leave you with UFOs (UnFinished Objects) that are discouraging to look at. If it's clear that a particular craft didn't "take" or a project just isn't going to make it to completion, get rid of all the paraphernalia and perhaps pass it on to someone else who'd love to see it finished.

Another reason projects become UFOs is that we put them in such an inaccessible place that it's just too much of a hassle to dig them out. If you discover a UFO and it still appeals to you, put it in your crafts area where you can see if it sparks your interest again. If it doesn't, ditch it.

Beware of the special gadgets for crafters out on the market. They're a lot like the unused tools in your kitchen (does anyone ever use a mushroom brush more than once?). Identify which tools you absolutely need to get started and add new ones only as your interest in a specific craft grows. To begin beading, for example, all you need are some beads, the right thread for stringing, a couple of needles, and a few other odds and ends. If there's serious interest, branch out and buy more advanced tools as you go along, like pliers and looms.

Are You Collecting Crafts or DOING Crafts?

Be careful not to use crafting as an excuse for collecting, rather than actually creating crafts. It's easy to do. There are so many books, videos, magazines, crafts sheets, new products, doodads, gadgets, and thingamajigs on the market you could fill, well, a whole STORE with them!

Make an honest assessment of which crafts you and your child really enjoy. It may take some time to figure that out and you may end up with some stuff you really don't use. Purge your crafts supplies periodically and pass on the projects that just didn't fly with you to someone else who'll soar with them.

Now that you've set up your crafting area and have a place for storage, you could probably use some ideas on how to store both general and specific items. Here are a few suggestions:

➤ Some hobbies are self-contained; almost all the supplies fit in one box or carry case. An embroidery project can fit in a tote. I have a special travel case for my beading supplies and most of them fit in there, with a few additional plastic compartmentalized boxes to hold more beads. Look for totable bags or boxes that are especially designed for your craft and others that can be adapted. Fishing tackle boxes or toolboxes work well for some.

Another advantage to having a portable craft case is that you can keep it where you're most likely to pick it up as moments present themselves, plus you can easily take it with you when traveling.

➤ A rolling cart with drawers is a good place to store often-used tools and supplies. You can keep the cart in your crafts area and roll it to wherever you're working. You can usually find these carts in the closet department of your favorite discount or department store, and I've seen them at wholesale clubs, too. Be sure yours is very sturdy, though. I find that once they are filled, sometimes the drawers don't move as well. Since I use mine all the time and it works well for me, I'm planning on buying a more substantial wooden version from an art supply store.

➤ A plastic box or bin works well for some materials, especially those that may be affected by light and moisture. Keep this in mind when storing anything—light, dampness, dust, and "critters" can destroy your supplies, so make sure they're protected and be careful where you put them.

➤ When shopping for storage containers, check out the hardware store as well as crafts and department stores. Sometimes I find the hardware store has storage boxes intended for nuts and bolts or tools that work ever so well for crafts and are a lot less expensive. They may be a less funky color, but I don't mind when I can put more money back in my pocket and spend it on crafts!

➤ Some crafts items or projects might be best stored rolled up in a clean, covered trash container. Certain pieces of artwork or even quilt tops lend themselves well to this. Use a cardboard tube to roll the work on. (Be sure to label the trash can, so no one gets the wrong idea!)

➤ Power tools and other tools can be mounted on pegboard up and out of reach of your children.

➤ You might want to slip paints into individual zip-lock bags before storing them in whatever container you've chosen. This is double protection against spills and accidents.

➤ Always clean paintbrushes thoroughly and wrap them in newspaper or rags before them putting away.

➤ Often patterns don't fit back in their envelopes once they're used. If you have a filing cabinet for your crafts, you can put patterns in individual folders and store them there. If not, have larger envelopes on hand and store them in a portable filing box. Be sure to include all instructions and the original envelope, and label each so you don't have to open them to see what's inside.

➤ Borrow storage solutions intended for other purposes when they seem to suit your crafting needs. A cardboard shelf unit, for example (available in any business supply catalog or store), might make a good system for storing quilting fabric squares. Dish pans or kitty litter pans can be labeled and lined up on shelves to hold fabric, paper, small tools, scrap wood, almost anything. If your Tupperware is languishing in a kitchen cabinet, get it out and use it to store crafts odds and ends.

➤ A sturdy folding banquet or card table might be a solution to finding a work surface when you need to spread out. Banquet tables are heavy, so you don't want to be putting them up and taking them down every day, but they make a good temporary setup for a project that takes more room than you've normally got. I've seen them at wholesale clubs for around $30 or $40. Besides, you can use them as extra dining tables in a pinch!

➤ Keep crafts materials close to where you use them. A centralized hobby/crafts area works best if you have the space, but if you don't, try to locate your supplies near where you and your child work most. If that's not practical (say, you work most often on the kitchen table), then have a mobile unit that you can move close to you. You want to spend time crafting, not gathering your supplies.

As you develop your crafting, you're sure to come up with your own customized storage and organizing solution.

Take Your Crafts on the Road

Remember how boring long trips were when you were a child? Know how frazzled your nerves get traveling with kids now? Well, since you and your child have discovered crafts, this doesn't have to happen ever again! Before a long trip, put together a craft box for traveling. You'll be amazed how much shorter the miles seem.

Certain crafts lend themselves to traveling. Crocheting and knitting, embroidery, beading, plastic canvas, lanyards, and certain paper crafts immediately come to mind. As you go through the chapters in this book and explore different crafts, you'll think of others that work.

You can also create a travel kit with homemade games and simple crafts. You might want to throw in some activity books, card games, self-contained puzzles, and anything else that's not messy and doesn't have a lot of small parts. Keep it in the car and it will become a welcome distraction for your kids if there's a long wait at the doctor's office or some other unexpected delay. Replenish and change the contents periodically, so there's something new to grab your child's interest.

If you and your child are pursuing a craft together, you might want to have a "take-along" project for each of you. If your craft is portable, you may just be able to grab your storage case and be off. It can be a special event to shop for a new traveling project just for the trip. Make sure it's travel-worthy and let your child choose something he's really interested in. I've actually done lap quilting with a small portable frame and beading in a plane seat without too much difficulty, so try different setups to see what works.

The Least You Need to Know

➤ Crafts supplies can end up being just more clutter. Use basic organization principles to keep your crafts materials in order.

➤ There are lots of storage solutions for crafts supplies, many of them using free recyclables from your household.

➤ Make a Kids Crafts Kit that your children can play with any time they want to entertain themselves. This should be filled only with safe materials your child can handle without close supervision.

➤ Store all toxic, messy, or dangerous materials in a separate storage container that's clearly marked "Adults Only."

➤ Having crafts projects for travel, and even a special busy box in the car, can make trips more fun for everyone.

Chapter 4

Safety First

In This Chapter
➤ How to protect sight and hearing
➤ Working safely around electricity
➤ Safety around flames and heat
➤ What to wear (and what not to wear) when you craft
➤ The right ways to handle chemicals

There's no reason why children can't work with a wide variety of crafts materials and tools and not get hurt. But it's your responsibility as a parent, teacher, or caregiver to know the hazards, handle tools safely, and teach your children to do the same.

This chapter will alert you to some of the potential dangers involved in the crafts we're going to explore throughout this book. It offers tips for avoiding accidents and gives you lots of resources for more information.

General Rules for Safe Crafting

Although most of the basic rules for working with art and crafts materials just seem like common sense, they bear repeating. Remember, too, that things you take for granted might not be obvious to a young child. Take some time before beginning a project or learning a new craft to review both basic safety procedures and those specific to the craft you're doing.

First, observe these general rules:

➤ Read directions thoroughly before beginning any project. That includes both the directions for the project and any labels on products you may be using. Always read labels! Check expiration dates, too.

➤ Make sure you have all the materials you need in one place. Accidents can occur when you're hurriedly looking for something or leave the room to get something you've forgotten.

➤ Arrange all your tools near you. Spreading things out in a semi-circle usually works well.

➤ Make sure you have enough room to work safely and efficiently. Cramped spaces can be dangerous.

➤ Always have adequate ventilation when working with chemicals or projects that produce dust.

➤ Protect your pets and keep them away from the crafts area while you're working.

➤ Don't leave young children unattended with dangerous tools or toxic materials even for a few minutes.

➤ Don't eat, drink, or smoke while using art and crafts materials.

➤ Don't use dyes or paints on the skin (for face painting, for example) or in food, unless the products you buy are specifically meant to be used that way.

➤ Don't transfer materials to other containers, since you'll lose the information you need provided on the package. If you must, be sure to cut out the important information and include it in the container.

➤ Use the right equipment for the job and make sure tools and equipment are in good working order. Don't work with questionable tools, especially power tools. If the cord is frayed or something else doesn't seem right, fix it or replace the tool.

➤ Keep your work area clean and continue picking up as you go along. Don't leave scraps of material or tools lying around.

➤ Keep your work area dry. Water on the floor, counter, or table can be an electricity hazard or cause a fall.

➤ Make sure you have an up-to-date, complete first-aid kit on hand.

➤ Wash your hands after crafting.

➤ Don't hurry. Make sure you have adequate time to do a project before starting it.

➤ Don't work when you're tired.

➤ Minimize distractions. Turn off the TV or the radio if it's distracting. Safety requires concentration.

Now that we've covered the general rules for safe creating, let's move on to some more specific safety features.

Eyes and Ears: Protecting Your Sight and Hearing

When it comes to the precious gifts of sight and hearing, it's better to be extra-cautious than risk injury, so make frequent use of eye and ear protection when crafting.

You can buy a good pair of safety glasses or goggles at any hardware store. Make sure they fit your child properly and comfortably, so he's not tempted to take them off. Keep them clean and store them properly, so they won't get scratched and impair vision. Use safety goggles to protect eyes from dust, stray particles, chemicals, and anything that might possibly fly up and hit the eye.

Adults with hearing loss can often trace the cause back to repeated exposure to loud noises when they were younger. In most cases, hearing loss can easily be prevented with inexpensive hearing protection.

The amount of protection might vary depending on the noise level, but since you probably won't be using heavy power tools around your child, simple foam ear plugs will usually do the trick.

Safety Signals
During crafting or any activity, if the noise level is uncomfortable, chances are you're risking hearing damage and should be wearing ear protection.

Shockless! Working Safely With Electricity

Most of the crafts in this book don't involve the use of power tools, but some may, especially woodworking or advanced glass techniques. Even if you're not using a tool that requires electricity, you may still be plugging in extra lights or simply working around power outlets and switches. We don't want any accidents or injuries here, either! So observe these general safety rules for working with and around electricity and power tools:

➤ Read the manuals that come with any power tools carefully before using them. Make sure you understand how to operate the tool and follow all safety precautions. Explain to your child what you will be doing and keep him clear while you operate the tool. If your child will be operating a power tool, make sure he understands the directions completely.

➤ Before using any power tool, make sure it's up to full operating speed. (Someitmes, when turning the tool on, it takes a few seconds to be rotating [or whatever its function is] at full speed.)

➤ Don't leave power tools unattended. Turn them off and unplug them before leaving the area. If you're done, put them away.

➤ Use all guards and safety devices when using power tools.

➤ Unplug power tools when replacing or adjusting blades or bits.

➤ Never force a tool. If it hangs up while drilling, sawing, sanding, or whatever, remove it and try again. If it still won't do the job, you may need a more powerful tool or a different one.

➤ Don't reach over or behind a cutting blade.

➤ Keep cutting tools sharp. Dull tools can cause injury. Replace blades often.

➤ Be sure power tools are properly grounded.

➤ Never drive nails, staples, or other metal objects through electrical cords.

➤ Be safe with extension cords. Use the right cord size for the appliance or tool you're using, don't curl an extension cord up on the floor, don't wrap it around a nail or tack it up with staples, don't put it where you can walk or trip on it, and don't put anything (boxes, clothing, magazines) on top of the cord.

➤ Be careful of multi-plug adapters. These may overload a circuit and cause a fire if you're using too many tools or appliances on one circuit. Work in an area where there are enough plugs (you may need to think about having more convenient permanent wiring done). If you're going to use a multiple outlet device, use one that's UL-listed and has a built-in circuit breaker.

➤ Make sure there are cover plates on all plug receptacles and switch boxes.

➤ Never try to defeat a circuit breaker by holding it open with tape or other means. Make sure fuses are the correct size for the circuit they protect and do not bypass. Keep the fuse box or circuit breaker box clear of storage and debris.

➤ Water and electricity don't mix. Keep your work area dry. If you're going to be working with water, do it away from electrical outlets, switches, and wires.

Follow these rules yourself and review them with your child and your crafting need never be a shocking experience.

The Heat Is On: Using Care Around Hot Tools and Flame

There are some crafts in this book that require the use of a stove or a hot tool like a soldering iron. You'll need to judge if your child is old enough and capable enough to do these crafts safely. Since this book is primarily for children age five through 10, you should expect to be supervising your children during these activities at all times.

In the case of handling a hot soldering iron or glue gun, I suggest watching your child practice with it BEFORE you plug it in, to see if it's a comfortable size and to give him a chance to find the proper position for holding it safely. Make sure you also have a place to rest the hot tool when you're not holding it that's out of the way and where it's not in contact with anything that can burn or scorch. You can buy stands to hold tools when not in use, or use a large ceramic tile.

Coming Up for Air: Ventilation

Fumes and dust can be hazardous. Even substances that don't smell bad or wouldn't cause a problem in a large room can be dangerous in a small space. When you plan a project, read the labels and look for any cautions about ventilation. (It's a good idea to work in a well-ventilated area anyway. It's more pleasant and helps keep you alert.)

> **Crafty Clues**
> Glue guns are a particularly hazardous crafting tool—they can cause lots of serious injuries, and even adults need some practice using them. There are so many glues on the market, though, that you can often avoid using the glue gun altogether.

In some cases, however, special precautions need to be taken with regard to ventilation. Wood dust, for example, may seem harmless, but in large quantities it can be harmful. Power tools like sanders often come equipped with dust catchers and these should be used. Certain hardwoods and plywoods actually contain toxic chemicals and a special mask should be worn when working with them. Ask questions about safety precautions where you buy your lumber.

Another ventilation hazard you may not think of is the dust from dry clays. Some of these are toxic as well. Again, know your materials and read labels carefully. If you're not sure about any materials you're working with, contact one of the organizations listed later in this chapter and find out.

When evaluating any ventilation system, you need to make sure it works two ways—that it takes out old air AND brings in fresh air. The best solution is to work outside. Windy conditions would be unsafe, of course, but on a nice day, sanding, sawing, painting, mixing, and dyeing are best done outdoors. If you must work indoors, an open window might be enough. Just make sure you have a source of fresh air and a way to remove hazardous fumes and dust from the air.

Keep your work area clean and remember to vacuum (not sweep) the area when you are finished. You don't want to kick up any more dust than necessary. A wet mop can also be used to clean up fine dust.

Safe Handling of Paints, Solvents, and Chemicals

Most of the crafts in this book use non-toxic substances and in many cases, there are non-toxic substitutes for many toxic materials. But how do you know which is which? Well, the Art and Creative Materials Institute (ACMI) has instituted a voluntary labeling program that makes it easy for consumers to identify non-toxic products. Look for one of the labels shown in the following figure and you can rest easy.

Look for one of those labels and rest assured the product is non-toxic.

CONFORMS TO ASTMD-4236   CONFORMS TO ASTMD-4236

If you will be using materials that are toxic, you'll need to observe some safety precautions each and every time:

Safety Signals
If you are a teacher or purchaser of arts and crafts materials for a school, you may be prohibited from purchasing any material with a chronic hazard warning label for use in pre-kindergarten through grade six. Check all labels carefully.

Saftey Signal
If your child appears to be having an allergic reaction to a substance, discontinue use and remove him from the area. Observe and if symptoms do not subside, or if they worsen, call your physician immediately.

➤ Make sure you use the right substance for the job. Never mix chemicals without first knowing that it's safe to do so.

➤ Read labels carefully and pay special attention to any safety precautions listed.

➤ Ventilate the area well. Take frequent fresh-air breaks.

➤ Wear eye protection when handling chemicals and know what to do if any chemical you are working with gets in the eyes or on the skin. Generally, you'll need to flush the eyes thoroughly with water, so keep some fresh water nearby or work near a water source.

➤ Cover the skin. Wear rubber gloves. Wear long sleeves and pants. Be aware that some substances are only irritating to people who have allergies. What may not bother you may bother someone else, and children are especially susceptible. Look for symptoms such as sneezing, watery eyes, itching, or rashes.

➤ No smoking while crafting!

➤ Open and close containers carefully. Always replace the cap after you've used a material.

➤ Pay attention to proper storage instructions. Usually directions will say to keep chemicals in a cool place out of reach of children and pets, but read the label for your particular product.

➤ Buy only what you need, so you're not storing a lot of chemicals.

➤ Pay attention to symptoms of exposure: eye irritation, dizziness, light-headedness, and/or headache. If they appear, discontinue use of the substance and leave the area. Call a physician if symptoms persist or worsen.

➤ Dispose of toxic materials according to the directions given by the manufacturer. If you're not sure, contact your local waste disposal contractor or agency. Make crafting safe for you, other critters, and the environment.

➤ Have the name and number of your poison control center and physician posted in a convenient place and in large, readable print.

➤ If you'll be using a mask, make sure it's the right type for the substance you're using. The wrong type could do as much or more harm than using none at all. Check labels on both the substance and the mask.

➤ Protect cuts or wounds by using bandages and covering them with gloves or clothing.

➤ Don't store flammable materials near heat, sparks, or flame.

➤ Don't heat any substance above the temperature specified on the label.

➤ Some crafting materials, like ceramic glazes and paints, contain lead. If you'll be working with children, look for substitutes that don't contain lead. If you must use lead-containing products, make sure you know how to use them safely and handle them yourself.

There's no reason you can't use chemicals in crafting if you're careful and follow these common-sense precautions.

Clothes Make the Crafter

I bet you never thought there were fashions just for crafters. Well, not exactly, but you and your child can dress for safety. Safety glasses, ear protectors, and dust masks are fashionable crafting accessories we've already discussed, but there's more. Here are a few simple things the well-dressed crafter will want to keep in mind:

➤ Be careful of loose-fitting or flowing clothing. You'll want to be comfortable, but extra material can get caught in things or knock things over.

➤ Don't wear jewelry that dangles, like long earrings, bracelets, or necklaces.

➤ Tie back long hair so it can't get tangled in anything and keeps hair out of the eyes. Even short hair can get in the eyes when leaning over. It may be necessary to put hair back with a hair band or barrettes.

➤ Don't wear ties or scarves while crafting.

I'll talk a bit more about crafting fashions in the next chapter, but when it comes to safety, observing these rules will keep you and your child lookin' good.

What I've given you here are some of the more general safety precautions you'll need to take with your child when crafting together (or alone, for that matter). This should get you thinking in the right direction, but it's up to you to assess each individual project or craft, get product and equipment information, and provide a safe environment in which to work. You can expect occasional cuts, bumps, or bruised fingers, but avoiding any serious injury is your responsibility. (Also, by teaching your child to think about safety, you'll be providing her with an important life skill.) If you use common sense, prepare properly, read labels, and observe precautions, you should have a happy and safe crafting experience.

On occasion, you may need to get additional information. Here are some good sources for more information about safety with arts and crafts materials:

> Art & Creative Materials Institute, Inc. (ACMI)
> 100 Boylston Street #1050
> Boston, MA 02116
> (617) 426-6400
> e-mail: dfanning@aol.com
> Web site: http://www.creative-industries.com/acmi/index.html

This is a non-profit association of manufacturers of art, craft, and other creative materials, and they have a certification program for children's art materials, ensuring they are non-toxic and meet voluntary standards of quality and performance. Look for the ACMI seals on product labels: either CP (Certified Product), AP (Approved Product), or HL (Health Label). The ACMI publishes a list of products that have been certified through its program.

> ACTS: Arts, Crafts, and Theater Safety
> 181 Thompson Street #23
> New York, NY 10012-2586
> (212) 777-0062
> e-mail: ACTS@CaseWeb.Com
> Web site: http://www.caseweb.com/acts/

This organization offers free art and theater hazards information by phone, mail, and e-mail, including health and safety counseling for art workers and hobbyists, copies of educational materials, information from an extensive technical library, and referrals to physicians and other professional sources. They even have a newsletter, *ACTS FACTS*, with the latest information ($15 for 12 issues/year; back issues are available). Data sheets on wax, dyes and pigments, paints, ceramic ware, glassmaking, resins, and many other topics can be ordered for 25 cents a page.

> Center for Safety in the Arts
> c/o New York Foundation for the Arts
> 155 Avenue of the Americas, 14th Floor
> New York, NY 10013

Performing Arts Hazards Data Sheets, General Data Sheets, and Conservation Hazards Data Sheets are available for 50 cents each. There's also an Art Hazards Library, and a subscription to *Art Hazards News* keeps subscribers up to date on new materials.

If you want to look up a particular material, you can search on the Material Safety Data Sheet (MSDS) Search Page. You'll get some information that may be more technical than you need, but sift through it down to the Health Hazard Data and you'll find what you need to know. You'll also find information on disposal.

The MSDA Search Page is located at: http://research.nwfsc.noaa.gov/msds.html.

Two books that cover the subject of art and crafts safety quite thoroughly are:

➤ *The Artist's Complete Health and Safety Guide* by Monona Rossol
➤ *Artist Beware* by Michael McCann and G. Watson

See Appendix A for more information about these books.

The Least You Need to Know

➤ Safe crafting takes a combination of common sense, information, and vigilance.
➤ Reading labels and following directions are probably the two most important safety precautions.
➤ Proper clothing and ventilation are essential to safety.
➤ Always protect sight and hearing while crafting.
➤ Not only do you need to watch out for your child, but pets can also be at risk from crafts materials and tools.

Chapter 5

How to Avoid Messes (and Clean them up Quick!)

In This Chapter

➤ Setting up your craft space to minimize cleanup

➤ Seven steps to avoiding messes

➤ Striking a balance between dirt and creativity

➤ A short course in stain removal

One of the greatest deterrents to getting into a crafts project is the prospect of making a mess. Of course, kids rarely think of this aspect, but you may be reluctant to get started on something if you think it's going to mean an hour of cleaning up afterward.

Well, take heart! With some forethought, preparation, common sense, and the information I'm going to provide here, you'll be ready to craft on a moment's notice completely undaunted, because you'll make less mess—and when you do, you'll know how to clean it up fast.

Let Your Craft Area Do the Work

One of the best ways to keep cleanup to a minimum (and this goes for all kinds of cleaning, including your regular housework) is to use materials that either don't get dirty easily, don't show dirt much, or, when they do get dirty, are easy to get clean again. You can actually design minimum maintenance into your crafting and living space.

When picking a place to pursue crafting with your child, you've got two options. You can choose a particular area BECAUSE it's low maintenance, or you can choose a convenient area and MAKE it low maintenance.

I'm fortunate to have a designated area in my home for doing crafts. Unfortunately, when we bought the house, that area was already carpeted, although the carpet is a good, sturdy, darker-colored industrial-type carpet with a very low pile.

Still, if I had the opportunity to design the room from scratch, I would have picked either ceramic tile or vinyl flooring, since it's easier to keep clean. When the carpet needs replacing, you can be assured it's not going to be with more carpet!

A Room of One's Own: Choosing Your Crafting Space

It's a good idea to have at least one place in the house where the kids don't have to worry about making a mess. This is where they (and you) can do crafts.

If your basement or attic is full of old junk, consider making it something more enriching to your family. If space is really at a premium, think about converting part of the garage. A spare bedroom that only gets used by guests once in a while is probably better used by your family. (You can always turn it into a guest room if you need to.)

> **Crafty Clues**
> Keep air vents and filters for exhaust fans (and heating and cooling systems) clean. This is all part of general ventilation system maintenance, but if your craft involves the creation of dust, you may have to clean or replace these filters more often. If you have some design leeway in your crafting area, install an exhaust fan if there isn't one. They can be installed in any room, not just a kitchen or bathroom.

Wherever you choose, make sure your crafting area has these essentials:

➤ *Adequate lighting.* It's easier to avoid accidents when you can see what you're doing!

➤ *Adequate ventilation.* Pick a place with windows and, ideally, an exhaust fan. To increase ventilation, you can add a window fan to either bring fresh air in or suck old air out, depending on which way the fan is pointed. Cross-ventilating with two windows is a great idea.

➤ *Fire safety.* Wherever you decide to do your crafting, make sure you have a smoke alarm and a fire extinguisher nearby.

➤ *Nearby storage space.* If you have a clearly defined, easy-to-reach space to store your crafting materials, you'll be much more likely to put them back when you're done with them.

➤ *A water source.* A regular sink will work, although a utility sink (a large, deep sink; also called a slop sink) is ideal if you'll be using dyes, pigments, or anything else that will stain. If you're planning on using a garage or basement area, see if you can install a sink.

➤ *Garbage disposal.* Have an adequate trash can or cans near your crafting area. Plastic cans are usually best, since they are lightweight, can't break, and are easy to clean. Use the trash can often and clean up as you go along.

➤ *Room to spread out.* Having enough room to work also helps avoid messes. How many times have you knocked something over because you were working in too close a space? If you can, pick a space that isn't in the middle of everything. If that's not possible, choose an area that's not in use every day; for example, part of the family room or den.

With your work area carefully chosen, we can move to the process of outfitting it for the easiest cleanup possible.

Your Crafting Table

Not only do you want efficient space to work, but while you're at it, why not make your work surface easy to clean?

If your work table is wood, which is porous and prone to scratching, think about covering it with some kind of plastic laminate (the shiny or almost-shiny kinds are easiest to clean) or several coats of polyurethane.

Consider putting a piece of glass over a non-scratch- or soil-resistant surface to create an easy-to-clean surface for crafting.

Remember, if you pick the kitchen table as your crafting area, you know you'll have to pick up and clean everything before the next meal.

Crafty Clues
For convenient crafting tables, invest in a couple of six- or eight-foot folding banquet/conference tables. (I bought mine at the wholesale club.) They're extra-sturdy and you'll find a zillion other uses for them.

Four Walls and a Floor

Once you've chosen a place for your crafting table, make sure the surfaces around it are easy to clean:

➤ Note how close your work surface is to the wall. If necessary, consider covering the wall with vinyl wall covering or laminate.

➤ Get rid of the carpet and put down some vinyl flooring if you can.

➤ A waxed floor is easier to keep clean and safer. Wax provides a protective shield and gives a smooth, even surface to sweep or mop. So if you're working on vinyl or linoleum flooring, wax it before you craft next time.

➤ If you're crafting in the garage, go to the extra trouble of sealing the floor with a commercial concrete sealer. Sealing concrete makes it much easier to keep clean.

➤ Avoid tracking stuff from the crafts area into the rest of the house by putting mats down on the floor in the doorway of the area. Make sure they're good-sized mats (the Astroturf-type mats seem to work the best) and shake and clean them often. Preventing dirt is one of the easiest ways of cleaning without cleaning!

Analyze the work surfaces and adjacent areas in your crafting area for cleanability and you'll undoubtedly find still more ways to make your crafting life easier.

Stashing Your Stuff

Another way to keep your crafts area clean is to encourage all the crafters in your family to put crafts tools and materials away when they're not in use:

Crafty Clues
Keep in mind that clutter makes everything harder to clean. The less clutter around, the less mess you'll make. If you are crafting in the kitchen, for example, look for ways to get things off the counters and stored away while you're working. (You may be so pleased with your clutter-free kitchen that you'll decide to keep it that way even after your crafting is done!) By keeping your work area uncluttered, you'll cut down your cleaning time.

➤ If you can, put up lots of shelving and places to hang tools. You can outline with a permanent marker or paint the tools as they hang on pegboard or plywood to help encourage everyone to put them back in the same place.

➤ Be sure you make storage for safe crafting materials low enough that your child can easily take things out and put them away. Make storage for unsafe or toxic items more difficult to get at (you may want to lock them away, if necessary).

➤ As much as possible, create a Crafts Control Center, one central place where crafting is done and supplies are stored. This helps keep the rest of the house clean, and encourages you to spend more time with your child crafting, since it's so easy to get started.

➤ Get in the "put away" habit. If you encourage your child to put all supplies and tools away after each crafting session, you'll both be more inclined to play together again, it'll take less time to get started, and things will stay in better condition. Plus, you'll be teaching your child some basic principles that will serve him throughout his life.

Pre-Crafting Cleanup Preparation

Now that you've got a neat, serviceable work area that's easy to maintain, you're ready to craft! Before you do, there are a few preparatory steps you can take to minimize cleanup even more.

Here are seven pre-crafting tips for minimizing cleanup:

➤ Keep all your crafts materials together and purchase them well in advance for the project you've selected. This not only saves time and helps maintain interest level, it also keeps you from tracking the mess from crafting to other parts of the house while you're looking for stuff.

➤ Clear up your crafting area. If you didn't tidy up after the last project (shame on you!), clean up now. Put away everything not related to the project at hand.

➤ Plan your project and make sure you have adequate work area for everyone. If you need to, put up a folding table.

➤ Cover any surfaces you can with butcher paper, newspaper, plastic drop cloths, or whatever will make cleanup easier.

> **Safety Signals**
> Be cautious when using paper in your craft area. You don't want lots of paper around if you're working with flame or heat, for example.

➤ Dress for the job. Consider having aprons or smocks for you and your child. Constructing these can be a crafts project in itself, or you can purchase some ready-made aprons and personalize them with embroidery or appliqués. Choose fabrics that are easy to clean and sturdy. I have a heavy denim apron I often use. It has deep pockets for holding small items or tools and it covers me from under my chin all the way down to my knees. Protect hair with a hat or bandanna. Tie back long hair.

➤ If you're going to need special cleaning solutions, solvents, or tools, gather those together and keep them nearby. Have cleaning supplies handy and your kids will be much more likely to clean up after themselves. If the crafts area isn't near where you usually store cleaning stuff, make up a caddy with the essentials and haul it with you or store it in the crafts room. If you'll need a vacuum to clean up, bring it to the area before you begin.

➤ Keep up with the dirt as you go along. As cleaning guru Don Aslett says, "Dirt by the inch is a cinch; by the yard, it's hard." Check out some of his many books in Appendix A.

When you're ready to quit, take some time to clean up. You'll need a place to wash hands (and whatever else) when you're done. Keep some disposable towels at the sink to save your linens. Clean your tools and work surfaces for the next time, too.

Vacuum if you need to, making sure you have room in the vacuum bag to pick up everything. If you fill up the bag, replace it for next time. Do a floor patrol first to pick up anything that shouldn't go through the vacuum, such as nails or buttons.

Dirt Versus Dash

All this talk about keeping things clean isn't meant to make you or you child obsessive-compulsive...or even uptight. Once you have your crafting area carved out and have made it as maintenance-free as possible, the idea is to not worry about making some mess.

Messes are healthy. Messes are part of the creative process. Some of us like to craft BECAUSE we like making messes!

If your child isn't allowed to make a mess, she'll be less likely to find her own creative spark. The idea here is to make controlled messes and to keep them in one centralized, easy-to-maintain area.

So, by all means, make things easy on yourself by keeping your crafting areas neat and tidy. Definitely teach your child how to clean up her own messes. But do strike a balance between neatness and abandon.

Out, Out, Damned Spot!

Inevitably, there will be those times when all your best efforts will fail and someone will create a mess that needs special attention.

If you're armed with the right tools and the know-how, these mishaps can be taken in stride. It reminds me of the advertisement a few years back for the spray carpet cleaner where the kid spills grape juice on his mom's white carpet and she smiles, completely relaxed, and says "No problem." Well, I'm not sure it's quite that easy, but having a few dirt-killing weapons in your home arsenal, plus knowing what to use when, sure can give you a greater sense of confidence AND perhaps lengthen your fuse when it comes to the accidents created by other crafters in the family.

First, let's take a look at some of the most common crafting messes. Then we can talk about how to remove them.

The materials you'll most likely have to pick up, wipe up, scrape off, or get out of fabric or carpet are:

➤ Paper, wood, metal, or glass scraps

➤ Fabric and thread scraps

➤ Glue

➤ Paint

➤ Marker

➤ Ink

➤ Crayon

➤ Colored pencil

➤ Dye

➤ Wood and other dust

Immediately you can see why vinyl flooring would be easier to clean than carpet, especially when it comes to just picking up various scraps and dust. Materials like glue, paint, or marker create soil or a stain, however, on most any surface, and need to be removed.

The secret to removal of any kind of spill or stain is to get it when it's fresh, so act quickly. The longer the stain has had to penetrate or dry, the harder it will be to get off. (Just one more argument for having cleaning supplies nearby or toting your cleaning caddy to wherever you're crafting.) You'll want to remove as much as you can, as fast as you can, then apply the right cleaning agent and get up the rest.

But what if you don't see a stain right away and it has time to penetrate, dry, or harden? Fear not. Chances are there's a way to get it out.

These are the five steps to removing any kind of soil or stain:

1. *Identify.* You'll need to know what the stain is, and how long it's been there.

2. *Remove.* Get up whatever you can by blotting the stain with a dry, white absorbent cloth or white paper towels. Don't scrub! If the staining material is a semi-solid, scrape up what you can with a spoon or a spatula. If it's a solid, break it up if you can and vacuum up whatever's loose.

3. *Apply.* Put the right cleaning agent to work on the stain. The right one may be something as simple as water or as powerful as an industrial cleaner or solvent. Generally, you'll want to use the gentlest cleanser you can to do the job. Not sure which one to use? I'll give you some resources a little later in this chapter to help you find the right one.

4. *Wait.* Give the cleaner time to work. It'll give you more of what you paid for and save you some elbow grease. If the stain is on a hard surface, you may need to rub the cleaner in a bit. If the stain is in carpet, don't scrub or rub it in.

5. *Remove.* You want to get up both the dirt and the cleaner. This may mean blotting, wiping, flushing, rinsing, or sucking it up with an extractor or vacuum. You'll want to get all the cleaning solution up as well, since leaving it in a surface like carpet may mean the area will get dirty again more quickly.

Remember, you may have to repeat these steps several times before the stain actually comes out. Be patient and keep doing it as long as you're getting some results.

Stain Kit

It's a good idea to put together your own spot removal kit and have it handy when you are crafting. A plastic container or caddy is good for this. I have mine, along with my stain removal manual, in the laundry room cabinet. Be aware that there's no one stain remover that will work on every kind of stain, so you'll want to have a variety of things on hand. Here's what I have in mine:

➤ Acetone

➤ Ammonia

➤ Baking soda

➤ Bleach

➤ Fels-Naptha soap (a heavy duty laundry bar soap ideal for prewash spot treatments made by the Dial Corp.)

➤ Dawn dishwashing detergent (this works especially well on grease or oil stains)

➤ A toothbrush

➤ Clean cloths

➤ Dry-cleaning solution/spot remover

➤ Enzyme solution (there are several on the market; I buy mine at a janitorial supply store)

➤ Stain stick

➤ Biz pre-soak

➤ Zud rust remover

➤ Sponges

➤ Turpentine

➤ White vinegar

➤ Rit color remover

If you're handling certain types of crafts materials on a regular basis and know there's a particular solvent or other substance you need to remove any stains, keep some on hand in your crafts area.

Hopefully, if you carefully plan the location and design of your crafts area, and if you take preventative measures before you craft, you'll have very little use for your stain removal arsenal, but it's good to know it's there—just in case.

What's Your Stain?

Although I don't have space here to cover all the possible messes you might have to clean, I've listed a few key stains that might commonly come up when you craft:

➤ *Glues.* Some glues dissolve in water or can simply be peeled off (like rubber cement). Epoxies and resins are more difficult to remove. Look on the label for instructions on which solvent to use. Sometimes hardening the glue with ice first (or putting the stained material in the freezer, if it's clothing, for example) will make it easier to peel or scrape the glue off.

➤ *Paint.* You'll first need to know if the paint is oil-based or latex. The label may tell you the procedure to get stains out, so read it carefully. Your cleaning method will also depend on whether the paint is still wet or has dried. If oil-based and wet, flush the stain with mineral spirits. If latex and wet, flush the stain with a detergent solution. If dry, first soften the stain with lacquer thinner or paint stripper, then use the appropriate solvent.

➤ *Ball-point ink.* Sponge it first with a detergent solution and rinse. Saturate with cheap hair spray and blot. Try (in this order) alcohol, acetone or non-oily nail polish remover, and fabric-safe bleach. I've also found that soaking ink-stained fabric in skim milk can take the stain out of some fabrics.

➤ *Oil.* Sprinkle cornmeal or fuller's earth (available from your local pharmacy) to absorb the oil first, then sponge the stain with dry-cleaning fluid. If the stain isn't completely gone, sponge it with a detergent solution and then rinse.

➤ *Crayon or candle wax.* Scrape off as much as you can with a scraper or knife first. First try freezing or putting ice on the stain to help harden it and make it easier to take off. If that doesn't work, put a clean white cloth (a cloth diaper works well) over the area and iron it with a warm iron. This will melt the wax and force it into the cloth. If that doesn't take everything out, repeat the procedure and then finish up with some dry-cleaning fluid.

Crafty Clues
Remember to always test any stain removal method on an inconspicuous place, or better yet, on a sample of the fabric or surface. That's why it's a great idea to keep scraps of drapery or upholstery fabric, extra tile or pieces of flooring, and carpet remnants.

Safety Signals
When cleaning up hazardous materials like paint removers and solvents, use old newspaper and put outdoors where the liquid will evaporate more quickly. Dispose of the papers in a metal container with a secure lid. Contact your local sanitation department or waste disposal contractor for information on disposing of hazardous materials.

There's a real science to removing dirt and stains, and that's who you need to turn to when you've got a tough one—the scientists! Get yourself a good stain removal guide, like Don Aslett's *Stainbuster's Bible* (for details, see Appendix A), or turn to one of the many Web sites with detailed advice on how to remove specific stains:

➤ The Tide Web site (www.tide.com) has something called The Tide Stain Detective for fabrics. You select from a list of stain types and match that with the type of fabric and whether it's colored or white.

➤ The Spot Remover Computer (www.carpet-rug.com) is for carpet stains and is maintained by The Carpet and Rug Institute.

Crafty Clues
Binney & Smith, the Crayola people, have special tips for getting stains caused by just about any of their products out of any surface. You match up the product with the surface and it gives you the method to use. Check out their Web site at www.crayola.com/tips/.

➤ There are several Cooperative Extension Services (CESs) that have stain removal information available in their publications or on their Web sites. You may want to check with your local CES. You can also try the Mississippi State University CES at: www.ces.msstate.edu/pubs/pub/400.htm.

➤ If your stain is caused by a specific brand-name product, sometimes contacting the manufacturer is the only way to go. Or you may want to work the other way around and contact the manufacturer of the material you're trying to remove the stain from.

➤ Many manufacturers of home building, decorating, and arts and crafts materials also have Web sites, and you may be able to contact them online.

Sometimes the staff at your local home improvement store can help, since they have data sheets with information on some of the materials they sell. They may at least be able to help you with a contact.

If you don't have access to a computer, you can write or call the manufacturer. Most are more than willing to help. Sometimes the information you need is actually on the product label, so read it carefully.

The Least You Need to Know

➤ With some forethought, you can choose or design a space for crafting that's easy to keep clean.

➤ There are specific steps you can take before you begin a project that will minimize the need for cleanup.

➤ You'll need to strike a balance between neatness and the mess that sometimes evolves out of the creative process.

➤ Knowing the right procedures to remove stains, acting quickly, and having the right cleaning tools and products on hand will help keep lasting crafting messes to a minimum.

Part 2
The Nine Basic Crafting Materials: Creating Your Crafting Repertoire

You've got the right mindset, you know what tools you need, you understand the importance of having a good place to work, and you know how to get the glue out of the carpet (sort of). Now you're ready to make something.

The next nine chapters will give you an overview of the many crafts you can get your hands into, organized by crafting materials: paper, fabric and fiber, beads, leather, wood, metal, clay, plastic, and glass. Each individual material could take a lifetime to explore, so don't be overwhelmed. Just get ready to play with whatever strikes your fancy.

The chapters in this part offer a general introduction to each crafting material; I heartily encourage you to further explore the ones that most appeal to your child and to you. Not only are these crafts fun to do, but each crafting technique presented here has a rich and diverse history. Give yourselves time to learn more about their context as well as their content. Consider doing some extra reading and embarking on some of the field trips I've recommended. And, most of all, have fun!

Chapter 6

Paper Power

In This Chapter

➤ History, uses, and tools for working with paper

➤ The art of origami

➤ Paper cutting and stamping

➤ Designing and creating scrapbooks

➤ Paper making for beginners

Paper is easy to take for granted. We read from it, blow our noses with it, wipe up spills with it, make money out of it, write lists on it, and on and on. It's so plentiful and comes in so many forms, it's not surprising that we sometimes forget how important it is.

Paper crafts make us aware of some of the characteristics and forms of paper. Paper crafts are also generally easy for beginners, relatively inexpensive, and capable of producing stunning results.

Bonding Experiences

If you're working with a younger child, take a moment to walk around the house and point out all the different types of paper and paper products you both can find. Look at this paper as possible crafts material as well. You can talk about such things as shapes, thickness, form, texture, color, and other characteristics. Consider a field trip to a large paper store to further expand the child's appreciation of the variety available. If you live in a community where there's a paper mill, arrange a visit for an older child. Read more about the history of paper by checking the books listed in Appendix A.

Paper Particulars

Some of the kinds of paper you might use for crafting include:

➤ Acid-free paper

➤ Cardboard and corrugated cardboard

➤ Crepe paper

➤ Construction paper

➤ Tissue paper

➤ Newspaper

➤ Origami papers

➤ Gift-wrap paper

➤ Brown paper bags

➤ Posterboard

➤ Blotting paper

➤ Parchment paper

➤ Sketching paper

➤ Sticker paper

➤ Bond paper

➤ Paper lace

➤ Paper ribbon

➤ Handmade paper

Handiwords
Paper is a sheet of interlaced fibers (usually cellulose fibers from plants, but sometimes rags or other fibrous materials are used) formed by making the fibers into a pulp and then causing them to felt or mat to form a solid surface.

And these are just a few of the types of paper used in crafting. As you explore the world of paper craft, you're sure to find many more.

A Brief History of Paper

Although it's not absolutely certain, historians generally believe that paper was invented in A.D. 105 by a Chinese court official named Cai Lun. It was kept secret for 500 years before it spread to Japan and the Arabic world. The first paper ever, though, was most likely made by wasps. We now call them "paper wasps" for the building material they use in their nests, which is chewed pulp mixed with saliva and fashioned into a sturdy home.

The first mechanical paper-making process was invented in France by Nicolas Louis Robert in 1798; yet it wasn't until the 19th century that the world came to know and use manufactured paper. Today we have a variety and quality of paper that is unsurpassed.

Tools for Working with Paper

Some of the obvious tools you'll want to have around for crafting with paper are pens, pencils, scissors, and glue. But there are some other things you might want to add to your list: Paper punches, glitter, stickers, string, paper clips, paper fasteners, wire, and possibly a paper cutter (like the ones you used in school or at the office). Even a blender or food processor could be part of your paper crafting tool kit, especially if you decide to try making handmade paper.

A word about scissors: It is not always a good idea to use one pair of scissors for every job. Having a good pair of scissors exclusively for paper projects makes sense, especially when you get into more detailed activities such as fancy paper cutting. Cutting paper dulls scissors and makes them less than ideal for cutting other things such as fabric.

If you're serious about paper craft, you'll want to invest in a pair of hot-drop-forged steel scissors. These are scissors especially made for cutting sheets of paper, with extra-long blades. Fancy paper cutting (or *scherenschnitte*, as it's called) requires much smaller, more accurate scissors. Make sure whatever you buy feels comfortable in your hand. In addition to a good pair of scissors, you may want a craft or utility knife and/or a rotary cutter, depending on what you're planning to do.

I have a collection of specialty scissors. Each cuts with a different pattern and is used for creating decorative edges. These are especially useful for finishing off projects and creating scrapbooks and collages. I picked mine up at a wholesale club for a very reasonable price.

Remember to clean scissors after each use and periodically oil and sharpen them. Store them in the protective sheath they came in or hang them up on a nail or hook.

Safety Signals
Be sure to teach children how to handle scissors. I don't need to point out their dangers, but when approached with good sense and respect, even a young child can use them. Of course, you'll want to use the duller, blunt children's scissors when you're working with a very young child, but when a child's motor skills reach a certain level, you can train him or her to safely work with fairly sharp instruments.

Handiwords
Origami is the Japanese art of paper folding to form flowers, animal figures, and other interesting shapes.

From Birds to Airplanes: Come Into the Fold

One of the simplest, most entertaining, and least messy forms of paper craft is paper folding. This craft is known as *origami* in Japan, where it has been an art form for hundreds of years. The word itself, however, comes from two Chinese characters: *ori*, meaning "folding," and *kami*, meaning "paper."

Bonding Experiences

To the Japanese, origami is more than just an entertaining pastime. It has deep spiritual meaning. The various animals and other constructions that are made are symbolic. An origami crane, for instance, is a symbol of long life. A frog is symbolic of fertility and love. Research the deeper meanings of origami forms in the Japanese culture. Together, think of appropriate ways to include them in gifts, celebrations, and decorations.

There is a special paper you can buy for origami (see Appendix A), but you can substitute other common papers you might have on hand. The traditional paper used for origami is brightly colored on one side and white on the other. Gift wrap often has a pattern or solid color on one side only, so it makes a nice pinch-hitter. It's great for origami because it makes a nice, crisp edge. And usually, the cheaper the wrap, the thinner the paper, and the crisper the edge. So look for inexpensive wrapping paper in discount stores and stock up! Also try shelf paper, brown wrapping paper, or newspaper (which works great for a folded paper hat). Even waxed paper is interesting for some projects.

With most origami projects you will need to begin with a square. The size of your square will depend on what you want the final project to look like and how manageable you want it to be.

To make a square out of any piece of paper, follow this simple procedure:

1. Fold the upper corner of the rectangle over and down until it meets the opposite edge.

2. Cut off the excess from the bottom so that the two bottom edges are even.

3. Unfold and you have a perfect square.

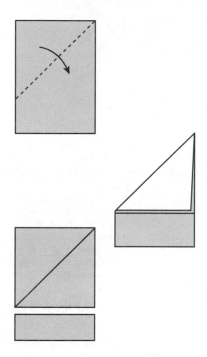

How to make a perfect paper square.

Origami is the ultimate traveling craft. No glue or scissors are needed—just paper squares and a hard surface to work on. It's also a great thing to do when confined in bed. Origami makes entertaining others or occupying yourself on a moment's notice a breeze, and it's always a big hit with small children. It should be required learning for all parents-to-be, baby-sitters, teachers, and grandparents!

The great escape artist and magician, Harry Houdini, was an avid paper folder and master of the craft. Other famous people who were into origami include Lewis Carroll, Leonardo da Vinci, and M.C. Escher. In the Orient, Spain, and Argentina, there are actually schools of origami and several countries have origami societies.

The paper cup project (see the next page) is one of several origami projects children enjoy, since they love containers to put things in.

Many other simple projects are included in *Origami for Beginners: The Creative World of Paperfolding* by Florence Temko.

Project: Paper Cup

Level: Easy

Age: 5 and up

Materials needed: Paper

Remember: Unless your cup is made from plastic- or wax-coated paper, liquid will seep through after a while, so drink quickly!

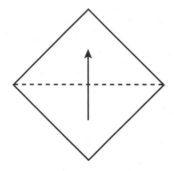

1. Turn paper square so it looks like a diamond and fold bottom point up to top point.

2. Fold the left pointed flap toward the right and right pointed flap toward the left.

3. At the top, fold the front pointed flap down and the back flap down behind the cup.

4. Squeeze the cup open and it's ready to hold anything from nuts or candy to cold liquids if made from fairly heavy paper.

Teaching Origami

What's the best way to teach origami to children? Here are some tips for making it a fun experience for you and them:

➤ Before making a figure, practice it several times until it comes out right every time. There's no better way to lose a kid's attention than to be looking back and forth at instructions while trying to teach.

➤ If possible, have the child sit next to you. If you're working with several children, stand in front of them, make the fold, and then turn around and hold it up so it's facing the same way they are.

➤ For best results, make sure you and the child are working on a fairly large, flat surface.

➤ Try teaching the process one fold at a time. You do a fold, then watch as the child copies you. You may want to do one all the way through first, then break it down step by step.

➤ Starting from a larger square is easier for younger children. Older children can be challenged more by working in increasingly smaller squares.

➤ Use newspaper for making a prototype yourself. Children like this, too, because they'll know it's "just for practice." Save a good sheet of paper for the second or third go-round.

➤ Consider contacting your local newspaper for some newspaper roll ends. That would give you some really BIG pieces of paper. Newsprint's a great, economical craft material.

Bonding Experiences

If origami really captures your child's fancy, you may want to get a membership in ORIGAMI USA (OUSA). This not-for-profit, educational arts organization has its home office at the Museum of Natural History in New York City.

Send a stamped, self-addressed envelope to Origami USA, 15 West 77th Street, New York, NY 10024-5192, (212) 769-5635, FAX (212) 769-5668. Membership benefits include a subscription to OUSA's newsletter, mailings, discounts on materials and books from the supply center, priority for convention and special sessions, and lower rates for classes and publications. The newsletter includes information on numerous origami organizations, as well as articles and diagrams for models.

Air-Craft: Paper Airplanes

Another popular form of paper folding is making paper airplanes. These lend themselves to outdoor fun, as well as all forms of decoration. Simpler airplanes only require folding, but more sophisticated versions can be cut in various ways to change their flight worthiness and quality of flight.

Bonding Experiences

One of the easiest ways to learn about flying and aerodynamics is by making and flying paper airplanes. You can make several different types of planes and rate how well they fly. See if you can figure out what makes one better than the next. Is it the size? The paper? The design? Try improving a particular design by bending the wings or trying different weighting techniques. Experiment! Then go for a glider ride!

Project: The Dart

Level: Easy

Age: 6 and up

Materials needed: Paper, tape

Here's how to make a simple paper airplane, known as The Dart. (Some people say this paper airplane originated at Dartmouth University to illustrate the "What goes up must come down" principle relative to the stock market):

Directions:

1. Start with an 8^1/$_2$ × 11-inch sheet of typing or printer paper. (You can experiment with heavier or lighter papers if you like.)
2. Fold the sheet in half lengthwise and make a sharp crease.
3. Unfold and crease corners A and B downward, as shown in the diagram, so the edges of the paper meet in the center.
4. Now fold corners C and D downward to meet the center line. Turn the plane over and fold along the dotted lines on side F.
5. Fold corners E and F up or down to make the plane fly more steady. See which works best.
6. Using tape, fasten the body of the plane together about a third of the way from the nose.

Project: Continued

7. Make a test flight.
8. Decorate!

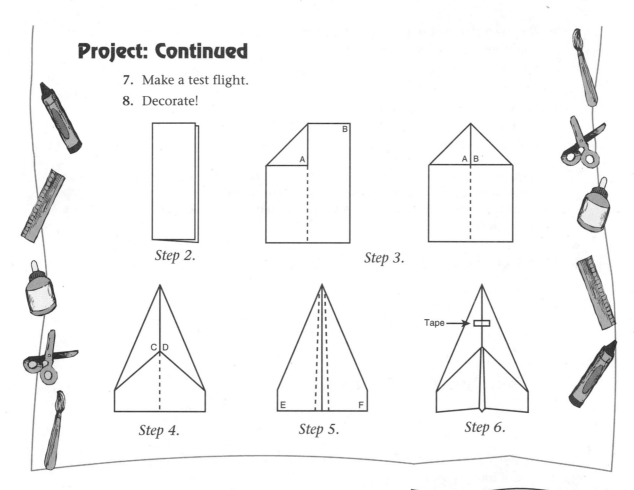

Step 2.

Step 3.

Step 4.

Step 5.

Step 6.

Now that you're an experienced paper airplane builder, you'll want to try more sophisticated models. There are lots of great books about paper airplane building (see Appendix A), and even a couple of computer programs that teach the basics and print out patterns. Try The Greatest Paper Airplanes software from Kitty Hawk (for more information, see Appendix A). It uses animation and illustration, and allows you to print out patterns, in color, on your printer.

Whether you're making a simple aircraft or one fit for the upper atmosphere, here are some tips for making better paper airplanes:

➤ Use light to medium paper. Heavier paper is appropriate for some types of paper airplanes, but it's hard for a beginner to fold.

Safety Signals
Even though these airplanes are made out of paper, they can actually cause injury if handled carelessly. So don't throw them at anyone, give a warning that an airplane is coming (it can startle someone and cause an accident), and count on their flight path being unpredictable.

➤ Accuracy counts. Make folds carefully and crease them with a fingernail or ruler. You want them crisp and precise.

➤ The first fold is especially important. It needs to be even or your plane will be off balance.

➤ Practice makes perfect. Make the same plane design several times. After you've mastered the basic procedure, try it with different weights of paper and experiment with slight variations.

From here, anything's possible. Once you've become a master paper airplane engineer, you may want to branch out into other forms of construction with paper, such as paper scale modeling (there are some sources for preprinted paper scale models in Appendix A) and kite building.

Teach Your Kid to Be a First-Class Cutup

Another paper craft with endless variations that's easily adapted to various ages and abilities is fancy paper cutting. You probably remember making snowflakes in school. Forgot how? Well, let's start with a snowflake review and go on from there.

Project: So, You're Flaky!

Level: Easy

Age: 5 and up

Materials needed: White paper (fairly sturdy, but not too thick). Computer paper or white bond will be just fine.

Directions:

1. Take a square of white paper (to turn a rectangle into a square, see "From Birds to Airplanes: Come Into the Fold," earlier in the chapter).

2. Fold in half. Fold in half again.

3. Now fold in half on the diagonal and keep going until you have a small triangle. Don't make it so thick you can't cut into it, though.

4. Make a variety of cuts in different shapes and sizes on all sides (angular cuts are usually easiest for smaller fingers). If you have interesting paper punches, you can try those, too.

5. Don't be afraid to cut away portions and make some deep cuts. Experiment and see what works best.

6. Add some silver glitter with some clear-drying craft glue if you like.

Kids can decorate a shelf in their room or the mantel in the family room. (This is an especially nice idea for open cabinets or bookshelves.) Kids love to decorate; this one's sure to please them.

Okay, now that you've had your kindergarten nostalgia experience and gotten in touch with your inner child, you're ready for another project.

Project: Shelf Borders

Level: Easy

Age: 5 and up

Materials needed: Paper (freezer paper, butcher paper, or newspaper), scissors

Directions:

1. Pick out some paper you'd like to use for a shelf border. White paper (try freezer paper or butcher's paper that you can get in huge rolls at a wholesale club) can be a great holiday decoration. You can also use plain old newspaper—kids especially like the comics section—or even brown paper bags. For now, let's start with newspaper for the first time around.

2. Fold a double sheet of newspaper in half horizontally, then keep folding it in half vertically as many times as you can and still cut comfortably. Be sure to cut on the fold, not on the open side or in the middle.

3. Try cuts similar to what you did on the snowflake, or you might attempt diamonds, hearts, squares, stars, or whatever you can dream up. The paper punches with shapes work well here.

4. When you think you've got it well snipped, open it up and cut the sheet in half. This gives you two shelf liners.

For more ideas for paper cutting, look into the German craft of *scherenschnitte* and the Victorian craft of *cutting silhouettes.*

Stamping and Scrapbooking

Rubber stamping has become one of the most popular hobbies in America. It's also one of the easiest of paper crafts, yielding some of the most fabulous results with the least effort. All you need to start is a couple of rubber stamps in shapes or motifs you like, a stamp pad, and a sheet of paper.

From there you can graduate to coloring in your stamped images once they've dried or using embossing powders, which give the image a raised effect. If you have artistic talent, you can cut your own stamps and mount them, or draw an image and have one of several companies make a rubber stamp for you.

One of the great things about rubber stamps and kids is they're infinitely adaptable to any age. A two-year-old can slap a rubber stamp onto a stamp pad and then onto a piece of paper. Magic! Yet an older child can embellish rubber-stamped projects to his heart's content.

Handiwords

Scrapbooking is the craft of putting photos and other momentos into albums in creative and meaningful ways.

Crafty Clues

There are lots of fun specialty scrapbooking products on the market, but frugal crafters can make fabulous albums using what's at hand. Cut up magazines and use various elements as embellishments. Think creatively…how about *Victoria* magazine for nostalgic images? Old crafts magazines yield some great usable clips, too. And if you have a computer, you can generate images and decorative lettering.

In Appendix A, I've listed several mail-order companies that have a good selection of rubber stamps and stamping supplies, although you're likely to find these items in your local crafts store. In some areas there are stores completely devoted to rubber stamping and its crafts cousin, *scrapbooking.*

Well into the 1940s, children and adults loved making scrapbooks. They included photos, postcards, pressed flowers, and other memorabilia in their books.

Today the scrapbook has really come of age. Called *memory books* or *memory albums*, today's scrapbooks don't look like the old versions with black paper, photo corners, and pictures all in a row. The new crop is embellished with stickers, stencils, paper frames, rubber stamps, embossing, special papers, pop-ups, and specially cropped photos.

The basic materials you'll need to make a memory book are:

➤ An album (sources for these are in Appendix A)

➤ Scissors, including specialty edging scissors if you have them

➤ A ruler

➤ Pen markers in an assortment of point types and sizes

➤ Colored paper

➤ Tape

➤ Glue

In addition, you might want to add decorative punches, decorative scissors, stickers, stencils, photo templates, paper frames, rubber stamps, embossing powders, clip art, computer-generated type, and just about anything else you can lay flat on a page and use to embellish a layout. Think, too, about adding sayings, poems, or phrases to particular pages. You can even turn certain entries into an expanded narrative and make more of a journal page.

You'll also want to select a material in which to cover your album. In their folder, *Memory Albums*, Suzanne McNeill and Lani Stiles show two cover versions. For more information, write or call Design Originals, 2425 Cullen St., Fort Worth, TX 76107, (817) 877-0067. I've also added a list of publications about rubber stamping and memory books in Appendix A.

Scrapbooking has lots of benefits for both kids and adults:

➤ It adds meaning to photos.

➤ It allows you to pare down to just a few of the best photos and display them, rather than keeping boxes of so-so snapshots that nobody ever looks at.

➤ It brings out the creative side of just about anyone.

Bonding Experiences

Use making a memory book as an opportunity to take a trip down memory lane. Maybe you could get out your child's baby pictures and make a ME album, reliving your favorite memories of his or her childhood.

Get Out the Blender and Make Some Paper!

Did you know you can make your own paper? It's easy, fun, and you get to use the blender for something other than milkshakes.

Handmade paper is stronger than many commercially made papers. It contains no chemicals or acid sizings, so it's gentle on things you might want to mount on it and it lasts longer. Do-it-yourself paper making is a nice complement to making memory books, too! And it's a great way to recycle scraps.

Always be alert when children are using a blender or food processor. You may want to do this part yourself if you are working with very young children. Don't put soggy paper pulp down the drain or you'll stop up the sink! Put it in a strainer, get out all the water, and then throw it away. Or you can add it to a compost pile, if you've got one.

Handiwords
A *mold* is a frame covered with mesh. It can be nylon or metal screening. A *deckle* is an open frame that sits on top of the mold, used to make paper edges straight and flat after pulp is spread on the mold.

Project: Paper Making

Level: Medium

Age: 5 and up with an adult using the blender or food processor

Materials needed:

    Paper scraps (computer paper and used envelopes work well)

    Water

    Large bowl

    Blender or food processor (clean it thoroughly after use)

    Large plastic dishpan

    Old newspapers

    Large spoon (wooden, plastic, or metal)

    Large sponge

    Mold and a deckle (you might want to buy them at a crafts store, but you can make your own)

    Water-resistant boards (Formica works well)

Directions:

1. Cover your work area with butcher's paper, plastic, or newspapers. Protect the floor…it's going to get wet!

2. Assemble all your materials. You'll want your mold, deckle, dishpan, and boards all in a row, so choose a place to work where you've got plenty of counter space or flat work surface.

3. Tear up scraps of paper into two- or three-inch pieces and soak them in water in a large bowl. Let them soak until the paper is good and soggy. Overnight is good, but it doesn't have to be that long.

4. Put warm water in the blender until it's about $1/2$ to $2/3$ full. Add some paper and blend on pulse or just turn on and off. If your blender seems to be straining, remove some paper or add more water. Blend until fairly uniform.

Project: Continued

5. Pour the mixture into the dishpan and repeat blending until the dishpan is about half full. Add enough water to fill $^3/_4$ of the dishpan. The more water you have relative to the paper pulp, the lighter the finished paper will be.

6. Stir the mixture with a spoon until the pulp is suspended in the water fairly evenly.

7. Put the deckle on top of the mold with the screen side up. Hold together tightly.

8. With a smooth motion, stand in front of the dishpan and hold the mold and deckle with your arms out as if it were a mirror in front of you. Scoop the mold and deckle into the mixture in one motion and turn them until they're horizontal while in the mixture. Lift the mold and deckle slowly out of the mixture and let the water drain out. Tip to each corner to get the rest of the water out. Put the mold and deckle down and remove the deckle, disturbing your paper sheet as little as possible. Put the deckle aside.

9. The next step is called *couching*. This is the process of transferring the wet paper sheet from the mold onto something absorbent, like a layer of newspaper with paper towels on top. (Later, if you get more into paper making, you'll want to use felt or old wool blankets.) Lay your absorbent material on one of your boards. Quickly turn over the mold onto the covered board. You can use a sponge to dab the back of the mold and remove any remaining water. Carefully peel one edge of the mold and pull it away. Your first paper sheet will be laying on your board. You did it!

10. To make more sheets, just start another layer of absorbent material in another place and repeat the process.

11. You can press your sheets between boards, which makes a flatter sheet and speeds the drying process, or let it air-dry, which gives it a more ripply effect. It'll take four hours or more for the paper to dry. Leave the sheets overnight and they'll be dry in the morning! When it feels dry to the touch, carefully peel the paper towels from your paper sheets.

For more interesting paper, you can add bits of colored paper to the blender when you first begin or add bits of confetti, thread, herb flakes, flowers, or grasses to the pulp while it's in the dishpan. Food coloring added in small amounts while the mixture's in the blender makes a good coloring method as well. Experiment!

Handiwords
In paper making, the process of transferring a wet paper sheet from a mold onto something absorbent is called *couching*.

Paper making is a great activity to do outdoors. One mother I met online uses a small kiddie pool as her mixing tub—there's no need to worry about making a mess of the kitchen!

For more information, Aunt Annie's Craft Page (http://auntannie.com/) is a great Web site that has a clear, detailed section on paper making, plus instructions on how to make your own deckle and mold.

The Least You Need to Know

➤ Paper folding is rewarding for beginners and advanced crafters, easy to take along on a trip, and always entertaining.

➤ Making paper airplanes is a fun outdoor activity and a good way to learn about simple aerodynamics.

➤ Rubber stamping is adaptable to even the youngest child and has many variations to make it more challenging for older children and adults.

➤ Memory albums take rubber stamping and paper craft to new heights and are a creative means of displaying your photographs and memorabilia in a meaningful way.

➤ With a blender and a few simple tools, you can make your own paper at home.

Chapter 7

Golden Threads: Crafts with Fiber and Fabric

In This Chapter

➤ Learn to weave using a simple handmade loom

➤ Sewing for beginners

➤ Basic embroidery and counted cross-stitch

➤ Quilting, crazy and otherwise

➤ Tie dyeing in your backyard

You'd give your kids the shirt off your back, right? Better yet, why not teach them how to make one? A shirt, that is. Or any other woven accessory or garment.

In this chapter, you'll get acquainted with the fabric of life, from the thread up. You'll learn to weave, sew, embellish, and then cut your creations up into pieces and put them back together again. Intrigued? Well, you're going to get warped, weave around, and then go crazy, all in the next few pages.

Get the World on a String

Start with a thread or a string, perhaps. What can you make with it? A loop. A bow. Weave it and you've got some cloth. Now there's no stopping you. You can start with making a beanbag and work up to anything at all. A magnificent robe or a wedding dress fit for a queen. Such is the power of a thread.

Children can learn any number of weaving, sewing, or needlework crafts, from the earliest ages, and these skills can provide them with a lifetime of enjoyment. Besides, everyone needs to know how to put on a button or put up a hem.

One of the most basic weaving projects you can do with a child is the God's Eye.

Project: God's Eye

Level: Easy

Age: 5 and up

Materials needed: Two popsicle sticks (or two straight twigs approximately the same size and thickness that have been stripped of any protrusions), scraps of yarn at least 12 inches in length

Directions:

1. Glue the two popsicle sticks together at the center in a cross.
2. Starting at the center, take one color of yarn and wrap it over (in front of) one stick and around the back and over to the next stick.

How to begin weaving a God's Eye.

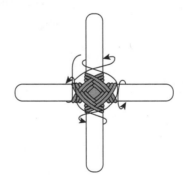

3. Repeat all the way around, making each pass above the last. Wrap around and around until you've used up one color.
4. Tie the next color yarn onto the first one with a tight knot and repeat the process until you've used several colors and filled up most of the cross shape.
5. End by tying a knot around the last stick. Make a loop with one piece of yarn and tie it or glue it to your God's Eye. Hang it up.

With a young child, work with fairly bulky yarn and fatter twigs. Older children enjoy working with finer materials. Try making one with embroidery floss and two toothpicks for a lovely Christmas ornament or pendant.

To learn more about making God's Eyes, which are also an introduction to lashings done in basketry, consult the book *New Lashings and Improvements to Old Favorites*. (See Appendix A for information.)

Dream Weaver

If you've ever braided a pigtail, you can learn to weave. And you don't need an expensive loom to make beautiful woven objects.

To get the idea of what it's like to weave fabric or fiber, pick up a potholder loom kit from a discount store, toy store, or yard sale. They usually come with a metal square with evenly spaced prongs and some stretchy fabric loops. Extra loops can be purchased separately.

If you're feeling ambitious, you can make a loom with a square frame and some nails. Just make sure you space the nails evenly in each direction (measure them out) and that they match up from side to side. Also be careful to make the loom no larger than the loops can stretch.

A simple loom can be made from inexpensive materials. I mean, how can you get more inexpensive than a discarded Styrofoam meat or vegetable produce tray?

Bet You Didn't Know
Weaving is believed to be the oldest craft next to toolmaking, and the intricacy of some of the earliest woven textiles are still the envy of the most accomplished modern-day weavers.

Handiwords
In weaving, *warp threads* are threads that run vertically, on which the weaving is worked. *Weft threads* run horizontally over and under the warp.

A *vertical slit* is a method of adding more than one color area by weaving from opposites edges toward each other, meeting and then returning to the starting point.

Project: Tray Weavings

Level: Medium

Age: 7 and up

Materials needed: Tracing paper, a pencil, a large-eyed needle, scissors, a ruler, a single-edged razor blade or utility knife, masking tape, yarn scraps in different weights, styrofoam produce trays, any size, thin white cord or string

This project can take several different forms, using different weaving techniques. I'll show you two, the tapestry weave and the spiral weave. As you learn more about weaving, you may want to try others.

continues

Project: Continued

Directions:

1. First you need to create the loom. Taking the razor blade or utility knife, cut out an opening in the Styrofoam tray, leaving a "frame" of Styrofoam around the opening.

2. Using the ruler, mark dots about $3/8$ of an inch from the inside edge and $1/8$ of an inch apart. You need to have an uneven number of dots and the dots need to have corresponding dots across from them in the same position on the opposite side.

3. Thread the needle with a long piece of white cord, which will become your *warp (vertical) threads*. Knot the end of the cord. Insert the needle from back to front at the first dot and bring it across the loom to the opposite dot. Then insert the needle from front to back. Come up through the back of the dot next to the one you just came through and bring the cord back across to the opposite dot (next to the first one you went through). Repeat this procedure until you've used all the dots. The warp threads should be taut, but not so tight that you pull the frame out of shape or begin to pull through the Styrofoam. Knot the end in back.

4. To begin weaving a tapestry weave, start on one side going across the warp threads. Go under and over each warp thread. When going back in the other direction with the same thread, alternate the warp thread as you go under and over.

5. To change colors, bring the first color out one end and when returning, start the new color. The loose ends can be worked into the finished weave later on.

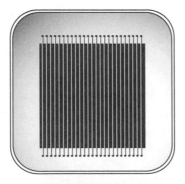

Setting up the tray for weaving.

Tapestry weave.

Project: Continued

To do a spiral weave, you set up the warp threads differently. Instead of threading across from each other, you work at a diagonal with all warp threads converging at the center. To begin weaving, start at the center and weave over and under the warp threads in a circle spiraling outward. Start a new color by doing what's known as a *slit*.

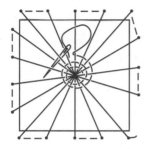

Spiral weave.

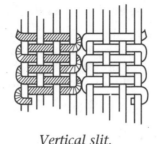

Vertical slit.

In the finished piece, the loom becomes the frame.

Looms come in different sizes. A simple loom called an *inkle loom* is easy to use and inexpensive. You can also make your own. This loom can be used to make an enormous variety of narrow strips. These can be used by themselves for belts or pulls, or they can be sewn together to make a wider woven piece.

Then there are *table looms*, which are just smaller versions of a four-harness loom. Four-harness looms can be of any size; some even take up a whole room.

Bonding Experiences

Check into various museums or craft shops that might have spinning, dyeing, and weaving demonstrations, or find a local weaver who might be willing to give you and your child a demonstration on a full-sized loom.

Make a field trip to a large, well-stocked yarn store. Look at all the different textures, colors, and blends of fibers. Feel them between your fingers. Look at any samples of finished pieces and note which kinds of yarns they were made from. Notice the ways the same yarn might make up using various techniques—weaving, knitting, or crocheting.

Other methods of making whole cloth out of yarn are knitting, crocheting, tatting, and macramé. These skills can be learned at an early age, too, and there are many excellent resources available to help adults get kids started.

One of the best primers on knitting, crocheting, embroidery, and tatting is a little booklet called the *Learn How Book*, put out by Coats & Clarks for decades. For more information, see Appendix A. You'll also find resources for learning macramé.

> **Crafty Clues**
> The major pattern companies all have Web sites you can visit. Check out Simplicity at http://www.simplicity.com/. Butterick and McCalls also have online catalogs at http://www.butterick.com and http://www.mccalls.com.

> **Handiwords**
> When you *embellish* fabric, you decorate it. You can add beads, buttons, trims, sequins, embroidery, appliqué and more to finished pieces.

> **Crafty Clues**
> Scale your embroidery patterns and tools up or down depending on the age of the child. Use larger cross-stitch patterns, larger needles, heavier threads, and looser-weave fabrics for younger children. Older kids can work with finer, more intricate patterns, smaller needles, and more delicate embroidery floss.

Sewing: Get It Together

One of the simplest ways to work with woven fabric is with needle and thread. Even a very young child can learn the basic principles of sewing by working with stiff paper that's had holes punched in it, a large needle, and some yarn.

An easy project is to make a beanbag. Use heavy felt, cut out a shape, put the two pieces together, and punch out holes that can then be stitched together with yarn and a large-holed needle. If the child can use a sewing machine, the pieces can be joined that way.

Fill with beans before completely closing the bag, then finish sewing. Bring the thread through the same hole several times to ensure it won't unravel.

If you're in a hurry or don't want to sew, there are amazing fusible webbing (such as "Stitch Witchery" or "Heat 'N' Bond") and glue products on the market that allow you to put fabric together with only an iron.

From the first steps of using a needle and thread or a sewing machine to make straight stitches, you can graduate to using a pattern to make a garment or accessory. Look for projects that use mostly straight stitching to start, like pillows or tote bags. Then you might try making a vest. There are several good vest patterns available from each of the major pattern companies.

A vest makes a great "canvas" to embellish, which I'll discuss next. Add appliqué, embroidery, charms, quilting, ribbon embroidery, beading, trims, or just fancy sewing machine stitches.

There are many different types of embroidery—crewel, cutwork, hardanger, and ribbon embroidery, to name a few. We're going to do a project with a technique called *cross-stitch*, one of the first kinds of embroidery children can learn to do.

Project: A Cross-Stitch Heart

Level: Easy

Age: 5 and up

Materials needed: Embroidery needle (size depends on age and medium used), embroidery floss or yarn, perforated canvas or cross-stitch material

Directions:

1. Look at the following pattern and notice the number of Xs in each line. (The first line has two Xs, followed by a space, followed by two Xs; that means you will complete two cross-stitches, skip one stitch, and then complete two more.)

2. Find a starting point on your perforated canvas or material and make a complete cross-stitch.

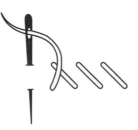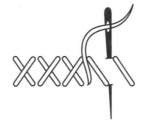

How to make a cross-stitch.

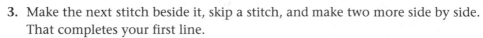

3. Make the next stitch beside it, skip a stitch, and make two more side by side. That completes your first line.

4. Follow the pattern for lines 2 through 5. You have now complete your first counted cross-stitch pattern!

line 1	XX XX
line 2	XXXXXXX
line 3	XXXXX
line 4	XXX
line 5	X

From here, the sky's the limit. You can learn to follow counted cross-stitch patterns in kits, magazines, or books. You can design your own patterns on graph paper or using computer software that lends itself perfectly to making your own counted cross-stitch designs.

To learn basic embroidery stitches other than cross-stitch, there are many good instructional sources. See Appendix A for more information on the following resources:

➤ I learned embroidery stitches with an inexpensive booklet from Coats & Clarks, *One Hundred Embroidery Stitches*.

➤ Cochenille Design Studio makes Stitch Painter for Macintosh, PC, and Amiga.

➤ Stitch Crafts Gold for Windows and Stitch Craft for Mac are available from Compucrafts.

For an overview of many software programs for needlework, check out http://www.wco.com/~kyder/software.html and the Software for Needlework page.

Quilting: Learning to Be a Cutup

Quilting involves taking whole cloth, cutting it up into pieces, and sewing it back together again. Then small stitches are taken through the pieced top, batting, and bottom in a specific design. The finished sandwiched together and sewn piece is then bound. Batting is a soft sheet of cotton or wool fibers sandwiched between the quilt top and bottom to add warmth and depth.

Quilted pieces can be used for bed coverings, clothing, wall hangings, window treatments...almost anything you can use regular fabric for.

There are many traditional quilting designs, known as *quilt squares*. These squares are designed individually, then sewn together to form an overall design.

Here are examples of some common quilt squares:

Handiwords
Batting is cotton or wool fiber wadded in sheets used as a filling in quilts or bedcovers.

To *quilt* means to stitch together two pieces of cloth and a soft interlining, usually in an ornamental pattern. The top layer may be made of small pieces of cut fabric sewn together in a design.

A *quilt square* is a design made from pieces of fabric sewn together to make a square.

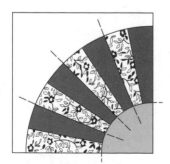

Grandma's Fan.

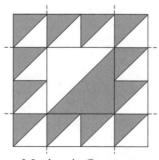

Mariner's Compass.

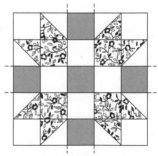

The Feathered Star.

One of the simplest forms of quilting is called crazy quilting. This is a patchwork created from odd-shaped pieces of fabric stitched onto a foundation in what looks like a random manner. It's easy because it doesn't require fitting pieces together.

Handiwords

A *crazy quilt* is a patchwork quilt made of irregular patches combined with little or no regard to pattern.

Project: Crazy-Quilt Sampler

Level: Medium

Age: 7 and up

Materials needed: $1/4$ yard each of several fabrics; one piece of muslin, 10×10 inches, embroidery floss in assorted colors; other embellishments as desired

Directions:

1. Cut your first piece of fabric in an odd shape, preferably one with four or five sides. Center it on your muslin square and pin it in place with the right side facing up.

2. Cut another odd-shaped piece from a different fabric. Put the second piece on top of the first piece with the wrong side up.

3. Match the raw edges along one side as much as possible and stitch through the two pieces and the muslin about $1/4$-inch from the raw edge. Open out the top piece. Repeat out from center until you've reached the outside edge.

4. Trim the pieces as you go along so they're in proportion to each other. Keep the sides straight when you cut the pieces, since straight edges are easier for a beginner to work with.

5. If there are any gaps or difficult areas to piece, appliqué a piece by hand over the area. You'll also be able to hide any imperfections with embroidery and other embellishment.

6. To finish your piece, embroider along the seams and add embroidery, appliqué (ornamented by different material or a piece of the same type, sewn on or otherwise applied), ribbon, beading, or anything else you like. Frame or complete as a pillow.

If you're looking for crazy-quilt kits and supplies, try Evening Star Designs (see Appendix A for details). A few more resources to try: For crazy-quilt embroidery stitch ideas, get *Crazy Quilt Stitches*. To learn ribbon embroidery, an especially sumptuous method of embellishment, see *The Art of Silk Ribbon Embroidery*. Other crazy quilt books you'll enjoy are *The Crazy Quilt Handbook* and *Crazy Quilt Odyssey: Adventures in Victorian Needlework*. For general information on learning to quilt, I recommend the *Quilter's Complete Guide* and *Quilts! Quilts! Quilts!: The Complete Guide to Quiltmaking*. For complete information, see Appendix A.

To Dye for

Dyeing fabric takes many forms, but one that can be done in your own backyard or kitchen is tie dyeing. The younger generation seems to have rediscovered "their father's T-shirt" from the tie dying craze of the 1960s. Everything that goes around comes around.

Project: Tie-Dyed T-Shirt or Cloth

Level: Easy

Age: 5 and up (with adult supervision)

Materials needed: All-cotton white T-shirt (or soft cotton, rayon, or silk fabric), liquid fabric dyes (Rit® will work, although experienced tie-dyers prefer Jaquard's Procion™ dyes), a large enamel or stainless-steel basin, a wooden spoon, rubber gloves, old towels, heavy mercerized thread, string, rubber bands, squeeze bottles (the kind used for applying hair dye work well)

This can be messy, so work outdoors (a picnic table is great if you can manage it). Or create a table with two sawhorses and a piece of plywood. Wear old clothes.

To get a clear pattern when tie dyeing, the tying and stitching must be very tight and firm. An adult may have to help with this if you are working with a younger child.

Directions:

1. Wash the fabric first to shrink it and remove any sizing. Read the directions on the dye packages to understand dyeing and rinsing instructions to obtain permanent colors.
2. On the part of the fabric where you want to create a design, pull up the fabric (one way is to use a closed fist and pull it up through the center.

Project: Continued

3. Wrap thread or twine around the end of the fabric you've pulled up as tightly as you can and knot it tightly. The fabric under the tied area will remain white after dyeing.

4. You can tie marbles, pebbles, bottle tops, or other objects into the fabric to create centers in your design. You can also stitch areas using a running or overcast stitch, gathering the fabric into tight puckers. This can even be done according to a traced design. Stitched areas will stay white. Try folding fabric in various ways, too. Experiment!

5. Wet the fabric before dyeing. Squeeze out excess moisture and blot with a towel.

6. Bring the dye to a boil and remove it from heat (or follow package directions if different). Dip the fabric in the dye solution. If you want sections to be more intense in color, leave them in the dye longer.

7. To dye the shirt more than one color, start with the lightest colors and proceed to the darker colors. Light colors will mix with other colors to give new tints, but a darker color will usually cover a light color. To avoid muddy colors, don't mix colors that are opposite each other on the color wheel, like blue and orange or red and green.

8. To distribute dye in more controlled amounts, use the squeeze bottles instead. You might also want to use color remover (a kind of bleach) in certain areas. You can purchase color removers in the same store where you got your dyes. Rit® makes one. Follow package directions.

9. Rinse the fabric in cold water. Squeeze out excess moisture and roll the fabric in a towel. Let it partially dry, then untie it and remove the threads and stitching. Shake out the fabric and let it dry completely, then press the fabric.

These are but a smattering of the many needlework, fabric, and weaving crafts you might want to explore with your child. The traditions of weaving, sewing, and needlework have been handed down from generation to generation, from ancient societies to today. They provide creative possibilities and a connection with our history that's hard to match.

For more ideas for tie dyeing, consult your local library. There is a videotape available called "Tie-Dye Made Easy" and a book called *Tie Dye, Back by Popular Demand* (see Appendix A for more information). Tie dyeing is a simple technique that has a lot of complex and challenging variations. Have fun with it!

The Least You Need to Know

➤ Weaving can be done with the most primitive of materials; you don't even need a loom.

➤ With a little patience and some practice, children can learn to sew by hand or on a sewing machine.

➤ Cross-stitching allows even the youngest child to embellish textiles.

➤ A crazy quilt made of fabric scraps is a canvas for all manner of needlework.

➤ Tie-dyed T-shirts are colorful and easy to make.

Bead It!

Beading is an ancient craft and one that is done in some form by nearly every culture. A real positive feature of beading is that it does not require any special equipment and can be pursued for very little money.

Of course, beading can become more expensive as you search for more rare or exceptional beads or perhaps start making your own glass beads, but this can come later.

All you really need to start beading is some thread, a few beading needles, and some beads. Add a pair of small needle-nosed pliers, some wire, and some *findings* (clasps, earring pieces, clamps, and all kinds of things), and you're all set. You can even start without these things, if all you want to do is glue some beads on a surface, but there's so much more! In this chapter, I'll show you many beautiful projects you can create with beads.

Beading Basics

Beads can be made out of almost anything you can imagine. Crystal, glass, bone, pearls, plastic, metal, stone, paper, papier-mâchè, clay, shells, wood, seeds, dried beans—you name it. Even broken necklaces and other pieces of jewelry can be transformed into exciting new pieces.

Beads can also be strung on other types of materials besides thread or wire. Heavier decorative cord can be used to string larger beads with larger holes, and leather thongs look good with more primitive-looking beads. You can also use elastic cord to string beads, which works well with continuous bracelets where you don't want to add a clasp.

Handiwords
A *finding* refers to anything in beading that is not a bead. This can include clasps, earring pieces, clamps, connectors, pin backs, separator bars, caps, and wire pins of various kinds.

Besides beads, beading needles, thread, and findings, you might use other equipment, like a bead board for laying out designs (see the following illustration), a magnification device (beading can be hard on the eyes), and, possibly, a bead loom for bead weaving. A partitioned container is helpful for sorting beads. (A used cardboard egg carton works great!) If you decide to try wire work, you'll need some additional tools that I'll describe later.

There are lots of ways to make beads yourself using a minimum of materials and tools. Try some of the following.

This bead board will help you lay out your necklace or bracelet design.

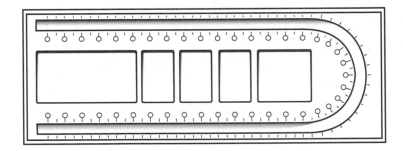

Polymer Clay Beads

Polymer clay, which is available at craft stores or through mail order catalogs, is such a versatile medium, once you get started with it, you'll think of a million applications. To make an easy marbled bead out of polymer clay, purchase two or three different colors of polymer clay (FIMO and Sculpey III are two brands to look for).

You'll need a craft knife or single-edged razor blade and a needle or skewer for making a hole.

Prepare your clay before you begin by rolling it in your hands and manipulating it to soften it; this will make it easier to work with. You can tell the clay is ready when you can bend it and it doesn't break off.

Take small pieces of each color clay you want to use for your bead and knead them together. Don't blend the pieces completely into one color, but distribute all the colors evenly.

Roll the clay out to make a snake-like shape, about $1/2$-inch in thickness. Use a craft knife or single-edged razor blade (adults can to do this for younger children) to cut the snake into equal pieces (you can measure with a ruler if you want to be precise). Then roll the pieces in the palm of your hand to create evenly sized, smooth balls. Pierce a hole through the center of the beads and bake according to the manufacturer's directions. You can also make cylindrical-shaped beads by simply cutting and putting a hole through the center without rolling the clay into a ball. Experiment with other shapes if you like!

You can read more about polymer clay in Chapter 12.

Handiwords
Polymer clay is actually plastic, but since is acts, looks, and can be fired like clay, it's called "clay." It can be fired at a low temperature in a home oven, which makes it versatile for the home crafter.

Crafty Clues
When beading, make sure that your thread, needle, or wire will fit through the bead hole you make. Sometimes you can make the hole bigger using an awl or circular file, but if you do this you risk damaging or breaking the bead entirely.

Paper Beads

Paper beads are also easy to make. This is a super recycling craft, too, since you can use scraps of gift wrap, junk mail, newspaper comics, and old magazines to create colorful and unusual beads.

Just cut long triangles out of any interesting paper. Experiment with different papers to see what kind of effect you get once your bead is wound.

Coat the surface of the paper with glue using a small paintbrush. Roll it up on a toothpick, skewer, or drinking straw, depending on the size of the hole you want. If necessary, add a bit more glue to secure the end of the paper and hold for a few seconds to make sure it's set.

If you're using a straw, just cut it off on both sides of the bead. If you're using a skewer or other item, gently pull it out. Let the bead dry. You can also use contact paper or self-adhesive wallpaper, and you can cut your paper in a rectangle instead of a triangle to get a cylindrical bead.

Ribbon Beads

Get some *grosgrain ribbon* in the colors you want (you can try other ribbons, too, but grosgrain seems to work the best), a knitting needle or wooden skewer in the size you want the hole to be, and some craft glue.

Cut off about eight inches of ribbon for each bead. Trim both ends of the ribbon straight across for clean edges. Roll the ribbon tightly around the skewer to make a bead. Spread some glue along the end of the ribbon on the underside and press the glued end down. Hold for a few seconds to set the glue. Carefully slide the bead off the stick and dab glue on both ends of the bead. Let dry.

String your beads on a piece of ribbon or sneaker laces. Add purchased beads in between, if you like, or make knots.

> **Handiwords**
> *Grosgrain ribbon* is a heavy, relatively stiff, corded ribbon made from rayon or silk. It can be purchased at craft or fabric stores.

> **Crafty Clues**
> You can buy a small microwave kiln that will raise the temperature of your microwave oven so it will fuse glass. Microwave kilns are not cheap (they cost from $70 to about $280), and you might outgrow the kiln if you become a serious beader. Still, kilns expand the possibilities for beads you can make yourself. These kilns require a fully grounded oven.

> **Handiwords**
> *Tiger tail* is wire that's been covered with nylon cable that comes in several thicknesses. Tiger tail is recommended for heavy beads or for pieces that will receive heavy wear. It can't be knotted like thread.

Dough Beads

Make bread dough using the recipe in Chapter 15. Make shapes out of small pieces of dough by rolling them in your hands or cutting them (see the earlier directions for clay beads). Bake according to the bread dough directions. You can then paint your beads and finish with fixative.

Glass Beads

Making glass beads in the traditional manner takes patience, practice, and more than a few dollars in equipment. However, you can make glass beads at home. Some interesting molded beads or pendant pieces can actually be made in your own microwave oven.

See Chapter 14 for more information.

Store-Bought Beads

Appendix A contains a list of sources for manufactured beads. Send away for some catalogs and visit some bead stores in your area (or when you're traveling!) to get an idea of all the varieties of beads available.

You can also paint store-bought wooden beads. Just clean them with white vinegar, let them dry, and then paint with acrylic paints. You can use permanent marking pen, too, especially for outlining to give definition to your designs.

Air-brushing works well, too. After the beads have dried completely, spray them with fixative.

Be aware that beads come in different sizes, which are expressed in millimeters (mm) even in the United States. This usually indicates the diameter of the bead, or the distance through the bead hole.

Handiwords
A *crimp bead* is a small, metal bead used to end pieces strung on a tiger tail. Sometimes they're also used as spacers.

As you and your child become more involved in beading, you may want to make beads out of items that aren't beads to begin with. Buttons, pieces of shell or bone, and other objects can all become beads if a hole is introduced. A small electric drill like a Dremel is handy to have (or you may be able to borrow one from another crafter).

Stringing Beads

Beads can be strung in a continuous string, or you can knot the string between each bead or at regular intervals. When you go to a bead store looking for material to string beads on, you'll likely find a few choices, such as nylon thread, silk thread, or a covered wire called *tiger tail*.

Tiger tail is actually wire, not thread, that's been encased in nylon. Since you can't knot it, you need to use small metal open bead-like findings called *crimp beads*, which are squeezed close and form a stop point. There's a special pliers you can buy just for crimping, but I wouldn't recommend it unless you're going to do a lot of beading. If you are, however, it's a handy tool to have. You don't need a needle when you use tiger tail, because it's stiff enough to poke through the beads on its own.

Crafty Clues
Don't store pieces made with tiger tail (or raw tiger tail, for that matter) in a way that will tangle the piece. This will produce a kink in the wire that will never come out and your finished jewelry piece won't hang right. It will stretch out if it's hung. So lay your tiger-tail pieces flat and coiled with the clasp open.

You may want to purchase some beeswax (available in bead or craft stores) to aid in your beading projects. By pulling your thread across a piece of beeswax, you'll put a fine coating on it. This keeps it from kinking up, prevents fraying, and makes it less likely to get cut from sharp beads. It generally strengthens and protects the thread and makes it easier to handle.

For your first stringing project you'll create a flowered bracelet. This project also allows you to do some freehand weaving. To make the bracelet, you'll need nylon thread, not tiger tail. You can use any beading needle that fits through your bead's hole, but I prefer using wire beading needles with collapsible eyes, because they're easier to thread. These come in various lengths. For this project, you'll want a fairly short one.

Project: A Flower Beaded Bracelet

Level: Medium

Age: 7 and up

Materials needed: One beading needle (fairly short), one 7-mm jump ring, one 7-mm spring clasp, green, white, and yellow seed beads (2-mm size): green for stems, white for petals, and yellow for centers, three feet of nylon beading thread, super glue

Directions:

1. Form a loop with eight white seed beads. Run the needle through this loop twice to make it extra strong and tie a knot. That's what you're going to add the jump ring onto.

2. Run the needle through eight green beads. Make a daisy by adding eight more white beads. Run the needle through the first white bead. Pull the thread tight to form a white loop.

3. Run the needle through a green bead, then through the fifth white bead of the loop. Repeat procedure until you've attained the desired length. End with eight white beads and make a loop.

4. Run the needle through again to make it extra strong and tie a knot. Clip off excess thread. Use a needle-nosed pliers to add your spring clasp and the jump ring on the other end. Secure all knots with a little glue.

Follow this diagram for making your daisy bracelet.

NOTE: If your thread breaks, back up a few beads and knot a new thread. Resume beading. Tie the thread tails in an inconspicuous place and clip the ends closely. Add a drop of glue to secure the knot.

For other beaded bracelet ideas, see *Beaded Bracelets, Friendship Bracelets,* and *Crosses and Friendship Chains, Seed and Bugle Beads.* Both books are available from Design Originals.

To learn more about knotting, measuring, and designing, I recommend *Pearl and Bead Stringing with Henrietta.* See Appendix A for more information on beading resources.

Bead Weaving

Bead weaving can be done free-hand, as in the flower bracelet you made earlier. For more complex weaving, you'll want to get a bead loom. Inexpensive plastic beading looms might be adequate if you just want to explore the process without spending a lot of money, but I believe that even beginners should have good-quality tools. I think you're more likely to have a good experience with a new craft if you have tools, equipment, and supplies that serve you well.

The best bead looms are made of wood and are fairly large. They are easy to manipulate and last longer than either plastic or metal looms. Wood looms should be sturdy enough to maintain good tension.

If you don't want to purchase a new loom, you may be able to borrow a well-constructed loom from a more experienced bead weaver or find a used one at a garage sale or thrift shop. You'll need to know how to set up your loom. If you buy a used one and have no instructions, ask an experienced beader to help you set up and string the loom.

One form of freehand bead weaving is called *peyote*. Peyote is the stitch most frequently used in those beautiful amulet bags you've probably seen around. This stitch requires some coordination, but with practice a fairly young child can master it. Sometimes it helps to use a form, like a paper tube, to learn. You can make a napkin ring in peyote stitch by weaving around a toilet-tissue tube. You can make your own designs in peyote using a kind of graph paper just for that purpose and using colored pens to represent the different bead colors you want to use.

> **Handiwords**
> *Peyote* is a type of bead weaving using the peyote stitch, which is a honeycomb network beadwork stitch worked spirallly to produce a beadwork tube.

To learn more about peyote, I highly recommend *Peyote At Last!: A Peyote Beadwork Primer.* See Appendix A for ordering information.

Blending Beads and Fabric

Just about anything you can do with embroidery you can do with beads. Beads add another dimension to needlecraft creations, plus they add color that no ordinary thread can.

If you're ever in the bridal salon or the bridal department of a major department store, look closely at the dresses and you'll likely see tiny seed beads, crystals, and sequins added to the contours of the lace and trim. This is one simple way of learning bead embroidery, which is also often used to embellish sections of crazy quilts. Many luxurious fabrics like damasks, paisleys, and jacquards have woven patterns that can easily be embellished by bead embroidery.

Usually bead embroidery requires a single thread, unless you have especially large beads that need to be reinforced. If you are working with a design that's already woven into the fabric, pick a shape in the design that's fairly large and defined. Then pick some small seed beads that are nearly the same color as the fabric (you might want a bead with added iridescence) and use the following three-bead technique to enhance the design.

To start, knot your thread and draw it up with a needle from behind. Add three beads and bring the needle back through the cloth along your design. Bring the needle up again between the second and third beads. Go through the third bead in the same direction you're working in and add three more beads.

You might want to try embroidering your own design next. You and your child can practice drawing or tracing designs on cloth that's been stretched in an embroidery hoop. If you'd like to explore the world of bead embroidery further, there are two books that should help you: *Beaded Clothing Techniques* and *Embroidery With Beads*. See Appendix A for details.

Handiwords
Wire work is a way of connecting individual beads or groups of beads using wire bent into shape.

Crafty Clues
If you are interested in wire work, definitely invest in good tools. I recommend buying them in a bead store, rather than a hardware store, to make sure you get tools with the right size and construction for bead work. Make sure you get pliers with box joints rather than screw joints. They will be more durable and work more accurately.

Wire Work

Another way of making jewelry with beads is linking them together with wire. This technique is called *wire work*. Wire work greatly increases the options you have for creating interesting beaded jewelry. In fact, jewelry can be created entirely with wire. See Chapter 11 for more details.

You only need a few tools to get started with this technique and they are highly portable. All you'll basically need is a small wire cutter, a needle-nosed pliers, and flat-nosed pliers.

Kate Drew-Wilkinson, the author of the *Complete Guide to Wire Work for Bead Jewelry* (see Appendix A), also recommends a bent or curved chain nose pliers, which I must confess I don't have in my beading toolbox. But after reading her description of the tool's uses (attaching hooks to earrings, closing crimp beads, etc.), I think I'll add it!

The findings you'll need to do wire work include the head pin, the eye pin, and the jump ring. You'll also need to familiarize yourself with various earring findings (for both pierced and unpierced styles), and clasps.

We're going to do an extremely simple wire-and-bead project called the Wire Bead Star. This can be a Christmas ornament or simply something pretty to hang anywhere you want a celestial reminder.

Project: Wire Bead Star

Level: Medium

Age: 7 and up

Materials needed: 20-gauge wire, round-nosed pliers, flat-nosed side cutters, beads of your choice (rocailles, tri-cuts, and crystal beads work well)

Directions:

1. Cut a 12-inch length of 20-gauge wire. Make a small loop at one end with a pair of pliers.

2. Each side of the star will have seven beads. To create the first side, put on seven beads and push close to the loop on the end.

3. Bend the wire at a sharp angle and thread the next seven beads on the wire. Bend sharply. Repeat the process until you have a five- or six-pointed star.

4. Close the other end of the wire with a loop. Lay one loop over the other and align the two loops. Make a hook out of wire or use a pre-made one, inserting the bottom of the hook through the two wire loops of the star. Close the loop.

5. Hang the star. You can make your own hook out of wire, use an ornament hook, or hang it with thread.

This project can be made as a five- or six-pointed star. Using clear or blue glass beads will make it look most star-like.

In addition to Kate Drew-Wilkinson's book, I also recommend *The Best Little Beading Book*. This is a comprehensive guide to beading and has some good projects using a variety of wire work techniques, plus peyote, stringing, and anything else you might want to try. See Appendix A for information.

You can take metal jewelry still further, if you like; we'll talk about that a bit in Chapter 11.

Hair Wrapping

Hair wrapping is all the rage and a big hit with boys and girls alike. With a little practice, your children will be dressing up all their friends' hairdos!

Try this on a friend first. Take a small section of hair and braid it into a very fine little braid. Braid it until you reach the point where you'd like to add a bead.

Bend a small piece of beading wire (about three inches long) in half to look like a hairpin. Wrap it around the hair (between the folds of the wire). Put the two ends through the center of the bead and, using the wire, draw the hair through the hole in the bead.

Remove the wire "needle" and begin braiding again.

You can also wrap and bead hair with embroidery floss. For more bead wrapping techniques, try the book *Hairwrapping Techniques: Creative Jewelry* or the book-and-kit combination *Top Knots!: The Ultimate Bracelet and Hair-Wrapping Kit.* See Appendix A.

Bonding Experiences

There are many ways to learn more about the history of beads with your child. Most art museums have jewelry exhibits that show a variety of beaded work. (There's even a bead museum in Prescott, Arizona!)

The History of Beads: From 30,000 B.C. to the Present is a good book about the history of beads. To learn more about Native American beadwork, read *Beads and Beadwork of the American Indians: A Study Based on Specimens in the Museum.* African beadwork is covered in *Africa Adorned.* For information on these and other beading books, see Appendix A.

There's also a fantastic magazine for beaders (and button fanciers) called *Bead and Button.*

If you and your child are computer-oriented, there's no end to the number of Web sites, newsgroups, and mailing lists you can hook into on the Internet. I suggest you start with one of Simone Oettinger's two Web pages, The Bead Fairies Page at http://www.mcs.net/~simone/beadfairies.html or http://www.mcs.net/~simone/ beadnet.html.

Now that you and your child have gotten a taste of bead mania (and believe me, it can become an addiction), "bead it" to your local bead store and continue stringing, twisting, wiring, weaving, knotting, and enjoying yourselves.

The Least You Need to Know

➤ Beads have a long, lustrous history and are a highly versatile medium.

➤ You can make your own beads from a variety of materials, including clay, glass, and paper (gift wrap, junk mail, and newspaper comics).

➤ You only need a few simple tools to get started in beading, but good-quality tools will ensure a happier experience and better results.

➤ Beads can be strung, put on wire, embroidered, and even glued.

Fancy Leather!

Chapter 9

Lessons in Leather

In This Chapter

➤ Leather-working tools you'll need

➤ How to choose the right leather for your project

➤ Ways to cut leather

➤ Using leather stamps to embellish leather

➤ Carving, sewing, and lacing

➤ The basics of dyeing and finishing leather

For most people, the smell of leather conjures up images of thoroughbred horses or the Old West. But leather is actually the oldest material used in permanent clothing known to man. Garments of animal hides are believed to have been made by our Stone Age ancestors at least 25,000 years ago.

Leather goods are known for their durability, good looks, and usefulness, presenting many possibilities for creative design and decoration.

Besides being used to make saddles and tack, boots and shoes, holsters, belts, carrying cases, and clothing, leather can be used to cover, carry, and protect just about anything. Other uses for leather, both past and present, include for wine and water casks, boats, tents, bows and quivers, slings, sheaths, helmets and shields, powder horns, hinges (yes, leather makes a great hinge), and upholstery.

Leather is an animal hide or skin that's been preserved by a process called tanning, which helps prevent it from decomposing, drying out, or rotting when exposed to water. Tanning also keeps the leather porous, soft, and pliable. The North American Indians tanned leather using a combination of vegetable (wood) tanning and oil tanning. The Eskimos used oil tanning because of the abundance of fish oils, and the Chinese used a mixture of mud and alum salts. Some Mexican leather is even tanned with cattle urine.

In this chapter, we'll use one project, a flat leather decoration for a key ring, and show you how to make it plain or embellish it. We'll also discuss additional ways to embellish leather. You'll learn how to finish your leather project using dye, paints, or leaving it natural, and how to seal and protect it.

Tooling Along

With a minimum of tools and experience you can create a wide variety of personalized leather products that will give you years of service. But remember, although leather-crafting basics are fairly simple, leatherwork requires time and patience, and your results will reflect the care you use in all phases of the project. It is also a craft that can accommodate the most artistic and complex variations—one that's almost impossible to outgrow.

Although there are many leathercrafter's stores, one I recommend is The Leather Factory of Fort Worth, Texas, which has outlets throughout the country. They provide a vast variety of uniform, quality products, including different grades of leather, at reasonable prices. Call 1-800-433-3201 for the toll-free number of their store nearest to you. I will be referring to different tools and related products throughout this chapter. For ease of identification, whenever I mention a tool I will include The Leather Factory part number with each item. (Note: There are many grades and prices for leather-working tools. I've referenced the most cost-effective for the beginner.)

The first category of tools the leatherworker needs to be familiar with is cutting tools. Generally, the process will be to trace a pattern on the leather and then cut it out in some fashion. Sometimes the best way to cut out your pattern is with a special *leather knife*; other times special *leather shears* are used. The rule of thumb is to use a knife for heavier leather; a shears for lighter leather. A utility knife with replaceable blades can be used in place of a leather knife, but the leather knife is more solidly constructed and tends to work better, especially when cutting thick leather.

The Leather Factory cutting tools I recommend are their leather shears (#3051-00) and beveled edge skiving knife (#48490-000). You'll also see in catalogs or at leather supply stores a knife with a rounded blade that looks something like a half-moon. This is something you might want to invest in later, but you may not need it at all, depending on how much and what type of cutting you do.

Handiwords

A *leather knife* is a special knife with either a round or an angled blade used for cutting leather, especially thick leather. *Leather shears* are large, heavy-duty scissors used for cutting leather.

Stick to projects that use lighter-weight leather when working with younger children so that they can use shears. Older children can learn to use a leather knife, especially if a template or other guide, such as a steel rule or square, is used. The project I've chosen for you to do in this chapter is best cut out with shears.

Another specialized type of leather cutting tool is a *strap cutter*, which is used to create uniform leather straps for belts and purse handles. The strap cutter is a wooden tool made up of two ruled crossbars that slide through a handle. The bars house a replaceable blade at one end and a *thumb screw* on the handle is used to set the desired cutting width. Cutting is done by inserting the leather between the crossbars, flush against the handle, and the tool is pulled to cut a strap of uniform width.

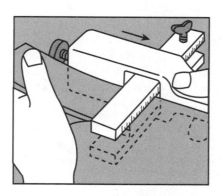

> **Crafty Clues**
> A heavy pair of kitchen shears might work for cutting leather, but whether you decide to buy a pair of leather shears or use something you already have on hand, you should plan on dedicating that pair of scissors or shears exclusively to cutting leather. Avoid serrated-type scissors, as they produce fuzzy edges when used on leather.

A strap cutter being used to cut out a uniform leather strap.

Leather can be sewn by machine or by hand. Leather sewing machines are special heavy-duty machines and are too expensive for the average home crafter, so you'll most likely be stitching your leather projects by hand.

Stitching leather requires some specialized tools that you'll want to know about. To create uniformly spaced holes in the leather through which a needle and thread will be drawn, you need first to mark them in some way so that they're evenly spaced, and then punch the holes through the leather. One method for marking the leather for punching is with a *stitching wheel* (sometimes called an overstitch spacer). A stitching wheel (recommended: #8091-00) is usually made with

> **Handiwords**
> A *strap cutter* is a wooden tool made up of two ruled crossbars that slide through a handle. The bars house a replaceable blade at one end. A *thumb screw* on the handle is used to set the desired cutting width and the leather is pulled through the cutter.

a wooden handle and a metal shaft that holds a removable wheel with small dull points evenly spaced apart. The wheels come in several different sizes, but the most commonly used are five, six, and seven holes per inch.

A stitching wheel is used to mark even spaces for punching stitching holes.

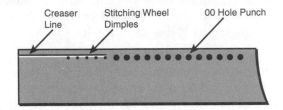

Creaser Line   Stitching Wheel Dimples   00 Hole Punch

Another method for making evenly spaced stitching holes is to create a groove even with the edge with a tool called a *stitching groover*, which is a tool with a wooden handle and a long thin shaft that holds an L-shaped piece at an angle that both measures and gouges the leather in one step. A *stitching punch* is then fit in the groove and struck with a rawhide mallet, then moved along the groove until all the stitching holes are punched. A stitching punch is a heavy metal tool that looks something like a fork with thick tines. The type used for creating holes for the most commonly used leather stitch, the saddle stitch, is called a *diamond hole punch*, and comes as both a single-prong or a four-prong punch, with different spacing available.

A tool similar to the stitching punch is used to produce the larger holes needed for threading lacing through. This is called a *thonging punch* and is used in the same way as a stitching punch.

A final way of making both stitching and lacing holes is by using an awl, after marking the holes first with a stitching wheel. An *awl* is a small, pointed tool for making holes in wood, leather and other materials, and is something that's handy to have in the home toolbox, even if you're not planning on working with leather. The awl is pushed partially through the leather to make a smaller hole for sewing and all the way through to create the larger holes needed for lacing. This is a less accurate way of getting your holes punched, but gets the job done, nevertheless.

For the actual process of hand-sewing leather, you can use two different kinds of needles. Thin leather is sewn with a *glover's needle*, which has a sharp point. A *harness needle* is used for thicker leather. Both kinds of needles come in different diameters and so does the thread. You'll want to

Handiwords

A *stitching wheel* is a wooden-handled tool with a metal shaft that holds a removable wheel with small dull points evenly spaced apart. Pressure is applied and it is rolled along the leather to create uniform impressions that can later be used as a guide for punching holes for stitching.

Handiwords

A *stitching punch* is a heavy metal tool that looks something like a fork with thick tines that when struck with a rawhide mallet punches a hole through leather for stitching. A *thonging punch* is similar to a stitching punch, except that the prongs are larger and it creates the larger holes needed for lacing leather.

match your needle and thread diameters, which are then matched to the diameter of the holes you're punching to accept the stitches.

There are two different kinds of thread for stitching leather, nylon, or waxed linen. My husband, who is a professional leatherworker, prefers waxed linen thread, because he says it doesn't stretch and it doesn't cut into the leather.

To do most kinds of lacing, you'll need a special two-prong lacing needle that actually holds the flat lacing between two metal strips that wedge in place against the prongs.

> **Handiwords**
> A *glover's needle* is a sharp-pointed three-sided needle used in hand-sewing thin leather. A *harness needle* is a blunt-pointed round needle used for hand-sewing thick leather. The round shape makes it slip easily through pre-punched holes.

There are several stitches you can use for sewing and lacing leather. Sewing stitches most commonly used include the single running stitch, the double running stitch, and the saddler's stitch.

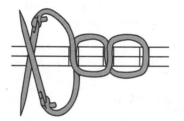
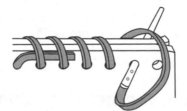

The two whipstitches used in lacing: the single whipstitch and the saddler's stitch.

There are special tools for stamping and carving leather, plus tools you'll need for dyeing, painting, and finishing leather, which we'll cover later in this chapter. But now that you have some basic familiarity with the leather-crafting tools used for cutting and stitching, let's move on to the basics of choosing the right leather and then tackle your first project.

Choosing Good Leather

Leather is usually purchased by weight in ounces and by the square foot. For example, one-ounce leather weighs one ounce per square foot, two-ounce leather weighs two ounces per square foot, and so on. Although many grades of leather may be available, buy the best unblemished leather you can (Tennessee Oak from the Leather Factory is a good choice) in the weight specified for the project. It's always a good idea to work with the best materials you can manage, even when working as a beginner, since inferior tools and materials often mean inferior results and a loss of interest.

Some suppliers sell whole skins, others sell only half hides or parts such as backs, bends, and shoulders. As you work with leather more frequently, you'll become familiar with the different cuts of leather and which suppliers have what.

The project you want to do will dictate what weight and what part of the hide you will need. Follow the instructions for your specific project and purchase the correct weight, or, if you're not sure, consult with your leather supplier and ask what weight would be best for the project you intend to do.

For smaller projects, you may be able to find a piece of inexpensive scrap leather that will do the job nicely. Often a supplier will have a large bin or several bins divided by different weights. Ask your sales clerk to direct you. For the project outlined in this chapter, scrap leather will do fine. You may need to ask your supplier to help you pick out a piece of scrap leather that's six to seven ounces in weight, since you may not be familiar enough with leather yet to know which weight is which.

Cut It Out!

The first step to any leather project is deciding on a pattern that is used to construct what you want to make, cutting it out, and assembling it, if needed. You'll then want to decide how you want to embellish it or even if you want to embellish it at all.

In this project, we'll simply cut out a leather shape to decorate a key ring. We'll discuss the best way to cut it out, then you'll learn how to clean the piece to prepare it for dyeing or painting, or simply sealing and protecting it.

Project: Basic Leather Key Ring Decoration

Level: Easy

Age: 5 and up (with some adult help for the youngest ones)

Materials needed: One pair of sturdy shears (#3051), one 12-inch ruler, one brown fine-point marker or pen, an awl, a piece of leather scrap (six to 7 ounces in weight)

Directions:

1. Pick a size and a shape for your key ring decoration. A size that's not too big but large enough to pick it out easily in a purse or school bag is about two to three inches long and an inch or two wide. It can be an oval, a circle, a square, a rectangle, or any other shape you'd like. Circles and ovals are harder to cut accurately, so you might want to choose a square, rectangle, diamond, or other angular shape for this project. Just remember you're going to be punching a hole into it and suspending it from a key ring.

Project: Continued

2. Next you need to get your shape onto your leather. You might want to trace around an object, drawing the shape on tracing paper first to get it right. Then lay it on top of the leather and pressing down with the pencil, go over the drawn shape.

3. Cut around the outside edges of the shape completely.

4. Decide where you want the hole for the key ring to be. Mark it with a dot and punch it at the dot with your awl.

At this point you may decide you'd like to embellish your key ring decoration. If so, follow the instructions in the next project box. If not, move on to the section in this chapter called "Finishing Up" to consider your options. When you're done, insert the key ring into the hole you punched and you've finished your first leather project!

Stamping Around

There are several techniques for decorating leather. You can carve it (sometimes mistakenly called "tooling"), which takes more tools and skills than the scope of this chapter allows us to cover. I've listed some resources in Appendix A if you'd like to explore this aspect of leatherworking further. Leather can also be painted, and, again, I've given you resources for further study in Appendix A. But the simplest method of decorating leather is with the use of stamping tools. These are held upright, then hit sharply with a rawhide mallet to make textured impressions on leather that has been moistened.

There are many stamping tools available and they can be combined to produce an unlimited variety of designs. To familiarize you with how these tools are used, I've given you a design that only employs three of them to embellish the key ring decoration you made earlier. You should add the stamped design before you dye and seal your key ring decoration.

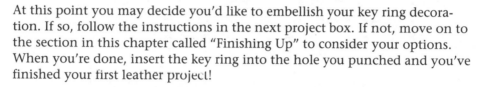

Crafty Clues

If you don't want to get involved in cutting at all, there are pre-cut leather pieces in all shapes and sizes and practice pieces available from the leather suppliers I've listed in Appendix A.

Now that you know something about how stamping tools are used, perhaps you'd like to try your hand at it. Using only three stamping tools, you can make a lovely decorative border—or if you're feeling creative, try some design variations of your own. If you'd like to add an initial or two (or even three), I've given you the part number for a letter stamping set you can invest in or you can choose one of the many larger decorative stamps that come in a variety of patterns as a centerpiece.

Bet You Didn't Know
Border stamping has been used for hundreds of years to dress up all sorts of leather gear, from belts to saddles to hat bands.

Choose from an eagle, flower, butterfly, horse's head, wolf, dolphin, cowboy, Cub Scout symbols, or any other number of interesting and beautiful designs. Refer to your Tandy or Leather Factory catalog or store for choices and part numbers.

Project: Stamping Your Key Ring Decoration

Level: Easy

Age: 5 and up, with adult assistance

Materials needed: One stylus, a metal ruler, one veiner (#V708), one seeder (#S932), one camouflage tool (#C426), one optional letter stamping set (#8130—^{1}/$_2$", #8131—^{3}/$_4$", #8132—1", or other larger decorative stamp), a sponge, a bowl of cool, clear water, rawhide mallet

Directions:

1. If you haven't already done so, create the key ring decoration outlined in the first project box in this chapter.

2. Along the edge of your key ring decoration, using your metal ruler, mark at regular intervals a quarter-inch from the edge with a fine-point marker. Then use the ruler to mark a line along the entire edge, which will then be a quarter inch all around.

3. Practice making the following design on a piece of scrap leather that you've moistened lightly with a sponge on both sides. You'll be stamping the design on the smooth side, not the rough side. Once you feel you can duplicate it fairly reliably, moisten your leather key ring decoration and make the design along the line you've marked using the stamps and your mallet. Again, you'll be putting the design on the smooth side of the leather.

Project: Continued

If the leather starts to dry out, re-moisten it. You don't want the leather too wet, though. One way to tell: If you put the stamp on the leather and press down, and water comes out of the leather, it's too wet. Just let it dry for a few minutes and then proceed with stamping.

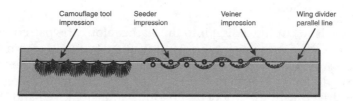

Camouflage tool impression   Seeder impression   Veiner impression   Wing divider parallel line

Border stamping patterns.

4. Decide where you want your initials and whether you want just one initial, two, or three (the size and shape of your key ring decoration may dictate how many you can use). Using the appropriate stamp and your mallet, embed your initials into your key ring decoration. If you've chosen a different decorative stamp, follow the same procedure.

5. Let your leather dry thoroughly. You can now finish the key ring decoration using one of several shades of dye, or you may decide to leave it in its natural state and simply apply some Saddle-Lac to protect it and keep it from turning color. You can finish with a coat of wash and a vigorous buffing. For more information on how to do these finishing steps, refer to the section called "Finishing Up" later in this chapter.

A Cut Above

The most elegant way to embellish leather is to carve it. This requires a great deal more skill and time than simple stamping, but the results are most rewarding.

Hand-carving leather is a technique used to produce a special "relief" design on the surface of a leather product. The design is usually hand-drawn and reflects the leathercarver's ideas of beauty, whether it be a simple design of flowers, leaves, and scrolls, a picture of an animal, or the writing of someone's name. There are also many pre-drawn carving designs available from leather-crafting stores that you can transfer directly onto your leather piece or adapt to your own design.

Once you've either drawn or purchased your carving design, the first step before actually carving is to get the design onto the leather you want to work with. This is done by attaching the leather by the corner tips only to your carving surface (it should be very smooth and hard, like a marble-top table, marble tile, or half-inch-thick Masonite), using some clear tape. Next, carefully align your tracing paper with your moistened leather and carefully tape your pattern in place. Then, using the pointed tip of your stylus, gently (trying not to tear the paper) trace your carving pattern through the paper and onto the leather surface. When you're done, remove the tracing paper and the tape from the leather and you're ready to carve.

The next step is to cut the design into the leather along the pattern lines you've embedded into the leather with your stylus. Most instruction books recommend the use of a tool called a swivel knife to do this, and you may want to experiment with this first. However, world-famous leather artist Bob Brown recommends using a simple, $3/8"$ flat-blade screwdriver, with the wooden or plastic handle removed and the blade sharpened like a mini chisel. Held like a pencil and rotated between the fingers and thumb for sharp turns, the simple screwdriver can produce incredible results with little training at a very modest cost. As skill increases, smaller screwdrivers can be used for more delicate work. Other professional leatherworkers have found this tool useful as well.

After the design is cut, a beveling tool is used to press down the edge of the cut, so that one side is compacted and the other side is raised. This is what gives leather carving its depth or "relief."

There are many books available with hundreds of pre-drawn carving patterns. They're relatively inexpensive, easy-to-use, and can be adapted to almost any project. A book that can help you further explore leathercraft is *The Leatherworking Handbook: A Practical Illustrated Sourcebook of Techniques and Projects* by Valerie Michael (see Appendix A for complete information). Most leather-crafting stores also offer classes in carving leather in which parents and kids can learn all about the wonderful world of leather.

Finishing Up

When you first cut out your leather, you'll find the edges are rough and need some sort of cleaning up. There are several ways to accomplish this, but the simplest is to simply sand the edges with fine sandpaper.

You may find it easier to wrap the sandpaper around a small wooden block for a better grip. Sand it until the edges are relatively smooth and even.

There are additional ways of finishing the edges of leather, which require additional tools and other materials. If you decide to pursue leatherwork as a hobby, you'll want to learn about these.

If you plan to dye your leather key ring decoration, this is the point at which you'll want to do that. Dyes come in a variety of colors and types. There are water-based dyes, which are non-flammable and recommended for use in schools. The type professional leatherworkers use, however, is an oil dye, which is deep-penetrating and gives a rich, strong color.

For your leather key ring decoration, a four-ounce bottle of professional oil-based dye will be enough to complete your project.

The dye is applied with a dauber, which comes free when you purchase your dye. Protect your clothes, and make sure you have plenty of newspaper down on your work surface. If you don't want to walk around for a while with dye on your hands, you may want to wear plastic gloves.

Apply the dye evenly with your dauber until it's saturated. Let it dry for several hours or overnight.

Once the dye has dried thoroughly, apply Saddle-Lac, which comes in a spray can (#2201-00), and then buff the leather piece with a soft cloth to give it a nice shine and prevent it from darkening or streaking. To further protect the leather, you may want to apply a finishing coat of some kind of wax. Clear shoe polish, available in any grocery store, will do the trick. Apply the polish evenly, then buff it with a clean cloth.

There are lots of kits available from The Leather Factory and Tandy, including key cases, coin purses, wallets, pocketbooks, wristbands, and barrettes. Doing some of these kits is a great way for beginners to learn different techniques, such as sewing, lacing, stamping, and carving, plus you can become familiar with some of the principles of constructing things from leather.

From there you can graduate to creating your own patterns and decorative designs. You'll also want to learn when and how to glue leather, and the various hardware that's used in leather projects and how to install it—for example, decorative spots and conchos, grommets, snaps, and buckles.

There are some excellent videos available from The Leather Factory and Tandy Leather. For example, a series of videos called "21st Century Leather Crafting with George Hurst" includes "Traditional Western Leather Carving," "Basketweaving and Geometric Stamping," and "Dyeing and Finishing," to name a few.

In this chapter I've only touched on the most basic skills needed to work with leather. With only these skills, you and your child can spend many hours crafting beautiful and useful leather projects for yourselves or to give as gifts. If you choose to add other skills to your leather-working repertoire, you'll increase the possibilities and the enjoyment of this rewarding craft.

The Least You Need to Know

➤ Leather is one of the oldest fabrics known to man.

➤ You should start with the best grade of leather you can find to make your efforts worthwhile.

➤ There are several ways to cut leather, but using leather shears is generally the best method when working with children.

➤ Stamping designs into leather is done after the leather is moistened with water, by tapping a metal stamp into the leather with a rawhide mallet.

➤ Leather can be dyed or painted or left plain, and then finished to preserve and protect it.

➤ Practice and patience are required in leathercraft, but it is a skill that produces many useful items that are both durable and beautiful.

Wondrous Wood

My earliest recollections of working with wood are of helping my father by holding tools and making little pencil lines on a piece of wood that he was going to cut after measuring carefully. It always amazed and delighted me that a flat piece of plain wood could become so many useful, decorative things.

You can enjoy this time-honored craft with your own child, beginning with a few basic tools and inexpensive materials. Woodworking is not only enjoyable, it teaches practical applications of simple mathematics better than any textbook.

Woodworking is a great craft for teaching measuring and marking skills. Even a very young child can help map out a project using a ruler and a pencil.

Tool Time

If you have any intention of working with wood on a regular basis, you'll need some tools. Many of these tools can be found in any basic home repair tool kit, so they're not something you have to buy especially for this craft:

➤ Yardstick

➤ Metal tape measure (the retractable kind is nice)

➤ Metal ruler

➤ Level

➤ Sharp pencil

➤ Pliers (slip-joint pliers are probably best to start with, other types can be added as needed)

➤ Pencil compass

➤ Crosscut saw—add other types (keyhole, coping, miter) as needed

➤ Awl

➤ Saw guide

➤ Sawhorses

➤ Safety glasses

➤ Hammer—start with a curved claw hammer and add other types as needed, such as ballpeen and tack hammers

➤ Nail set for recessing nails into wood

➤ Nails

➤ Screws

➤ Screwdrivers (both Phillips and regular)

➤ Rotary hand drill (this looks like an egg beater; it eliminates the need for a power drill and bits)

➤ Bar of soap

➤ Wood glue

➤ Vise (this jaw-like device is mounted to a surface and used to hold an object firmly while working on it. It's a good idea to use a vise when working with children who are cutting, sawing, or drilling; it helps with painting, too)

➤ Sandpaper (in various grades, from fine to rough)

Crafty Clues

When you buy power tools, consider buying one of the newer systems that works off an interchangeable rechargeable power pack. That way there's no cord to trip over and the tools are completely portable.

Some power tools you may want to have that you'll use yourself (or supervise an older child with) are:

➤ Power drill for drilling holes. Some can also be used to drive screws into wood or remove them

➤ Circular saw for cutting wood

➤ Power sander for finishing wood and preparing for paint or stain

Don't even consider buying low-quality tools for your child if you're in any way serious about creating an interest in woodworking or carpentry.

Instead, buy high-quality tools you can adapt to a child's use. For instance, screwdrivers come in various handle lengths. Buy some with shorter handles so your child can hold them easily. Let your child use a tack hammer for driving small nails. (You may have to drive larger nails with a full-sized hammer until your younger child is able to handle a full-sized claw hammer.) Don't assume children can't use a tool until you show them how and give them a chance to practice. You may be surprised!

Safety Signals
Teach your child to be careful when carrying tools. She should always hold the sharp edges or points downward and away from her body. When handing a tool to another person, hand it to him handle first.

Bonding Experiences

Take a field trip to a good hardware store with your child. Make sure it's one where the sales personnel won't mind spending some time answering your child's questions (and yours, for that matter!). Look at all the different types of tools available. Spend time in the hammer aisle, for instance. Let your child hold different hammers in her hand and see what feels comfortable. Learn their names. Ask what each type of hammer is for. Browse through the nail and screw aisle and examine the different sizes, shapes, and materials they're made out of. Ask lots of questions.

Nail It

There are many different types of nails and screws and it's a good idea to be at least familiar with some of the differences. The most commonly available nails are the common nail, box nail, casing nail, and finishing nail.

Different types of nails are useful depending on your project. The box nail is thinner than the common nail and less likely to split your wood. Casing or finishing nails (also called

Bet You Didn't Know
The penny nail's name comes from the days when nails were sold by how many you could get for a penny. A two-penny nail meant you could get two for a penny. A sixty-penny nail meant a penny bought sixty of them. As you might guess, the higher the number, the smaller the nail!

brads) are useful when you don't want the nailhead to be visible, since they are easy to push below the wood's surface with a nail set. You can then fill the small hole with wood putty and sand it smooth, or fill the hole with a crayon that matches the paint and buff it smooth with a cloth.

The unit of length for a nail is called a *penny* and is abbreviated with the lowercase letter "d." Size ranges from 2d to 60d, which is one inch in length to six inches in length. You can commonly find nails made of steel, bronze, copper, iron, aluminum, or stainless steel.

The general rule for deciding which nail length to choose for a project is to use a nail three times longer than the thickness or type of the top material being joined. When working with materials of different sizes, you'll also get the best results if you nail from the thinnest material into the thickest.

When to Use Screws

Crafty Clues
To help prevent nails from splitting wood, make sure they're not too sharp. You can blunt the point of a very sharp nail by tapping it a bit with a hammer. Also, don't hammer a series of nails along the natural grain of the wood. Stagger them instead.

Crafty Clues
If you're having trouble driving a screw, rub soap or wax on the threads and it will go easier.

Wood screws come in three shapes and two head styles. The head can be round, flat, or oval-shaped and you'll either be using a slotted screw or a Phillips head.

Size is determined by the length of the screw (in inches) and the diameter (gauge). Generally, you'll see screws that range in length from $1/4$-inch to 6-inch and gauge numbers from 0 to 24. They're usually made from mild steel with a zinc chromate finish, nickel or chromium plate finish, or brass. You'll want to use screws whenever you need greater holding power than a nail will provide.

When using screws, you'll need to create a *pilot hole* to get the screw started. This is usually done with a drill. For a short screw you can use an awl or punch to make the hole.

You will probably want to follow the same rule for screw size that you did for nails. Your screw should be two to three times longer than the thickness of the top material being joined, but not less than twice as long. You want to be sure it's long enough to hold securely, but not so long that it will come through the other side. Screw from the thinnest material into the thickest. Match the screwdriver size and type to the screw head you're using, otherwise the screwdriver could slip and you could cause injury to yourself or your child.

Start with a Shape

If you're working with very young children and just want them to get the feel of working with wood, emphasize the finishing work (like sanding, painting, and sealing) rather than some of the more difficult operations like cutting and drilling. Perhaps the best way is to start with a pre-cut shape or a kit you can assemble.

Binney & Smith, the Crayola crayon people, have a birdhouse kit that actually slides together with a series of slots, so there's no cutting AND no nails or screws. It's recommended for children age 5 and up and is called the Crayola Birdhouse Kit. If you have trouble finding it in your local craft or department store, call (800) CRAYOLA.

For this project you don't need any tools; everything is provided, including the sandpaper to smooth rough edges and a whitewash stain to rub into the wood when you're finished. Kids can then decorate to their heart's content with crayons, also provided in the kit.

You can also find pre-cut wooden shapes in craft stores for making ornaments, pins, and refrigerator magnets or for incorporating into other projects like wreaths or other wood projects.

For example, a pin back can be glued on a wooden heart and worn as jewelry. Or glue a magnet on the back—now you've got a pretty magnet that can hold notes or photographs up on your refrigerator. (Make sure your wooden piece is light enough to be supported by the magnet.)

Carving Yourself a Niche

Carving and whittling are two of the oldest forms of woodworking and require next to no tools. Whittling means to cut, trim, or shape a stick or piece of wood by taking pieces off with a knife. Carving is similar but can also involve simply carving decorations into wood and can employ other tools. Whittling is best described as the simplest, most primitive form of woodcarvings.

Wild Wood

Woods generally used for carving are balsa, basswood, white and yellow cedar, butternut, apple and cherry, hazel wood, birch, pine, cottonwood, red mahogany, redwood, poplar, and walnut. Some of these woods are hard to find, and some are best for specific projects. Basswood is considered one of the best woods for carving. Kiln-dried pine is also suitable.

To pick out wood for carving, there are a few things to look for. You'll want a straight grain and very little change in color, since changes in color indicate changes in hardness. The grain of wood is the pattern created by its fibers. You can test hardness by pressing on the wood with your thumbnail.

You can get wood from your local lumberyard or home improvement store, but craft wood might be easier to find at a crafts store or through mail-order sources (see Appendix

A). You can also ask your local lumberyard if they have a scrap bin. Sometimes you can find some wood suitable for carving in the scrap bin—and best of all, it's usually free!

A word about lumber: The size you ask for at the lumberyard or home improvement store is different than the actual size of the wood. You may ask for a "one-by-two" or 1-inch by 2-inch board, but its actual size may be $^3/_4$-inch by $1^1/_2$-inches. ALWAYS measure everything and never assume the size is right without checking.

Tools for Carving and Whitting

Carving and whittling requires few tools, yet those tools must be sharp. Children need to be taught how to use sharp tools without injuring themselves. Mostly this is the result of practice, but in the meantime, expect a few cuts along the way. You need to supervise carefully in the beginning and be ready with some iodine and a Band-Aid.

You may think sharp tools are dangerous when working with children, but it's actually a blunt instrument that is most likely to cause injury, since more pressure needs to be applied to make it work and it's more likely to slip.

To carve anything you'll need some knives. You'll always want to select knives made of high-quality steel so they'll stay sharper longer. A simple three-bladed pocket knife is a good start, since it gives you one large blade for heavier cuts, and two smaller blades for finer work. When buying a folding knife, get one with a lockable blade so it can't collapse while you're whittling or carving.

Other carving and whittling knives include one called a *sloyd* or short-bladed sloyd knife, which is used for rough cutting, and the *whittler's knife*, which is especially designed to be useful to the whittler. A craft knife with interchangeable blades, such as those made by X-Acto, is nice to have for fine work. X-Acto makes a whole line of whittling, carving, and craft knives, as well as knife sets.

You'll want to keep your knives sharpened using an oil stone (moistened with oil) or a whetstone (moistened with water). Even a new knife will need to be sharpened, since it has a chisel edge. Finish the job by stroking the blade up and down on what's known as a slickem stick, which is a piece of planed wood with abrasive cloth attached to it, or a leather strap also known as a strop.

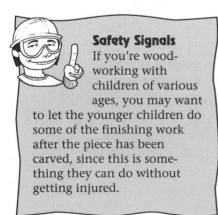

Safety Signals

If you're wood-working with children of various ages, you may want to let the younger children do some of the finishing work after the piece has been carved, since this is something they can do without getting injured.

Knife Moves

Carving is done by holding the knife in a particular position. Use your thumb to steady your hand and grip the knife in the rest of your hand and draw it toward the thumb. (Be careful not to use your thumb to stop the blade. Ouch!) Deeper cuts should be made away from you, with the knife gripped in your whole hand (see the following figure). Some of the deeper cuts might best be made by a child while the wood is held in a vice. Use a cloth or some leather wrapped around the piece to keep the vice from crushing the wood.

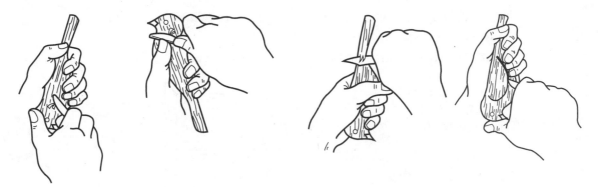

How to hold a knife while carving.

You'll also need some rasps and files for finishing off your carving and smoothing out grooves. A rasp is a coarse file that has conical teeth. A file is a long narrow tool of steel or other metal that has a series of ridges or points on its surfaces for reducing or smoothing surfaces of metal, wood, and so on. You can make sanding sticks by covering wood dowels (a small, round wooden rod) of various diameters with sandpaper, using glue to hold the sandpaper in place.

Project: Carved Boat

Level: Easy

Age: 7 and up

Materials needed: Block of balsa wood, coping saw, carving knife, fine sandpaper

One of the easiest projects to whittle is a small boat. You can even add a mast and a sail if you like, but we're going to concentrate on the boat itself.

Directions:

1. Draw a boat the size you want as if you were looking at it from the top. You'll want your wood to be as thick as you want the boat deep.

2. Cut out the basic shape with a jigsaw (an adult will have to do this) or by hand using a coping saw.

continues

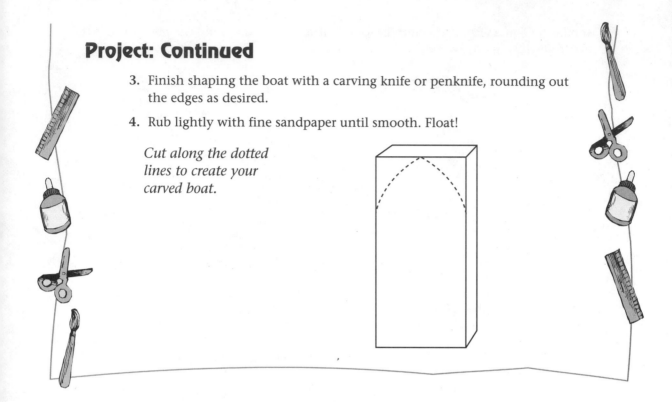

Project: Continued

3. Finish shaping the boat with a carving knife or penknife, rounding out the edges as desired.

4. Rub lightly with fine sandpaper until smooth. Float!

Cut along the dotted lines to create your carved boat.

This New House: Birdhouses

One woodworking project that can be made ultra-simple or super fancy is a nesting place for our feathered friends. Birdhouse designs can be simple (a box with a lid and a hole in the front for the bird to enter) or complex (a Victorian cottage with gingerbread trim—see "Gingerbread: Not Necessarily for Eating!" later in this chapter—and all sorts of decorative elements).

Before you decide what kind of house to build, consider the age of your child, your collective woodworking skills, and how much time you want to put into the project before you can actually hang it outside and have your first birdie housewarming party.

Another consideration is what kind of bird you're building a house for. It would be a shame to discover the house you thought you were building for mother robin and her babies has been invaded by sparrows instead!

You can choose the right dwelling for your backyard birds—and learn more about backyard birding and birdhouse construction—through your local Agricultural Extension Office. Look in your phone book in the State Pages section under Cooperative Extension or Agricultural Extension for a number. You can also access Extension offices over the Internet. Enter the words "coorperative extension" or "agricultural extension" in your search engine (be sure to enclose in quotes). There is also a site called State Partners of the Cooperative Research, Education, and Extension Service with state links at http://www.reeusda.gov/new/csrees.htm.

Local wildlife centers or resources can also help. Again, the Internet can offer a wealth of information. One of the most extensive sites I found on birdhouses is the Northern Prairie Wildlife Research Center's site at http://www.npwrc.org/resource/tools/birdhous/birdhous.htm. Not only are there plans for a variety of birdhouses, you'll also learn how to build a bat house, nest boxes, and shelf feeders for a variety of birds. If you have a list of birds common to your area, you'll know whether a particular house will attract the birds you want.

Another great site, which lists nest box dimensions for 28 different birds, is the Homes for Birds site sponsored by Baltimore Bird Club. They have the entire contents of the U.S. Fish and Wildlife pamphlet "Home for Birds" at http://www.bcpl.lib.md.us/~tross/by/house.html. For another great birding site with tons of links for kids and parents, check out http://birding.miningco.com/msubkids3.htm.

You're going to build a birdhouse that requires only five pieces and no special cuts. This design is a favorite of the American Robin and Barn Swallow and is actually more of a shelf with a roof than a true house. I chose this design because even urban dwellers will find robins in their neighborhoods.

Crafty Clues

When building birdhouses, one size definitely does NOT fit all. Know which birds are common to your area and find plans for a house that will suit the birds you wish to attract to your yard.

Crafty Clues

Paints, varnishes, and polyurethane come in various types; each leaves a different finished look. Matte finish dries somewhat dull, semi-gloss (also called a satin finish) is slightly shiny, and gloss finish is very shiny.

Bonding Experiences

Make a project out of learning about one species of bird that flocks to your area. Make a house that that species will use. Find out what nesting materials they need and make sure they're available in your yard; provide plenty of the food they prefer. Make or buy a bird bath so there's always a source of water nearby. Research their habits. What are their migration and nesting patterns? Make sure you have a good pair of binoculars and a notebook to write down your sightings. Make friends with a bird!

Project: Robin or Barn Swallow Nesting Shelf

Level: Medium

Age: 7 and up

Materials needed: One piece of good quality lumber, 1 inch by 10 inches by 4 feet, 2 to 2½-inch flat-head screws or nails, hammer or screwdriver, hand-held drill, paintbrush, paint or wood stain, polyurethane finish coat (matte, gloss, or semi-gloss), sandpaper, medium abrasiveness

Directions:

1. Using the pattern and dimensions in the following figure, cut out your pieces using a hand saw or power saw (adults should do this).

   Cutting diagram.

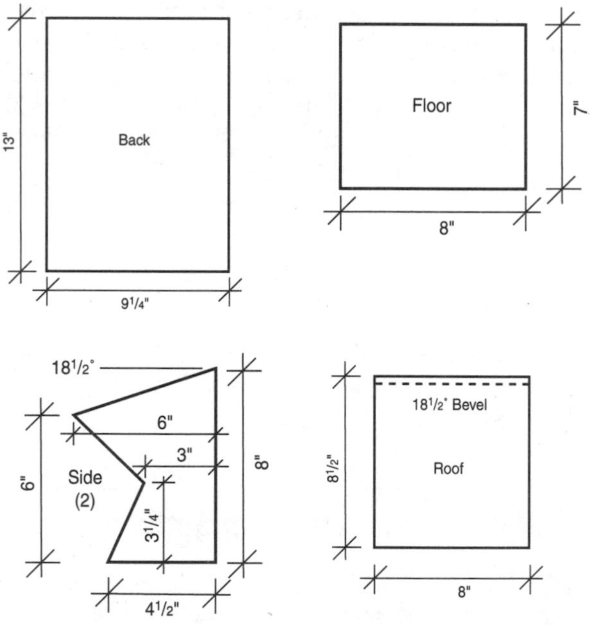

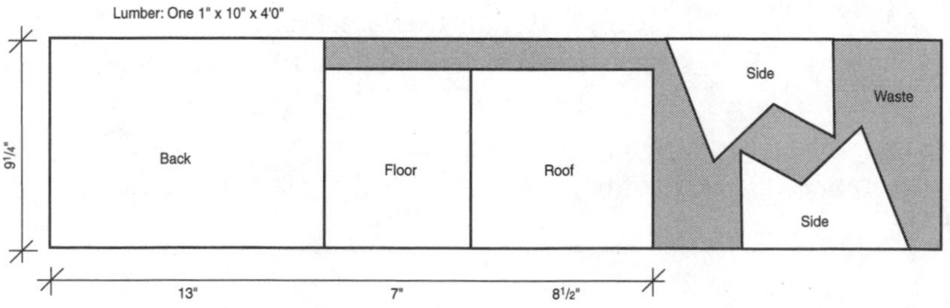

Project: Continued

2. Sand each piece thoroughly. It's best to paint or stain all your pieces before you put them together, since moisture will be less likely to get into joints and rot the wood. So, decide if you want to paint or use a wood stain product on your house, then put on a finish coat of polyurethane. You'll need to let the pieces dry between coats.

3. Line up the edge of one side with the roof. Draw a line along the inside edge. Mark where you want to put your nails or screws and make a dot. That's where you're going to drill your pilot holes.

4. Drill through the roof piece, then line it up again with the side and put a long nail through the hole. Tap it lightly to create a mark. That's where you'll make another pilot hole, so your screw can go through the roof and into the side easily. You'll do this for both sides and then again when attaching the back to the assembly.

5. Nail or screw your nesting shelf together, attaching the two sides to the roof first, then attaching that assembly to the floor, and finally putting the back of the house on. One way to make it easier to line things up is to bring your screws through one piece of wood so they just protrude a little on the other side. Then use the screws to help you line up the holes on the piece of wood you're joining to.

Hang your nesting shelf on a wall or tree trunk and wait for the birds to come. Place your birdhouse near a window where birds can be seen throughout the nesting season. Try to get it at least six feet off the ground. Ten feet is even better.

*Finished nesting
shelf.*

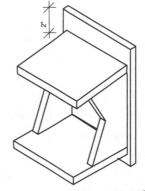

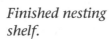

If You Wood Like to Decorate

You can simply stain your robin house and finish it with a coat of polyurethane and it'll be very functional and attractive for years to come. In some ways, a wood stain blends more with the natural environment. But if you want to make your woodworking more decorative and try your hand at painting or stenciling wood, go ahead and have some fun! There are lots of techniques you can use to spruce up the place!

Sponging

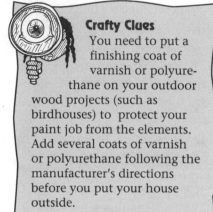

Crafty Clues

You need to put a finishing coat of varnish or polyurethane on your outdoor wood projects (such as birdhouses) to protect your paint job from the elements. Add several coats of varnish or polyurethane following the manufacturer's directions before you put your house outside.

Sponge painting involves using a natural sponge (not the cellulose kind you find at the grocery store, but the critter in its natural state, available at paint and craft stores) to apply colored paint to an already painted surface. There are sponge kits available at craft and home improvement stores, if you want to have everything conveniently packaged in one place.

A sponge finish can be left as is or you can add more decorative painting on top of it with a brush and some acrylic paints. How about some interesting border designs or some simple flowers?

If you'd like to learn more about sponge painting, plus some additional techniques, check out the book *Brush Sponge Stamp: A Creative Guide to Painting Beautiful Patterns on Everyday Surfaces* (see Appendix A for information).

Stenciling

Stenciling is one of the quickest ways to get a design on wood without having a great deal of drawing skill. Basically, you take a sheet of plastic out of which a design has been cut, place it on the surface you wish to decorate, paint over it, and then remove the sheet (called a stencil). You're working with someone else's design (although you can make your own stencils) and simply painting through a pre-cut pattern onto the surface you want to decorate using a special brush or a spray-paint can. Some basic equipment you'll need to stencil are:

➤ *Stencil brushes.* These are available at art supply or craft stores. They have blunt tips designed to give a sharp-edged image through your stencil.

➤ *Sponges.* Using a sponge creates a different effect than a brush. Natural sponges, which are available in paint stores, craft stores, or art supply stores, work best.

➤ *Stencil paints.* You can use special stencil paints or artist's acrylics, which come in tubes. Acrylics can be thinned before using. Make sure whatever paints you use are appropriate for your application (outdoor or indoor use).

➤ *Stencils.* You can buy pre-cut stencils or cut them yourself from acetate. (I recommend buying stencils if you're working with younger children, since this eliminates the need to work with a sharp knife.) More complex patterns are achieved by using a *partial stencil*. With a partial stencil, you can use more than one color in a design by partially masking out the pattern with one stencil and filling it in with the next. You need to let each color dry before applying the next one.

You can try a *reverse stenciling* technique, which is created by cutting a shape out of adhesive paper, applying it and painting over it, and then removing the sticky paper.

Other stenciling techniques include *ombre stenciling*, which is shading from one color to another; *dry-brush stenciling*, which gives the look of old, faded decorations; *spatter stenciling*, which gives a mottled look and is done with thinned paint and an old toothbrush; and *dimensional stenciling*, which gives a three-dimensional look and is done with various shades of the same color.

For more information on stenciling, Kathy Fillion Ritchie's book *Stencilling; How to Create Clever Paint Effects on Wood, Ceramics, Paper and Fabric* is a great place to start. See Appendix A for more information.

> **Handiwords**
> *Stenciling* produces a design using a thin sheet of plastic or other impervious material. This sheet, called a stencil, has perforations through which paint, ink, and so on applied on one side will pass through to form the design on a surface against which the stencil rests.

> **Crafty Clues**
> To create multicolor stencil designs, simply block out part of the design with masking tape and paper while you color the rest; then remove the tape and paper and color the covered section a different color.

Decorative Painting

Decorative painting—the art of creating flowers and leaves (among other things) with simple brush strokes—is enjoying a renewed popularity in the crafts industry these days. There are lots of books, videos, and classes around to help you and your child learn. Experienced decorative painters make a rosebud with just a few flicks of the wrist and dabs of several colors on their brush. Abracadabra, it appears before your eyes.

These fine painting techniques aren't the only way to paint designs on wood. Geometric shapes and simple flowers or animals are easy to paint, even for a young one or beginner.

The best thing to do before attempting to paint a design on your painted birdhouse is to practice first on some scrap wood. Let your child get the feel of the brush and consistency of the paint. You'll probably want to first draw the design lightly in pencil on the fully dried painted surface. It may be easier to do your decorative painting before assembling the birdhouse, because it's easier to work on a nearly flat surface.

For more information on decorative painting, try the book *Acrylic Decorative Painting Techniques: Discover the Secrets of Successful Decorative Painting* by Sybil Edwards (see Appendix A for information).

You can also apply decals, adhesive paper designs, or use rubber stamps (ones you've purchased or ones you make out of clean rubber sponges) to decorate your wood.

Gingerbread: Not Necessarily for Eating!

Gingerbread is the term given to fancy trims and moldings that were used on houses in the Victorian era. These can add a more finished look to your birdhouse or make it into a fantasy cottage, depending on how far you want to go.

These moldings come in different scales, so you'll need to match the scale of the molding to the size of your finished house. One source for dollhouse trims and molding is Northeastern Scale Models in Massachusetts; see Appendix A for contact information.

Bonding Experiences

Find some books about Victorian architecture in your local library or bookstore. Look for pictures of houses with interesting trims and moldings. I recommend any of the *Painted Ladies* series of books by Michael Larsen and Elizabeth Pomada. (See Appendix A for more information.)

Who knows, building a birdhouse may be the perfect introduction to the whole world of miniatures and dollhouses! To explore further, check out *A Beginners' Guide to the Dolls' House Hobby* and *The Ultimate Dolls' House Book*. You'll find more information on these books in Appendix A.

The Least You Need to Know

➤ A few basic tools are needed to do beginning woodworking, but these are tools you probably already have in your basic home repair tool kit.

➤ Sharp knives are essential for good results in whittling or carving wood, and they are actually safer to use than blunt knives.

➤ Making a birdhouse is a good starting project for the beginning woodworker. It can be made as simple or as fancy as you desire.

➤ Before deciding on which birdhouse to build, make sure your design is appropriate for the birds you want to attract.

➤ There are many ways to decorate your birdhouse, including adding fancy moldings or trims, sponge painting, stenciling, or using decorative painting techniques.

Heavy Metal

Put the guitar away—this isn't a chapter on rock music. It *is* about the many useful and durable items you can craft from metal. Besides, you don't need an "ax" to work with metal, just a few tools you'll find in your toolbox and other household objects you might not even think of as metalworking tools.

You can use sheets of various metals and work from the raw material or you can use one of the most plentiful free materials in any household—tin cans. I'll show you how to do both in this chapter.

Cut, Punch, Pierce, and Join

The activities you'll most find yourself doing when working with metal are cutting it, making holes or small slits through it, making impressions in it, joining pieces together, or affixing it to other materials. Some metalworking tools you'll want to be familiar with (and perhaps add to your toolbox, if you don't have them already) are:

➤ Pop riveting tool and rivets

➤ Soldering gun and soldering supplies

➤ Rubber or leather mallet

➤ Metal snips, serrated and plain-edged

➤ Pliers, round-nosed and long-nosed

➤ Vise

➤ Ball-peen hammer, 6- or 8-ounce weight

➤ Awl

➤ Can openers (both the kind that opens the can from the inside of the rim and the kind that cuts from the outside below the rim, or one that can do both)

➤ Hardwood board for hammering

➤ Chisels for making decorative impressions

➤ A wooden bowl, like a chopping bowl, used to hammer metals into a curve

➤ Steel wool of various fineness (from very coarse to very fine)

➤ Decorative upholsterer's tacks

➤ Screwdrivers of various sizes

Crafty Clues
When you start collecting tin cans for use in metalcraft, examine the inside of the cans as well as the outside. You'll find different colors and finishes. Some cans are shiny; other are frosted or even patterned. Colors may vary from silver to a rich gold. Collect both beaded cans and those with smooth sides, since both are handy for different projects. Save the lids, too.

Crafty Clues
Handle tin carefully. Hold it lightly by the edges to avoid leaving fingerprints, which can mar the surface of the metal.

You'll also want a variety of tin cans and lids in different sizes and shapes. (For instance, don't overlook the cans used to hold canned hams or sardines.)

You can also get cans from commercial sources like restaurants and bakeries. Since these establishments usually buy food items in bulk, you can usually get larger cans from them, as well as cans with unusual shapes.

The advantages of working with tin cans is that they often have ribbing that can be both decorative and act as a guide for cutting or punching. You may even end up hammering the ribbing (or *beading*, as it's called in the tin can business)

out, but the marks will still be there to serve as a guide. It also eliminates the need for soldering in some cases.

Besides tin cans, you may want to use sheet metals for some of your metal working projects. A sheet of aluminum, brass, copper, galvanized iron, iron, tinplate, or zinc that's up to 3/16 inch thick is referred to as *sheet metal*. You can buy sheet metal in hardware stores, craft stores, or jewelry supply stores in various sheet sizes. It is sold by gauge number. The higher the gauge number, the thinner the metal.

If you've never done any soldering or riveting before, you might want to familiarize yourself with these new tools and practice using them before you attempt a metalcraft project. (Depending on what projects you decide to do, you may not even need to bother with soldering or riveting.) The projects I've given here don't involve any joining, but if you want to explore the true versatility of metalwork, eventually you'll want to learn how.

Safety Tips for Working With Metal

In addition to observing the basic safety rules discussed in Chapter 4, there are a few special considerations you should keep in mind when working with metal. Yes, metal is sharp, but that needn't stop you from pursuing this craft with your child. You'll probably get a few minor cuts in the beginning, but nothing a Band-Aid can't handle. Here are a few simple metal-specific rules to observe to make your metalcrafting experiences safe and sound:

➤ Don't grasp metal pieces tightly. A light grip will prevent cuts and slices.

➤ Never run your fingers along the raw edge.

➤ When using a tin snip or other cutting tool, keep the cutter deep in the cut as you move along. Avoid making short cuts and creating small burrs along the cut line.

➤ Beginners might want to wear gloves for protection, but you can get a better feel for metalcraft without them, so as soon as you're familiar with the tools and materials you'll probably want to work bare-handed. Start your child out with gloves and when she appears to be ready, let her try working without them.

➤ Whenever possible, use a well-mounted vice to grip your piece while you're working on it. This may not always be practical, but consider it whenever you can. Use a rag or piece of scrap leather to cushion the metal and keep from marring it.

➤ Don't brush scraps of metal into the trash with your hands. Always use a brush or even a piece of stiff cardboard to push them along.

➤ Don't rush yourself. Take your time and you'll be less likely to injure yourself or your child.

➤ Work with adequate light. If possible, use both natural and artificial light. Metal shines, which makes it difficult to see clearly under certain lighting conditions.

➤ Invest in good tools. A pair of good tin snips is worth the investment. Expert metalworkers recommend aviation snips, even though they may cost a bit more, and stress the need for quality tools for beginners as well.

Now that you've got your metal working tool kit assembled and have familiarized yourself with the more unusual tools, you're ready to begin your first project.

Piercing and Punching

Metal piercing is a craft commonly used to make Colonial furniture in America as well as in other countries. You've most likely seen it decorating panels in cupboards, pie safes, cabinets, and shutters from the colonial era. Unlike some metalcraft, metal punching is suitable for children as young as five or six. When applied to metal, the term *punching* is sometimes misused. To punch metal actually means to use a tool to make an impression, but not to go all the way through the metal. This creates a raised design on the other side. *Piercing* is using a tool to go all the way through. You may see the terms used interchangeably for piercing. But you know better!

There are punching sets you can purchase, and these are called "punching sets," but they're actually piercing sets. Remember, punching uses a tool to make an impression, not a hole.

Piercing tools come in different styles to make fine, medium, and large holes. You can also use various-size nails or an awl to create your holes. By piercing a series of dots through the metal, you can create almost any pattern, from basic geometric shapes to intricate pictures.

Make a piercing pad by taking several layers of newspaper and placing a piece of plywood underneath them. This will protect your work surface and help absorb the sound made by hammering against metals.

Use tape to secure the metal to the plywood (duct tape works well for this) so it doesn't slip or buckle. Then you can tape down whatever pattern you're working with, centered on the metal, with masking tape. You should remove the pattern when you're completely done piercing, but do it a little at a time, checking the holes as you go and making sure they all went through.

Handiwords

When applied to metalcraft, *punching* means to create an impression on metal by striking a tool on one side and raising the metal on the other. *Piercing* refers to making a hole through the metal, usually with an awl, nail, or other similarly sharp tool.

Crafty Clues

You and your child should practice piercing on pieces of scrap metal to get the feel of the material and the hammer and tools. As you practice, you'll be able to better control the size and spacing of the holes.

Painting and Antiquing

Painting a finished pierced metal piece can add interest and color to your craft. You can use various paints and finishes to get different effects. Glass stain gives a glossy, transparent look that resembles enameling. It's applied with a brush. (You can add a second coat to deepen the color, but be sure to let the original coat dry first.) Acrylics give a denser look. Two coats is usually best, and antiquing can be added on top of acrylic paints after they dry. All you need to clean up after using glass stain or acrylics is water.

Antiquing gives metal an aged look (bet you guessed that, didn't you?). You can use antiquing to emphasize the holes you've made with piercing, or to enhance the metal surface. An oil-based paint is used for antiquing. Any kind of artist's oil paint in a darker color or antiquing product will work. Apply it with a soft cloth into the holes with a circular motion. Clean up with *mineral spirits*, a petroleum distillate solvent you can buy in any paint, hardware, or crafts store.

You can also give your piece an antique finish using acrylics—just thin the acrylic with a water-based varnish and brush it into the metal. Wipe it off right away while it's still wet. If you get more color than you wanted, let it dry and then use steel wool to remove some of the color.

After your project is completely dry, protect it by spraying it with clear acrylic paint or varnish. Then you can mount it and frame it, if you like. Choices for mounting are infinite as long as the surface suits your finished piece and can be adhered to.

If you choose to mount your project, you can glue it down on a mounting board and decorate it with upholstery tacks. Make a hole first all the way through your metal piece and into the mounting surface with a hammer and nail, then add some glue on the back of the tack and hammer it into the hole. If you're using a thin mounting board which the tack would go through, cut the shank with a heavy-duty wire cutter. Don't rely on the tack to hold the metal piece down.

The following project shows you how to use a pierced metal picture to decorate a rustic basket.

> **Safety Signals**
> *Mineral spirits* is toxic, so handle carefully, use only in a well-ventillated area, store according to label directions, and wash you hands after use.

> **Crafty Clues**
> Oil-based paints dry more slowly than acrylic paints, so you can play with them more, but they're toxic and not as easy to clean up. Acrylic paints are non-toxic and clean up with water, but they dry very quickly, so there's not as much time to experiment. Make your decision on which to use based on your needs and your knowledge of your child.

Project: Pierced Metal Picture

Level: Easy

Age: 5 and up

Materials needed: Tin or copper sheet, medium gauge (.010-inch thick: large enough to accommodate the design you've chosen), piercing design made up of dots, hammer or mallet, metal-piercing tool, piercing pad (can be made out of plywood and several layers of newspapers), tin snips, work gloves, duct tape, masking tape, fine steel wool (2/0, 3/0, or 4/0), E-6000 glue, white craft glue, oil-based paints (optional), acrylic paints (optional), glass stain (optional; Delta is one brand), clear acrylic or varnish in a spray can

Directions:

1. Using your snips, cut your metal sheet to the desired size, large enough to accommodate your design with a little room to spare for framing or mounting.

2. Trace or draw your pattern onto tracing or other thin paper.

3. Center your pattern on the sheet of metal and use masking tape to secure it in several places.

4. Tape the metal along the outside entire edge with duct tape to your plywood piercing pad to keep it from buckling.

5. Using your mallet and your metal-piercing tool, pierce your design, making sure the hole goes all the way through.

6. Remove the paper design on one edge and check to see that all the holes have gone through. If not, reposition the pattern and complete. Repeat this procedure for each section of the pattern.

7. Completely remove the paper pattern.

8. If you decide you'd like to paint or stain your finished piece, use fine steel wool to clean the metal and rough it up for accepting paint or stain.

9. If applying glass stain, use a brush and clean up with water. You may need two or more coats to get a deep color. Allow to dry between coats.

10. When you want to give a solid section of your design some emphasis, you can use acrylic paints. This will give it a dull finish and can be antiqued after it's allowed to dry.

11. Protect your finished metal with a coat of clear acrylic or varnish spray after you're sure the paint or stain is completely dry.

Here's another piercing project, this time using a tin can to create a lantern that will cast a pretty pattern when a candle is placed inside. The kids and I have used these outside in the backyard on a summer's eve and even when we've gone camping.

Tin is an extremely versatile crafting material. Although tin was in use as early as the 5th century B.C., the tin can wasn't invented until 1810. When tin is combined with a small amount of copper, a stronger metal called bronze is formed. When tin is combined with a small amount of lead, it makes pewter.

Project: Pierced Tin Can Lantern

Level: Easy

Age: 5 and up

Materials needed: Hammer, nails in assorted sizes, tin cans, 16-gauge wire, masking tape

Directions:

1. Pick a used can with a shape you like. Peel off any labels and wash and dry the can thoroughly. Fill it with water and freeze. (You'll use the ice to keep the can from collapsing.)

2. Decide on a design and either put it on paper and tape it to the can or draw the design on wide masking tape after you've applied it to the can. Pick a simple geometric design; for example, diamonds or hearts. The following illustration gives you some ideas.

Some patterns you can use to pierce your tin can lantern.

3. Lightly pound in the nails. Use different sizes to create different-size holes, or use one size for all the holes. Make two holes near the rim of the can on opposite sides for the handle.

continues

Project: Continued

4. Cut a length of 16-gauge wire and bend it into an even U-shaped handle. Turn up each end to form a hook. Attach the handle to the lantern and put a votive candle inside.

5. Lanterns can be hung or carried. (Remember to always observe fire precautions with lighted candles.)

Finished tin can lantern.

A variation you can try is to make some cuts in the metal in addition to the holes. Use a sharp chisel to add some diagonal cuts and push the peaks in.

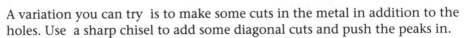

Cut-Ups

Now let's cut some metal. Don't be afraid, it's really easy. Here's a project you and your child can jump right into.

Project: Cut Starburst Mobile

Level: Medium

Age: 7 and up

Materials needed: Eight can lids of various sizes, one large can with a rim approximately six inches in diameter (a three-pound coffee can works well), gold or silver cord, metallic ribbon or trim, tin snips, glue, a ruler, a non-permanent marker

Directions:

I suggest reading through these directions first, then trying several of the starburst designs on scrap lids before actually doing them on the lids you want to use for your finished mobile.

1. With a ruler and a non-permanent marker, divide your first lid into eight equal pie-shaped sections. Then measure approximately $1/4$ inch on ONE side of each section and mark with another line (see the following figure). Cut along each solid line up to $1/2$ inch from the center. That will give you eight wide sections and eight thin strips.

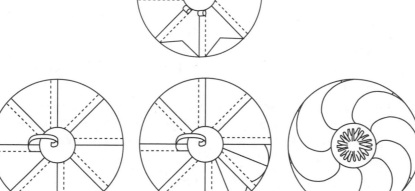

Measuring and masking for cutting your starbursts.

continues

Project: Continued

2. Now you can make variations on your starburst, depending on how you manipulate the wide sections and thin strips. You can cut the outside edges of the wide pieces into V shapes, round them into "petals," straighten them, or leave them as is. You can roll the narrow strips up tightly toward the center or more loosely (using a pair of round-nosed pliers). You can choose to crimp the narrow strips or twist them.

Swirl starburst design.

Rolled starburst design.

Another variation is to make a swirl design, as shown in the figure that follows. This has no strips in between sections. Just be careful to clip the sharp points of each section before moving on to the next one so you don't cut or scratch yourself. This can be left as is or rolled, as shown.

3. After you've got your starbursts cut and shaped the way you want, make a hole (use a metal punch if you have one) for hanging and suspend them from a frame made from the rim of the coffee can (or a wooden embroidery hoop).

4. Decorate the hoop or rim with metallic ribbon or trim. (See the following figure.)

Project: Continued

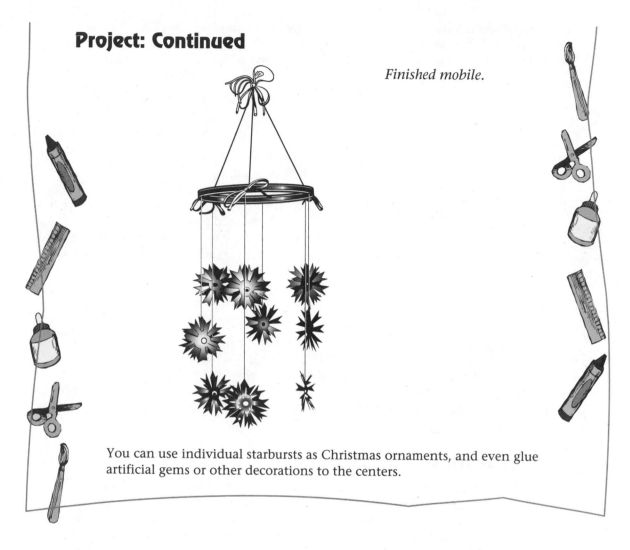

Finished mobile.

You can use individual starbursts as Christmas ornaments, and even glue artificial gems or other decorations to the centers.

Embellishing Metal

There are lots of ways to decorate metal. Painting it is always one option, and you can try your hand at applying various overall finishes or painting designs. Metal can also be enameled (which requires the use of a kiln) or etched with chemicals.

Some especially interesting and rewarding methods of embellishing metal involve creating designs right into the metal itself. These techniques are called *planishing*, *embossing*, *chasing*, and *repoussé*.

These operations are performed on fairly thin metal (sometimes called *foil*) which is generally 32-gauge or thinner.

There are metal styluses you can buy specifically to use in embossing and chasing work, as well as wooden modeling tools that are commonly used. But you can also use found objects, such as wooden popsicle sticks or orangewood sticks (used in manicures to push the cuticle back from fingernails; you can find them in a drugstore).

Handiwords

Repoussé is a metalworking technique that uses the combined techniques of embossing and chasing. *Embossing* means raising metal from the reverse side by hammering or pressing it to form a design on the front side. *Chasing* is indenting metal from the top side. *Planishing* refers to decorating metal by hammering it and overlapping rows of hammer spots to produce a faceted effect, which also hardens the piece. Planishing is done with a special planishing hammer.

You'll also need a work surface with some give, like a pile of newspapers or a fairly hard rubber mat. A vinyl floor tile works well, if you can get the kind with a cushioned back.

A simple project you might like to try is decorating the lid of a wooden cigar box with a foil piece into which you've embossed a design. You'll want to cut the foil to size first, then tape it down on your work surface so it doesn't slip or buckle. You'll probably want to work out your design on paper, then tape that over the foil and work through the design using your orangewood stick or other tool to trace over it. To make raised dots, use a pencil or a pen with the point retracted. You can turn the foil over and use an eraser or rounded tool on the front side to emphasize parts of the design.

You may want to practice a little foil work first, before you actually try this project. Try different designs. Apply tools from both sides and see what the effect is. Get foil in different gauges and work with them all, noting how each feels and responds to your tools. Start looking around for patterns that might lend themselves to this craft.

More Metal Ideas to Try

We already talked a little bit about making beaded jewelry with wire in Chapter 8, but you can learn to make jewelry entirely of wire. If you'd like to find out more, read *Making Wire Jewelry* by Helen Clegg and Mary Larom. You may want to learn more about other uses of metal in jewelry making and there's a book for that, too. Check out *Jewelry: Fundamentals of Metalsmithing* by Tim McCreight.

If you'd like to learn more about tincraft, take a look at these books:

➤ *Chasing* by Marcia Lewis

➤ *Tinwork* by Marion Elliot

➤ *Wirework* by Mary McGuire

➤ *Wire* by Suzanne Slesin

➤ *The Fine Art of the Tin Can* by Bobby Hansson

➤ *Tin Craft; A Work Book* by Fern-Rae Abraham

➤ *A Beginner's Book of Tincraft* by Lucy Sargent (This one is out of print, but worth looking for—I found a copy at my local library.)

Full information on all of these books can be found in Appendix A.

Some interesting Web sites you also might want to check out are those maintained by The ArtMetal Project, "a not-for-profit volunteer venture of a group of metalsmiths and organizations" whose goal is to pass on information about working artistically with metal. Try:

➤ http://www.wuarchive.wustl.edu/edu/arts/metal/ArtMetal.html

➤ http://www.wuarchive.wustl.edu/edu/arts/metal/Gallery/Gallery.html

➤ http://www.wuarchive.wustl.edu/edu/arts/metal/AM_res.html

The ArtMetal Project can also be reached at 505 Luther Road, Apex, NC 27502, (919) 362-0543; email: evaga@artmetal.pdial.interpath.net.

Of course, there's lots more you can do with metal than what I've been able to cover here. You can do poured metal casting, metal sculpture, enamel work, engraving, and more. I've only given you a start using beginning skills, inexpensive materials, and a minimum investment in tools, but once you've mastered these, the sky's the limit. Investigate ways of combining metal pieces with other materials. Metal and wood suggest some wonderful possibilities and metal pieces of various kinds are commonly used with leather.

The Least You Need to Know

➤ Metal is a craft material that can be safely used even with young children, if certain basic rules are observed.

➤ Tin cans make a versatile and free material for use in metalcraft.

➤ Pierced metal lanterns and lampshades are quite decorative and can be made by children of all ages.

➤ Cutting metal is best done with a good pair of metal snips, preferably ones used in the aviation field.

➤ Metal can be decorated in a variety of ways. Some of the easiest are painting, embossing, and chasing.

Chapter 12

Feats of Clay

In This Chapter

➤ The different kinds of clay

➤ Crafting with polymer clay: Basic to advanced techniques

➤ Working with ceramics

➤ A word about pottery: Coiling, slabs, and throwing

➤ Plastic casting and clay sculpture

Does your child love to play in the mud (you too, huh)? Well, then perhaps clay is the craft for you. If you like the feel of mushy stuff between your fingers (perhaps even your toes) and love rocking and rolling, then maybe you should rock n' roll down to your local crafts store and get yourself something worth kneading.

There are lots of kinds of clay you can work with, from those that need to be fired in a special kiln to those you can just let air dry. There are even some you don't let dry at all. In this chapter, I'll concentrate mostly on polymer clays, but I won't neglect to mention some of the other ways clay can enter your life.

The Ancient Art of Pottery

Pottery is an ancient craft that appears throughout the development of civilization and clay pots often tell us much about the way a people lived. Clay objects, specifically pottery, are very distinct from society to society, and clay pots were often buried with the dead.

Handiwords

A *potter* is a person who makes pottery by using a device called a *potter's wheel*, which has a rotating horizontal disk upon which clay is molded. The wheel can be manually or electrically operated.

Throwing is the technique potters use to shape the clay.

Handiwords

After a pot is made and left to dry, it is baked (or fired) at a high temperature, usually more than 2,000°F, in a special oven called a *kiln*. Kilns can be fueled by almost anything, but the most common heat sources are electricity, gas, coal, or wood.

Bet You Didn't Know

Native Americans apparently did not know of the existence of the potter's wheel, so most American pottery was made by building coils of clay using the hands alone.

Clay may have first been used to line baskets, so they would better hold water, small seeds, and grains, until someone discovered that baking clay makes a non-porous container.

In their natural forms, clays come in a great spectrum of colors (from pure white to jet black) and textures. They can be all one color or flecked, spotted, speckled, and streaked. Some clays are nearly see-through; others are completely opaque. Some are very moldable or elastic; others are more crumbly.

Modern *potters* (craftspeople who make pottery) work with several different types of clay, depending on the look they want, the finish they might be adding, and the use their finished piece is meant for. Generally, a potter works with a potter's wheel, a device that is either manual or electric consisting of a rotation horizontal disk, and performs an act called *throwing* or shaping on a potter's wheel, but this is the most difficult technique to master.

The potter's wheel can be operated by human power, called a kick wheel, or by a motor, called an electric wheel. Some potters actually prefer the kick wheel because they feel it is more sensitive and gives them more control over the process. The kick wheel is a crafting tool that has pretty much remained the same for 6,000 years.

If you are sincerely interested in pottery, you will need to make a fairly large investment of time and money to pursue it as a hobby. Not only do you need the tools and equipment to form the pots, but you'll also need a *kiln*, a kind of oven for baking clay, to fire them. I suggest that you and your child take a class first at a nearby arts and crafts center or school where you can use the studio's equipment and see if this hobby is truly to your liking.

If you don't want to invest heavily in equipment, you can try making *coiled pots*, which don't require a wheel, or learning the *slab method*, in which clay is rolled out kind of like pie crust, and then cut into pieces and assembled. You can then progress to learning about firing and glazing, perhaps buying time in a kiln owned by someone in your area.

Ceramics: Starting Out Ahead

Another way to begin working with clay is to learn *ceramics*. Ceramics is actually a general term referring to anything made out of clay and fired, but in this context it refers to those already formed in a mold and is sometimes called hobby ceramics.

Learning ceramics usually means working with something called *greenware*. These are pieces that are already formed from molds, which the crafter prepares, paints, fires, then glazes and fires again. You can probably find a local ceramics store and studio that gives classes and makes a kiln available to its students. Firing is a process of baking in a kiln at a particular temperature.

Baking pottery at a high temperature in a kiln makes it stronger and more durable. Firing is usually done in two steps, the first, or bisque, is at a relatively low temperature making the item safer to handle when a glaze is applied. At this point it is still porous. The second, or glaze firing, makes the surface hard and usually non-porous.

Again, this is a good way to get the feel for working with clay, although some people prefer working from scratch. There is a huge selection of ceramic greenware to choose from, from lamp bases and bowls to figurines, lighted Christmas trees, and decorative items. To find out more about ceramics, take a peek at The Ceramics Web site at http://apple.sdsu.edu/ceramicsweb/ceramicsweb.html.

Wonder Clay: The Polymer's

Polymer clay is a relatively new crafting material. It isn't a true clay. It's really more of a plastic, polyvinyl chloride suspended in a plasticizer, but since it acts like clay, looks like clay, and can be fired, I chose to include it here rather than in Chapter 13.

Polymer clay has taken the crafting world by storm. It comes in lots of different colors and consistencies, and you can work with two or more colors without having them blend together. Polymer clay is extremely pliable

Handiwords
Ceramics generally refers to the art of making objects of clay and similar materials treated by firing, but it is commonly used to refer to working with objects that have already been formed using a mold, where the craftsperson takes this "greenware," prepares it, paints it, applies glaze and then fires it in a kiln. This craft is often called *hobby ceramics*.

Handiwords
Greenware is an object produced by pouring runny clay (called slip) into a *mold*, which is a hollow form used to create a particular shape. Once the clay reaches a certain dryness, the mold is removed and the greenware is left to dry further. It is then cleaned of any seams or defects and then finished using any variety of painting techniques, underglazes and overglazes and fired one or more times.

A glassy coating, or *glaze*, is melted onto a piece of clay during firing, adding strength and beauty to the clay while usually making it non-porous.

Handiwords
Polymer clay is a modeling material made of microscopic plastic particles embedded in a grease-like base. Once the clay is heated to a certain temperature (which varies from manufacturer to manufacturer) the particles expand and fuse with each other.

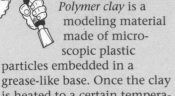

Bet You Didn't Know
Polymer clay was first developed in Germany in the 1930s. It comes from the same kind of plastic, PVC, that is used to make the plumbing pipes in most of our houses.

and you can fire it in your own kitchen oven. The color doesn't change when it's fired, either.

The names you'll hear most often regarding polymer clay are *Fimo, Sculpey, Cernit, and Promat.* Sculpey comes in three different types, Sculpey, Super Sculpey, and Sculpey III. Fimo and Cernit are made in Germany, Sculpey and Promat are made in the United States. The major difference between brands is stiffness. Sculpey tends to be softer, which means it's easy to work with and to put through various tools (more on that later). Promat and Cernit are stiffer than Sculpey, but softer than Fimo. Different brands are also stronger than others. As you get more into using polymer clay and decide what you want to do with it, you'll probably use different brands for different applications.

You also may end up mixing more than one brand together. Just make sure when you bake it, you follow the directions for the lowest temperature.

You can model polymer clay, press it into a mold, carve it, weave it, even turn it on a lathe. It can be made to look like ceramic, glass, ivory, plastic, wood, raw clay, and metal. For sheer breadth of possibilities, polymer clay really is a miracle crafting material.

Another great advantage of polymer clay is you really don't need any special tools to work with it, and what tools you may want to use you can make from objects you have around your house. It's good to work on a smooth, protective work surface, such as marble or glass, so you don't damage your table or counter. They're also easy to clean. You can also tape waxed paper down on a wood or plastic surface and throw it away when it gets soiled.

Claymates: Tools for Working With Clay

You'll probably want something to cut your clay with. You can use a single-edged razor blade or a serrated knife. (Just don't use the same knife for food— delegate one specifically for working with your clay.)

Crafty Clues
You may find your hands getting dry after working with polymer clay. After washing them thoroughly, apply a moisturizer.

Other tools you may want are a rolling pin, something to make holes in the clay (for beads), and a metal garlic press (this works great for making clay "hair" on figures or other textures). Many serious polymer clay crafters and artists use handcranked stainless steel pasta machines, not the extruder type, to make clay shape. Again, if you're going to use your pasta machine for clay, you have to be very sure it's clean before you allow it to come in contact with food. I have a feeling I'm going to have to make a choice about mine or simply get another one just for clay!

You can use your regular kitchen oven or a toaster oven to harden your finished product. If you use a toaster oven for your work with clay, use it in a garage or basement, so if you have an accident and the clay burns, you won't have to deal with the fumes and mess inside the main house.

Another luxury you might like to have is a dedicated food processor (look for one at yard sales). The same thing goes here, though…use it only for clay, and not for food.

And, finally, you may want to invest in a template to help you gauge sizes and keep your work consistent, especially if you're making beads or jewelry. A template is simply a sheet of plastic with various size holes in it. You use it to gauge size of beads and other creations.

You might check out the various clay extruders and guns available specifically for working with polymer clays. They're not required, but it's good to know they're there. Extruders and clay guns are just tools that you put clay in and the tool pushes the clay out in a particular shape. Kind of like the old Play-Doh factory, if you remember that.

Note: polymer clay is safe if people follow directions and pay attention to what they're doing. Anthing can be dangerous if people misuse the product and don't follow directions.

Crafting With Clay: Clay Projects

Before you can work with polymer clay, you need to soften it so it's of kneading consistency. You can do this by simply working it in your hands. (Some people put it in a plastic zip-top bag and put it in their pockets for a while.) You can also put it in a zip-top bag and lay it in some warm water (not too hot or it'll harden!), and I've even heard of warming it under a heating pad on the lowest setting.

Once the clay is warm and you can knead it, the fun begins.

Safety Signals
One thing polymer clay is NOT good for is to use to contain or serve food, because plasticizer can leach out even after it's fired. If you want to make cups, plates, and bowls and the like, you'll have to use a true clay. Although polymer clay is considered non-toxic, it is not a good idea to use the same utensils that you use with the clay in the preparation or eating of food without washing thoroughly. Wash your hands after working with clay and clean off any work surface you'll share with food. (It's better to work on a piece of glass, marble, or wax paper when you craft with polymer clay.)

Safety Signals
If you do burn your clay in the oven, get fresh air into the area immediately. The fumes can be hazardous to small animals. Clean the oven completely before using it again for cooking. Following the manufacturer's directions closely and keeping an eye on your clay in the oven should prevent a fire, but if you should have a mishap, make sure you and anyone around (including pets) are kept away from the fumes.

Clay Beads

Since I'm an avid beader, I already told you how to make marble beads from polymer clay in Chapter 8. Now you might like to try making some more advanced types of beads and other jewelry pieces. I recommend *Creative Clay Jewelry: Extraordinary Colorful Fun: Designs to Make from Polymer Clay* (see Appendix A) to take the next step and a few more besides.

To make a more advanced bead, try this project.

Project: Clay Beads

Level: Easy

Age: 5 and up

Materials needed: Polymer clay in various colors, rolling pin, knife, skewer

Directions:

1. Roll out a "snake" (called a *cane*) in a color you like until it's about $1/2$-inch in diameter and about two inches long. You can make it bigger or smaller if you want.

2. Roll out another color so it's flat, maybe $1/4$-inch thick or so. You can use a pasta machine to roll it out, or just use a rolling pin and try to get your "pancake" as even as possible.

3. Cut a square piece out of your pancake that's the same length as your cane and wide enough to wrap around it and just meet on the other side. Do this several more times using complimentary colors.

4. With a single-edged razor or very sharp craft knife, cut very thin slices from your cane. Apply this to a round bead you've already rolled in a complimentary color. Roll the whole thing between the palms of your hands until you have a smooth surface.

5. Make a hole the size you want with a needle or skewer and bake the bead according to the manufacturer's directions (check your oven's temperature accuracy with an oven thermometer). If you have several beads, you may want to string them before baking.

Experiment with this technique of making canes (they don't have to be round, either) and putting them together. You can try putting them side by side and wrapping them with an outer layer. The smaller the canes, the fancier the design.

Canes put together to form a design.

Try carefully compressing several canes so there aren't any spaces and stretching the composite snake, starting from the center and working out, until your "snake" is longer and thinner. Then begin making your slices. What does that do? Look at beads that have been made from polymer clay in bead stores and pictures and see if you can figure out how they were made. Play together.

Button, Button

A simple project using polymer clay to do with younger children is to make clay buttons. You can cut around templates with a craft knife, but small cookie cutters are even better to work with.

To make about 12 buttons, you'll need around one ounce of clay. Once you cut out the buttons, insert a toothpick or skewer to make the button holes (make sure the hole goes all the way through). Bake the buttons according to the directions on an aluminum foil-covered baking sheet. Then you can paint them with acrylic paints, finishing up with a coat of clear gloss lacquer or shellac. (Use a toothpick to hold the button for painting and to dip it into the lacquer or shellac so you get a good coat.) Painting a white base coat first will give your detail painting a better base. You'll need a #3 or #5 paintbrush for the overall painting and a #00 for painting detail. Ask at your cafts store for these sizes or look for them printed on the brushes.

Try cutting clay into different shapes, like hearts, cats, flowers (daisies or pansies work well), little cows, ice cream cones, fruits, and vegetables...the more whimsical the better. For younger children, use simple designs, like hearts and stars, that don't require much detail. Older children can get fancier.

Some clay shapes.

Bonding Experiences

Join the National Polymer Clay Guild, which will keep you up to date on the ever-changing world of polymer clay as an art and craft material. Write to them at Suite 115-345, 1350 Beverly Road, McLean, VA 22101. You'll get a subscription to their newsletter, the *POLYinforMER*, and can attend meetings in some localities. To hang out online with other polymer clay addicts, you can frequent Polymer Clay Central on the World Wide Web at http://www.primenet.com/~thayer/ or join a newsgroup by checking in at rec.crafts.polymer-clay.

Make Your Own Clay

If you skip ahead to Chapter 15, you'll find a recipe for salt dough. This is a kind of bread dough recipe that's only one of many that can be used for modeling. These doughs can be shaped, molded, embellished, baked, and sealed, and form the raw material for all kinds of inventive crafts products.

If pottery, ceramics, or polymer clay don't seem to do it, homemade doughs and clays are a great way to play with squishy stuff, use your collective imaginations, and barely feel it in the pocketbook.

For more recipes for clays and doughs, get yourself a copy of *Mudworks: Creative Clay, Dough and Modeling Experiences* (bibliographic information in Appendix A).

Once you've got your dough made and you're satisfied with the consistency, you can use a variety of techniques to shape it. Here's a list of ideas you can use with dough or polymer clay to get interesting patterns, shapes, and textures:

➤ Look for small and large cookie cutters (especially the small ones generally used for garnishes). Use them for cutting out uniform shapes.

➤ Reexamine your everyday kitchen tools. Garlic presses (holes vary in size) are great extruders for making hair or just thick strands. Graters and meat mallets can be used to create textures. Walk around your house and look for other everyday objects that you might be able to press into your clay to give it an unusual texture.

➤ Collect some items from nature—a few simple flowers, some leaves, an acorn—and examine their parts. See if you can duplicate them in clay or dough and assemble them. Try copying them first and then improvise.

➤ Do the same thing with fruits and vegetables (try larger foods with smaller children, smaller foods for older ones).

➤ Try duplicating different shells. You can look at pictures, but it's easier if you work from the real thing so you can hold it in your hand and look at it from all angles.

➤ Try using different makeshift tools (toothpicks, skewers, the tines of a fork, an old toothbrush) to create lines and grooves in your clay.

➤ Experiment with making textures. Pull netting tight over a piece of dough or clay and see what it does. Try a piece of discarded pantyhose. How about cheesecloth? Wire mesh? A cheese grater? What happens when you pull it harder? Lighter?

➤ Try using a real leaf (wash and dry it first) as a template on some thinly rolled clay or dough. Put some waxed paper over the leaf and roll over it to make an impression. Use a knife to cut out the edges. Remove the leaf carefully.

➤ Make braids with long "snakes" rolled out of dough. Use just two strands, then three. Braid them first and then twist the braid. See what happens.

➤ Make some flat, wider strips of dough and see if you can weave it so it looks like a basket. What happens when you use different widths? Different textures of strips?

Dough baskets.

➤ Use objects like bowls or baskets and form the clay over them, then peel the clay off carefully.

➤ Layer small pieces of dough or clay formed into shingles or petals to create depth and texture. Use a flat shape as your base. For example, try making a roof on a house using individual shingles, or a wreath using individually shaped leaves.

➤ There are punches and stamps used in leatherwork that make interesting designs. (Make sure the leatherworker says it's okay to use them though!) Broken jewelry findings make useful impressions as well. Try different objects and see what you get.

➤ Concentrate on one shape (a star or a heart, for example) and see how many variations in texture or decoration you can come up with. Create a sampler and either hang your variations as ornaments or mount them on a board and frame them.

If you just want to get your feet wet without spending a lot of money on clay, start with *The Incredible Clay Book* by Sherri Haab and Laura Torres. It comes with eight pieces of clay, one ounce each. Suggested projects include finger puppets, dinosaurs, beads, and more. See Appendix A for more information.

Put Yourself in a Cast

Now, don't break a leg! Instead, try *plaster casting*. Plastercraft is the art of creating things by casting them in plaster.

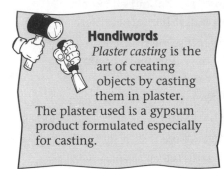

Handiwords
Plaster casting is the art of creating objects by casting them in plaster. The plaster used is a gypsum product formulated especially for casting.

Crafty Clues
To figure out how much plaster you'll need to fill a mold, pour water into the mold first and then measure how much water was required to fill the mold. That's how much plaster you'll need.

There are all kinds of molds you can use. Some are made out of plastic and are relatively rigid. These are used for making wall plaques and fairly flat objects. You can also find latex molds—some quite detailed—for figurines and statues. You can also buy castings already made, some of which are highly intricate, as in the case of military or fantasy figurines.

A simple bucket for mixing, a paint stirrer, a mold, and your plaster are all you really need to make a cast. (There are special plasters designed just for casting, although some are more durable and chip-resistant than others.)

You may need something to support the mold and hold it steady and level when you're pouring. (Try a couple of blocks of wood or a box full of sand.) You'll also need a sharp knife to trim the edges of the casting when you take it out of the mold and some cleaning sponges for the finer preparation stage.

Other handy (but not necessary) materials to have around include certain chemicals that make getting a smooth casting and removing it from the mold easier. These include a wetting solution that is sprayed inside the mold to help prevent bubbles, and a mold release agent, also sprayed inside the mold, that helps you get the finished casting out. There's also something called a *sliding agent* that's sprayed on the outside of a latex mold so that as you peel it off it doesn't stick to itself and tear. You spray this stuff on the outside of the mold.

To make a plastercast, follow the directions on the package of casting plaster and mix it up. Pour it SLOWLY into the mold, and tap the mold every so often to break up any air bubbles. Shake the mold a bit when you've got it nearly full to level it and add more plaster if necessary.

Leave the casting in the mold for the required amount of time, then remove it from the mold. Let it air dry thoroughly at room temperature. (An old wire baking rack works well, or you can recycle a wire oven or refrigerator shelf.) If you're not sure it's dry, put it on absorbent paper (like newspaper) for at least 30 minutes and see if the paper absorbs any moisture. If it does, your casting's not dry yet.

Once you've sealed your dried casting with a special plaster sealer, you can paint it. Use water-based acrylics or pastels for softer shading. You can also use various faux finishes like verdegris, stone, or marble. You'll then probably want to put on a finish coat to protect your piece and keep it from getting dirty. You can use a spray sealer in a matte, semi-gloss, or gloss finish, depending on the effect you're trying to achieve.

Painting a plastercast is a task that requires very fine skills and patience. It's more of a hobby for adults than children. However, you don't need a lot of tools to get started in plastercraft, and the skills required are fairly basic. If you start with a larger, less-detailed plaque or figure, even a young child can play along.

If you're planning on hanging your piece, you'll need some wire hangers to add before the plaster hardens. Make sure they are strong enough to hold your finished piece.

These are just a very few of the things you can do with clay, dough, and plaster. When you go to museums, art galleries, craft galleries, or craft shows, look for ways artists and craftspeople are using this medium. Ask questions and learn more.

The Least You Need to Know

➤ Pottery is a very old craft that has been raised to an art form by many cultures. It tells us a lot about how ancient peoples lived.

➤ There are many different kinds of clays. Some finished pieces made out of clay need to be fired at a high temperature to become hard.

➤ Polymer clays are among the most versatile clays available today and can be hardened in a home oven. They can't be used for objects that come in contact with food, however.

➤ Homemade doughs and clays can be used instead of commercial ones.

➤ To create textures, shapes, and patterns on clays and doughs you have only to look around you at everyday objects.

➤ Plastercraft requires few tools and is easy enough that even a young child can master it.

"I Have One Word For You, Son: Plastics!"

In This Chapter

➤ What is plastic and how can you use it in crafts?

➤ The sailor's art of lanyards and making braids

➤ Plastic canvas needlepoint expands needlework to 3-D

➤ How to make resin castings

➤ Other plastic materials and their possibilities

There's no doubt about it: Plastic is a miracle material. It lasts forever and doesn't break if you drop it. It can take quite a bit of impact and still hold liquids without leaking. Some plastics are incredibly strong and others can be made into objects that are amazingly delicate. And it's all around us.

As a crafting material, plastic is extremely versatile. Whether in sheet form, foam, mesh, or liquid, you and your child will enjoy exploring this modern craft material.

Plastics Primer

Plastic is the general name given to thermoplastic and thermosetting resins. We usually know the different types of plastics by their trade names, such as PVC (polyvinyl chloride), Styrofoam (polystyrene), or Plexiglas (polymethyl methacrylate). So when you say "plastic," you may actually be saying a mouthful without even knowing it.

There are several types of plastics that lend themselves to crafting. Some of the most versatile forms of plastics for crafting are plastic foam, plastic resin (used for casting), plastic lace, plastic canvas, and sheet acrylic. There are others, but these are the ones we'll concentrate on in this chapter.

In Chapter 19, you'll read about other ideas for recycling plastic products into craft materials. Here, we'll be dealing more with plastic as a raw material for crafts.

Can All Those Lifeguards Be Wrong? Lacing Lanyards

You've seen 'em. Every lifeguard worth his salt has a whistle hanging from a plastic laced lanyard around his neck. Plastic lanyards are used because they're durable, don't mind the salt water, and come in all those cool colors. Bird watchers and duck hunters wear them, too, to hold all those funny whistles and callers they use while traipsing around in the marshes. And if you ever were a Boy or Girl Scout, you probably made one.

Well, lanyards, or *boondoggles*, as they're sometimes called, are cool again. And they can be as basic or advanced as you want, depending on the type of weave you choose.

There are two lanyard kits with accompanying books that should help you get started. One, *The Lanyard Book*, comes with a book, plastic lacing in several colors, lanyard clips, key rings, and plastic pony beads. The second kit is called *Boondoggle: A Book of Lanyard & Lacing*. This one includes a spiral-bound book (which is nice because it lays flat when you're working) and comes with plastic lacing or boondoggle, a key ring, two lanyard clips, a bolo tie slide, and a metal bracelet blank. See Appendix A for more information about these titles.

You can use these kits or just buy the plastic lacing and metal accessories separately from a craft or hobby supply store (or one of the mail-order sources I've mentioned in Appendix A). In addition, you'll need some scissors, some big metal sandwich-type paper clips, some clear plastic tape, and perhaps some additional beads, buttons, or charms.

One braid that's generally taught to beginners is the box, and that's the one I'm going to describe here.

Handiwords
A *lanyard* is a small cord or rope for securing or suspending small objects, such as a whistle or key, around the neck, often woven of several flat strands of plastic, leather, or other material.

Handiwords
The word *boondoggle* was coined by Robert H. Link, an American scoutmaster. It means a braided cord worn by Boy Scouts as a neckerchief slide, hat band, or ornament. The word later came to mean a wasteful or impractical project or activity often involving graft. Who knew?

Project: Lanyard Key Chain

Level: Medium

Age: 7 and up

Materials needed: Two plastic laces in different colors (each about 24 inches long) a key ring, extra lace or string to make an anchor (long enough to wrap around your knee and tie comfortably)

Directions:

1. Fold each strand of plastic lace in half and make a crease, so you know where the center is. Cross the two strands of plastic lace at their centers.

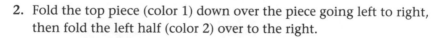

Starting your lanyard.

2. Fold the top piece (color 1) down over the piece going left to right, then fold the left half (color 2) over to the right.

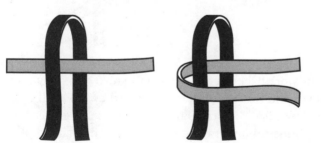

The next step in weaving your lanyard.

continues

Project: Continued

3. Fold the right-hand piece of color 1 back up and weave the top piece of color 2 over the nearest strand of color 1 and under the farthest strand of color 1. Pull everything tight.

How to finish weaving and what your finished box should look like.

4. Turn your work over and slip your anchor piece through the loop on the back. Tie it around your knee or on a doorknob or the back of a chair (or whatever is handy for you to pull against).

Inserting the anchor loop.

5. Turn your work back over and make the next "box" by folding the top piece down and the bottom piece down (they are both color 1), keeping them side by side. Then cross the left color 2 piece over the nearest color 1 strand and under the color 1 strand that's farthest away. Repeat with the color 2 strand on the right. Pull tight.

6. Repeat the process until your braid is the desired length. Tie a knot as shown in the following figure and then insert your key ring and do it again. Make sure your knot is tight.

Project: Continued

Finished knot.

7. Or, you can insert your key ring at the beginning and use your anchor through the ring, forming the first box braid around the ring.

Variation using the key ring to start.

Now that you've mastered your first lacing, try some of the other stitches, like the diamond, the zipper, the spiral, or the snake using the references I've given you in Appendix A. You can make woven covers for barrettes or bracelets. You can get glow-in-the-dark lacing for added fun.

Here are a few tips to keep in mind when you create lanyards:

➤ Don't be afraid to pull apart your lacing and try again until you get a particular braiding technique down.

➤ You may want to start off with manageable lengths (20 to 24 inches is good) before you try to weave something longer, just for practice.

➤ Snip the ends of your laces on a slant to make them easier to thread. Don't allow your laces to twist, but keep them flat. If they do twist, undo your lacing to where the twist is, then continue.

> **Bet You Didn't Know**
> *Ooooo...*
> Modern lanyards are the descendants of those created by cowboys, who made lassos and halters out of strands of leather; and sailors, who spliced and knotted ropes.

➤ Unravel your lacing and smooth it out before using, since it will probably come looped and tied or wound on a spool. That'll make it easier to work with. Keep tightening your work by pulling and coaxing strands together with your fingernail. Don't stretch too hard, though, or your lace may break.

➤ If you're a lefty, don't forget to reverse the directions!

If you decide you like lanyard lacing, I suggest you find a book or an expert to show you the more advanced techniques. They take a little practice and it's especially helpful to be able to see them done, rather than try to follow written instructions.

One of the great things about lanyard lacing is its portability. Make up a small kit with lacing in a variety of colors, some hooks and rings, beads, and photocopies of the instructions for a few different stitches. Throw it all in a zip-top plastic bag and you're all set. Kids can take it with them on a long car trip, to the beach, on vacation, or just to occupy a rainy day.

Bonding Experiences

Take your kids on a field trip to a tack shop (they sell horse and riding supplies) and look at all the different ways braiding is used. See if you can spot the types of braids you learned making your lanyards. Notice the different types of materials that can be used in braiding besides flat plastic lace and the differences they make in texture and design.

Needlepoint in 3-D: Plastic Canvas

If you've never worked with plastic canvas, do give it a try. This plastic mesh comes in various sizes and has a lot going for it when it comes to doing needlework crafts with kids:

➤ Plastic canvas is virtually indestructible, both when you're working with it and when a project is in its completed form.

➤ Plastic canvas comes in various mesh sizes (5, 7, 10, and 14), so you can use a bigger mesh (5 or 7 mesh) for younger children and graduate to a finer mesh. By mesh size, we mean the size of the holes.

➤ Plastic canvas is portable.

➤ Best of all, plastic canvas can be made into three-dimensional shapes and covered with colorful needlepoint stitches, which means it can be used for lots of useful as well as decorative objects. I've heard of plastic canvas used to make Barbie doll furniture, dollhouses, pull-toys, and, of course, the inevitable Christmas tree ornaments or refrigerator magnets.

➤ Plastic canvas is a great way to teach or learn needlepoint, since the canvas doesn't ravel and the finished product doesn't need to be blocked by stretching to correct and even out its shape.

➤ Plastic canvas is washable, which makes it perfect for place mats and coasters.

To work with plastic canvas, I suggest using the 7-mesh size to start. Four-ply worsted-weight yarn works well, but you can also buy a special plastic canvas yarn (Needloft is one company that makes it) that's designed to cover plastic canvas. You'll need a tapestry needle (size 16 is good). The only other tool you'll need is a pair of scissors or a plastic canvas cutter.

Here are a few tips to help you and your kids make wonderful designs with plastic canvas:

➤ Begin with simple shapes.

➤ Some people like to stitch their work first, then cut out the shape. Others like to cut their canvas first. Do whatever works best for you.

➤ When following a pattern for a plastic canvas project, remember to count the bars between the rows of holes, not the holes.

➤ Plastic canvas comes in clear mesh and in colors. You may want to use the colored mesh if you're not stitching the entire project and want some to remain see-through.

➤ You may want to draw the outline of your shape first onto the canvas with a non-permanent marker, then cut out the pattern.

➤ Cut in the spaces between the bars (not the bars themselves) and trim the corners, so the canvas doesn't show through.

➤ Clean the marker off with water and a cloth before you start to stitch.

To get the idea of using plastic canvas and yarn together, and to teach you a simple needlepoint stitch, start with the following bookmark project. Once you learn how it's done, you'll be making them for everyone!

Project: Plastic Canvas Bookmark

Level: Easy

Age: 5 and up

Materials needed: A sheet of 7-mesh plastic canvas (your finished bookmark will be approximately 1¼ inches by 6 inches), yarn in any color you desire (variegated works nicely), a size-16 tapestry needle

Directions:

1. You can cut out your shape first or work on a larger sheet and cut it out later. Start your yarn from behind, and instead of making a knot, leave some yarn and hold down until you've made a few stitches so the yarn won't pull through.

2. Using the Continental-tent stitch (see the following figure), work across your first row starting at the top. Always work to your left and from top to bottom diagonally.

Continental tent stitch on plastic canvas.

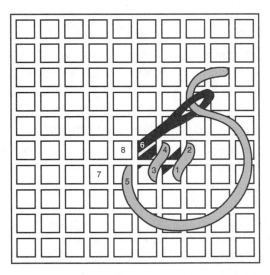

3. When you finish your first row, leave your needle at the back of your work and turn the canvas upside down, so the top is now at the bottom.

4. Come up with your needle just to the left of the last stitch you made, but in the next row (see the following figure), and stitch your next row.

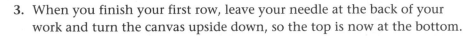

Project: Continued

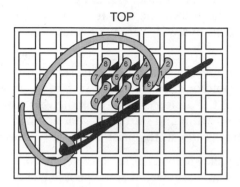

TOP

Stiching second row of project.

5. Keep rotating the canvas before you begin each row so all your stitches are worked in the same direction.

6. Repeat until you've completely covered the canvas in the correct dimensions. Work the loose threads on the back through the stitches so they're hidden. You can leave the back plain or cut a piece of coordinating felt just slightly smaller than the finished dimensions of your bookmark and glue it on the back.

With plastic canvas, you can design anything you want. You can purchase patterns from craft stores or find scores of projects in crafts magazines. There are even magazines devoted to plastic canvas crafts:

➤ *Plastic Canvas Corner*, six issues a year. Contact P.O. Box 420229, Palm Coast, FL 32142-0229, (800) 829-9159.

➤ *Plastic Canvas Crafts* and *Plastic Canvas World*, both published every other month. Contact *Plastic Canvas Crafts*, P.O. Box 9020, Big Sandy, TX 75755, (800) 829-5865; or *Plastic Canvas World*, P.O. Box 420235, Palm Coast, FL 32142, (800) 829-5865.

➤ *Plastic Canvas! Magazine* and *Quick & Easy Plastic Canvas*, both published every month. Contact 23 Old Pecan Road, Big Sandy, TX 75755.

There's a plastic canvas newsgroup on the Internet at alt.crafts.plastic-canvas. There are also plenty of Web sites, both personal and commercial, that can give you an idea of the versatility of plastic canvas.

Now it's time to try some new stitches and more complicated projects!

Friendly Plastic

Another plastic material that's easy to use with young children, yet sophisticated enough for use by adults, is called Friendly Plastic. It's a modeling material made by the American Art Clay Company, Inc. that's non-toxic and can be used to create toys, jewelry, masks, and even fishing lures. It comes in sticks in a wide variety of colors.

Crafty Clues
To contact the American Art Clay Company, makers of Friendly Plastic, contact AMACO, 4717 W. 16th Street, Indianapolis, IN 46222, (800) 374-1600).

Safety Signals
Children should be supervised while using an oven. Make sure they understand that surfaces are hot and teach them to use oven mitts to put pans in and take them out. Don't forget to remind them to turn the oven off when they're done!

Friendly Plastic can be softened in warm water or in the oven (follow manufacturer's directions) and then pressed into a mold or onto a textured surface to embed a design into it. If the design doesn't look the way you want, simply heat it up again and start over—but you need to work quickly, because as the plastic cools it will become hard.

Friendly Plastic looks different when it's baked, rather than softened in warm water. Some people like to use a potpourri simmer pot for softening it, others prefer a toaster oven set at 200 degrees, but watch your plastic carefully, since oven temperatures vary. If you're using a toaster oven, always line the oven pan with aluminum foil, since you don't want food coming in contact with any plastic residue.

As you work with Friendly Plastic, you're likely to get scraps. Don't throw them away. Just put them all together on a piece of foil and heat them in the oven. They'll melt together and you can cut new multi-colored shapes from your scrap sheet.

For more information about Friendly Plastic, look for books and materials at your local crafts store, or order it from Sunshine Discount Crafts (see Appendix A). Some books you might find helpful are *Friendly Plastic Step By Step* and *Friendly Plastic Wear With Flair: 16 Jewelry Designs That Shine.* Again, see Appendix A for more information.

Cast Your Treasures in Plastic Resin

A craft more suitable for older children (age eight and up) is acrylic resin casting. This craft allows you to embed or encase just about anything in a clear plastic shape.

Some items your child might enjoy casting are pieces of colored glass, coins, dead insects or other natural specimens, marbles, leaves, pressed or whole flowers, hardware or parts like nuts and bolts, rocks, seeds, beans, grains, shells, old jewelry or watch parts...as I said, just about anything.

Even paper, fabric, or photographs can be encased in plastic, but you'll need to seal them first to protect them. Coat them with a sealant known generically as a vinyl resin glue/sealer, allow it to dry, and then embed the object in the resin.

Here's what you need to begin acrylic resin casting:

➤ The plastic resin

➤ A catalyst

➤ An eyedropper to dispense the catalyst

➤ Some disposable (unwaxed) cups to mix it in

➤ Some popsicle sticks to mix it up

➤ A mold (available from your crafts store, or you can make your own)

➤ The items you want to embed

➤ Mold release to make it easier to get the hardened casting out of the mold (optional)

To begin experimenting with plastic resin casting, I suggest you buy your first mold at the craft store. I also suggest you start with a single-layer casting; smaller projects are probably the easiest to begin with. Here are the basic instructions:

1. Follow the instructions on your containers of plastic resin and catalyst and mix the exact amounts of casting plastic and catalyst for the first layer.

2. Stir well using your wooden stick. Try to "cut through" the liquid and introduce as few air bubbles into the mixture as possible.

3. Pour the liquid into the mold to form the bottom layer of the casting.

4. Let the first layer set until it's rubbery. Poke it lightly with a wooden stick to make sure it's ready. (Don't use your finger as you may embed your fingerprint!) It's ready when it is about as firm as set Jell-O and doesn't stick to the stick.

5. Carefully lay the objects you want to embed on the base layer. Before you place them, decide which side of the casting you want them to be facing.

6. Mix the plastic and catalyst for the next layer. The instructions for mixing the second layer may be different than the first, so read the directions on your containers carefully. The proportion of catalyst to plastic usually changes with succeeding layers.

Handiwords
A *catalyst* is a substance that causes or accelerates a chemical reaction without being permanently affected by the reaction.

Crafty Clues
When you're working with resin casting, make sure that you measure your plastic and catalyst carefully. If the directions say 45 drops, make it 45 drops! You may also have to make some adjustments depending on the room temperature in which you're working. Also, keep your work area clean. Dust will get into the mold and become a permanent part of your project. You can cover the mold with plastic wrap while you're waiting for the layers to harden to help minimize dust and debris. Make sure your containers and molds are clean, too.

7. Continue mixing, pouring, laying out your objects, and allowing the layer to set, according to package directions, until you're finished.

8. Let your casting cool completely (from four to 24 hours) and then pop it loose from the mold. You can tell it's set when it makes a clicking sound when you tap it with your wooden stick.

9. Smooth off any rough spots that may be left on the casting with a medium-grade file. Do this very gently.

10. Sand the casting with a very fine sandpaper by laying the sandpaper on a flat surface and moving the casting over it.

11. Buff the casting with a soft cloth (or buffing wheel) and plastic buffing compound.

Crafty Clues

Use a hair dryer to warm up the mold and dry the surface of your mold. Moisture in the mold could cause defects like white spots or even cracking in the casting. It's also a good idea to get all your casting products (plastic, catalyst, and additives) from the same manufacturer since they're formulated to work properly together. Don't mix products from different manufacturers.

Safety Signals

The chemicals used in casting could cause a rash. Wear rubber gloves when you and your child are handling the liquid plastic and try not to get any on your skin. If you do spill some on you, wash the area immediately with warm water and soap. Keep your work area well ventilated as well.

You can add dyes or pigments to color your resin casting, but only use those specially formulated for use with polyester casting resin. Dyes are usually transparent and pigments are usually opaque.

Be sure to clean your molds carefully (the same is true for all molds, including candle molds) so you can use them again. Don't use steel wool or scouring powder. Even a sharp fingernail can make an indentation in a soft polyethylene mold. If you do scratch or dent a mold, get rid of it and start with a new one. Always look molds over carefully in the store for imperfections.

If you want to move on to advanced casting, you can try creating your own molds. Molds can be made from a variety of materials: oven-proof glass (like Pyrex), certain rubbers and plastics (poly plastic molds are among the easiest to work with), metal, aluminum, and stainless steel. You can pour your mold so that multiple objects are all embedded on the same level, or do a multi-layer pouring, where you allow each layer to gel before adding more objects and pouring again. The multi-layer technique gives your piece a feeling of depth and interest.

Resin casting is a great way of taking what seems like just a lot of clutter, souvenirs, or small collections, and making them into something both useful and pretty to look at.

A good booklet to get you started with plastic resin casting is the *Castin' Craft Idea Book* by Casey Carlton (see Appendix A for information). Your local crafts store should have all the supplies you need, too. The ones I use are called Castin' Craft brand and they're from E.T.I. in Fields Landing, California.

Other Ideas for Plastic

Acrylic sheets known as Plexiglas or Lucite can be cut, joined, painted, and used for any number of crafts projects. You can drill them, glue them, or use tape to join edges.

Styrofoam is actually a brand name for plastic foam from The Dow Chemical Company. You may have used it as a base for Christmas ornaments or in the form of florist's foam for making flower arrangements, but Styrofoam has lots of other crafting uses. It makes a great wreath form and there are cone-shaped forms that are used for topiary. If you're looking for more ideas about how to use plastic foam, try the Dow Styrofoam crafts Web site at http://www.styrofoam-crafts.com/.

The relatively thin plastic foam you find in produce trays make great inkpad stamps (glued to an applicator, like an empty plastic film container) or stencils. This foam can be covered with various substances, like plaster, wallboard compound, gesso, modeling paste, or other wall texturing materials to give it texture. Use a low-temperature glue gun, as high temperatures will melt the plastic. You can paint it, too (use water-based paints, since paints made with solvents may cause Styrofoam to pit or disintegrate).

If you want to learn more about objects you can make with plastic foam, order the video "Styrofoam Wizardry" from Creative Pastimes in Video, P.O. Box 7, Walworth, WI 53184, (800) 327-5403.

Then there's soft craft foam, the floppy kind you sometimes see as a packing material for those luscious mail-order fruit baskets you get around the holidays. This plastic foam can be purchased in various size sheets, cut, and used to make all sorts of things. It makes a great (and safe) base for costume pieces like bunny ears or flower petals. Soft foam can be spray-painted (make sure your paint is safe for plastic foam) for an all-over color or painted with water-based paints for detail.

One of my next purchases is going to be a laminating machine. With this plastic sealing device you can seal

> **Crafty Clues**
> You can cut plastic foam by using a *coping* or *scroll saw* (a narrow saw mounted in a frame used for cutting curved ornamental designs) or running a serrated knife along an old candle so it's waxed to make it glide easier. Some people swear by an electric serrated knife. You can smooth out rough edges by "sanding" the foam with another piece of foam.

> **Safety Signals**
> Use caution when cutting plastic foam, as it may give off dust. (Denser foams don't give off as much dust when they're cut.) If you're going to be cutting a lot of foam, use a respirator and always use safety glasses to protect your eyes.

all your child's paper or fabric crafts in plastic so they'll last a lifetime. And you can also use it for laminating photos, recipe cards, and membership cards in between crafts sessions!

We've just barely touched the surface of the crafts you can make with plastics. New and better plastic products that are non-toxic, versatile, and easy to use are coming on the market all the time. Check out your crafts magazines and crafts and hobby stores to see what's new in plastics.

The Least You Need to Know

➤ Plastic is a general name for thermosetting resins and there are many forms of plastic suitable for crafting.

➤ Making lanyards is a craft that's adaptable to children of most ages and highly portable.

➤ Plastic canvas is a great medium for learning needlepoint and has the bonus of being rigid enough to use to make three-dimensional shapes.

➤ Resin casting is a fun craft best done with older children.

➤ Working with various plastic materials carries with it some safety considerations. Read directions carefully, use common sense, and observe safety precautions.

Chapter 14

Looking at Glass

In This Chapter

➤ Using glass you already have around the house

➤ How to cut glass safely

➤ Experimenting with stained glass

➤ Blown glass and lampwork

➤ Working in mosaic

Glass holds a fascination for almost everyone. It gleams, it glistens, it refracts light; whether colored or clear, it holds a special magic. Glass can be incredibly delicate and yet amazingly strong. In our homes, it keeps the elements out and the climate we create for ourselves in, yet it allows us to see the world as it passes by. And glass is a canvas or palette for some of the most exquisite works of art the world has ever known.

As craftspeople, we can melt it and mold it, twist it, blow it into gossamer threads, or make it into paper-thin crystal. We can use it for beads, eat off of it, drink out of it, and back it with silver and see our own reflection.

You and your child maybe itching to work with glass as a craft material, but you may be holding back because you think it's either too difficult or too dangerous for children. Well, think again!

You don't necessarily have to get into cutting glass to work with it creatively. Some projects involve painting, etching, or combining ready-made glass objects.

I'm going to talk about two different techniques: painting on glass and glass etching. With these techniques, you can create hand-decorated glass medallions, panels, small windows, containers, bottles, tableware, candle holders, and canisters for yourselves or to give away as gifts.

If you'd like to learn stained glass with your child, I'll give you some strategies and resources to get started. You can also create a stained-glass "look" with paint. I'll show you how to do that, too.

Bonding Experiences

If you can, visit a museum that specializes in decorative arts like the Metropolitan Museum of Art in New York City or the Smithsonian in Washington, D.C. Don't overlook smaller local museums, since they often display everyday objects. If you can't get to see these objects in person, trot on over to your local library and look for books about antique glass.

Glass Painting

Let's start with painting on glass. You can use both paints that do not need firing in a kiln and paints that do, and the results are different. I'm going to assume you don't have access to a kiln and would like to work with paints that harden on their own.

I recommend DEKA paints from Decart, Inc. You'll find DEKA-Transparent paint, a professional-quality, solvent-based glass paint; DEKA-Translucent, a water-based glass paint; and DEKA-Outline Paste, which is also water-based and used to create the "leading" for a stained-glass look. The outline paste comes in black, gray, silver, and gold. Make sure whatever you buy is specifically formulated for glass, and read the directions carefully for drying and cleanup. You'll need to know whether water is sufficient for cleanup or if you'll need a solvent.

For your first project, why not work with a free material you undoubtedly have an abundance of—used glass jars? Once you start looking at common jars as a crafts material, you'll start to notice the many shapes and sizes that are available and ideas for uses will suggest themselves. Large jars (mayonnaise or pickle jars) can become canisters; smaller jars (jelly or baby food jars) can be votive holders or hold cotton balls or cotton swabs on the bathroom counter.

Any glass jar you might use as a container can now become one you've decorated yourself.

Project: Painting on Glass Jars

Level: Medium

Age: 7 and up

Materials needed: Used glass jars and bottles, glass paints in assorted colors, outline paste (optional), an assortment of brushes (synthetic brushes, flat, round, and outliners)

Directions:

I'm going to give you some illustrations that should give you some ideas for designs, but I'm sure you'll come up with many more of your own.

1. Wash your jar in hot, soapy water and remove any labels. (If there's a glue residue left behind by the label and you can't get it off with just soap and water, try one of those citrus solvents formulated for this purpose.) Dry the jar completely.

2. Cover your work surface with newspapers and have whatever cleaning solution you'll need for your brushes already set up. Open a window or otherwise make sure you have good ventilation.

3. If you're going to do an outline, test the outline paste before you start to learn how much pressure you need to apply to get it to come out evenly from the tube. Remember, if you make a mistake with either the outline paste or the paints, it's easy to correct by wiping it off with a paper towel before it dries or scraping it off with a craft knife after it dries.

4. Paint your outline first. If you're working from an existing pattern, you can tape the paper pattern on the inside of the jar and follow it from the outside. Or, you can work freehand. Let the outline dry according to directions, then paint with transparent glass paints. Hold the jar up to the light periodically to see how it looks. It'll look different with the light coming through it.

5. Allow your design to dry thoroughly (this usually takes about two days).

To turn your glass jar into a lantern, put a layer of sand on the bottom and add a votive or tea light and a wrapped wire handle (20-gauge works well).

continues

Project: Continued

A handpainted glass jar.

The uses for handpainted glass are unlimited and jars are just the beginning. Look for clear-glass votive holders in bargain stores and at garage sales. The square ones are easier to paint on than the round ones, especially for younger children. Add some handpainting and they become a special holiday accessory, a decorative accent in your home or at the family table, or a special gift.

Safety Signals
If you'll be working with adhesive lead for more than one or two projects, you'll want to wear plastic gloves and make sure you wash your hands thoroughly before eating or drinking, since lead is poisonous.

You can handpaint glass globes that fit over lamps to give them a custom look. Or try using your child's handpainted glass as an accent to his own self-decorated bedroom. You can also paint the glass "chimneys" that go over colonial-style–candle lanterns or oil lamps. I've seen complete landscapes and scenes painted on these, which look wonderful when the light glows through them.

Even flat pieces of glass or medallions can be painted and then hung. The raw edges can be finished off with adhesive lead or metal foil tape, both of which you can get at craft or stained glass supply stores. You can use metal foil tape to put flat pieces of glass together, too, to make your own votives.

You can also stamp on glass using any enamel glass paint and either flexible stamps (you can get these in rubber stamp stores or your local crafts store) or stamps made out of sponges. You'll need a paintbrush or applicator sponge to get the paint on the stamp evenly. Press firmly over the entire stamp, especially over curved areas, and lift it gently off the glass. If you want to switch colors with the same stamp, just blot off the color on a double-thickness, damp paper towel.

Another word about paints: There are many different paints on the market and more are becoming available all the time. Next time you go to your local art supply or craft store, ask about glass paints. Experiment with different products, including those that need to be baked in your home oven. You'll find they have different characteristics that create different effects, and you may discover products you especially like working with.

Glass Etching

True glass etching is done by sandblasting, but there are etching creams on the market that simulate the sandblasting effect by producing a chemical reaction with the glass.

One brand is Armour Etch cream (from Armour Products in Wyckoff, New Jersey). Armour's starter kit includes rub-on stencils you can use. The cream is also available in separate bottles at hobby and craft stores. Another brand is Reddi-Etch from Plaid Enterprises, Inc. in Norcross, Georgia. Their Web site is http://www.plaidonline.com.

It's best to practice etching on an old piece of glass (good thing you've got that unlimited supply) and then try it on a special piece.

The basic procedure (follow the specific directions on your particular etching cream product) is to clean the glass first, put the cream on, and let it set for two or three minutes. Then you dunk the glass into a sink filled with water and remove the cream. You can use an old toothbrush to scrub it off. Then wash the glass in soapy water. That's all there is to it!

You may want to work with stencils, and there are lots to choose from (some brand names to look for are Peel 'n' Etch and Rub 'n' Etch) or you can make your own stencils from masking tape or contact adhesive paper. Just cut out the pattern with a craft knife, apply the stencil, apply the cream, then peel the stencil off after you've washed off the cream.

If you have any trouble finding glass etching supplies or want to learn more, check out the EtchWorld Web site maintained by Eastern Art Glass at http://www.etchworld.com.

Safety Signals
It's a good idea for you and your child to wear plastic gloves when using etching creams. Keep these products out of children's reach when not using them together.

Cutting Glass Without Tears

You may have tried to cut glass with a hand glass-cutting tool before and had it break or shatter. Believe me, so have I. Well, there are some secrets that will help you cut glass cleanly nearly every time. Of course, if you're going to get into serious stained glass, you'll be doing a lot of cutting and may want to get either a band saw outfitted for cutting glass or a professional glass cutter.

However, for most purposes, a hand glass-cutting tool will do the job (a well-known brand is Fletcher-Terry). These usually have a steel cutting blade.

There are more expensive cutting tools that use a tungsten carbide wheel for cutting. Although they run about $40, the replacement wheels are only around $9, and they last longer than steel cutting blades. Make sure you buy the kind with the ball on the handle or similar device for tapping glass to separate it. You'll also need some kerosene for lubricating the cutting wheel (it's a good idea to keep a jar with kerosene handy so you can dip your cutting wheel into it for lubrication periodically as you work). Or you can buy self-oiling cutters that eliminate the need to lubricate as you go along. These come with carbide steel blades advertised to last 25 times longer than conventional cutters.

Before you start, make sure you have a firm, flat, and level cutting surface. It should be at a comfortable height if you're standing, since you can get the best leverage from a standing position. Usually 34 to 36 inches from the floor is good, but you may have to adjust that depending on your height. Use a piece of plywood under several layers of newspapers to create a surface that has some "give," which helps make cutting the glass easier.

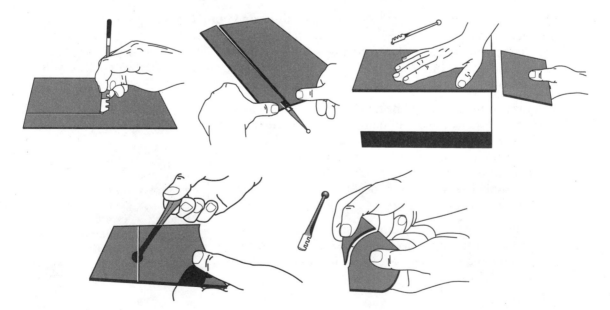

Sample glass cutting techniques.

Clean the glass first with water and dishwashing liquid. Your aim is to remove any dirt that may cause the cutter to skip and leave a gap in the cut edge, which can cause the glass to break. Use warm water, since warm glass cuts more easily.

Make sure the cutting tool is perpendicular to the surface. It can lean a bit toward you, but only a little, and be careful not to lean the tool sideways.

Begin at the edge farthest from you and pull the cutter toward you without stopping, pressing firmly. You should hear it make a scratching sound. As you near the edge closest to you, relax your hand a bit so you don't chip the glass at the edge. While you cut, apply adequate pressure from your shoulder, not your wrist. Don't lift the cutter before you're through.

Separate the glass IMMEDIATELY. The glass actually "heals" itself somewhat if you wait more than a couple of minutes to separate it, making it extremely difficult to separate the glass cleanly, if at all. You can do this with your hands or by laying the scored line over the edge of a table and snapping it down. If it resists a bit, use the ball on the end of the cutter to gently tap the glass from underneath along the score line.

Crafty Clues
When cutting glass, make sure you have your work surface fully set up so you won't have to stop while you're making a cut.

Safety Signals
Always wear eye protection when cutting or grinding glass.

You can work safely with glass without getting cut if you observe some basic safety rules:

➤ Never shuffle through pieces of glass with your bare hands. Remove pieces one by one from the top down and wear gloves where feasible.

➤ Watch for small slivers, especially along the edges of freshly cut glass. You can remove these by scraping the edge with another piece of glass or sanding it lightly under water.

➤ Keep a small table brush and trash can nearby so you can brush away glass shards. Clean up frequently.

➤ Cut glass in an area away from your pets so they can't accidentally knock over any glass or step on a shard.

➤ Always wear eye protection when cutting or grinding glass.

Now that you and your child have some experience working with the more simple glass crafts, you may want to "graduate" to the far more complex craft of stained glass. You'll have to gauge your child's readiness for this more difficult craft, but the rewards are well worth the effort and patience it takes to get started.

Handiwords
Came is a slender, grooved bar of lead used to hold together the pieces of glass in windows of latticework or stained glass.

Bet You Didn't Know
Stained glass was developed because glass manufacturers couldn't make glass large enough to fit the windows of Gothic cathedrals. Glass artisans devised a way to join small pieces of glass with strips of lead. Medieval glass windows became giant picture books of Bible stories for those churchgoers who were unable to read. Medieval legend has it that stained glass was made of melted rubies and emeralds, but this, luckily, wasn't true. Who could afford it?

Handiwords
Lampwork is the art of making beads or other objects by forming molten glass that has been heated over a special lamp.

Stained Glass

Perhaps you've seen beautiful colored glass windows in churches or old Victorian homes and wondered if you could learn this craft. Well, you can, and there are many ways to "get your feet wet" with stained glass without using expensive equipment and tools. Stained glass is a fairly difficult craft that requires some patience and skill, but older children can learn it, too.

One way to get started is to buy a kit with pre-cut glass. Some of these kits take only an hour to assemble and all you need are a few tools, some *solder, flux*, and lead *came* (a grooved bar that holds together the pieces of glass). The Delphi Stained Glass catalog offers several project kits (see Appendix A for information).

After doing a few of these pre-cut kits, you and your child should be able to decide if you want to get further into stained glass. If you do, I recommend you take a class. Not that you can't learn from a book (people do), but you need to learn how to handle equipment like a grinder and a glass saw, plus you'll need advice on what to buy. Check out adult education programs, community colleges, recreation centers, and stained glass suppliers and studios to find a class.

If you want to read about stained glass first, a few books recommended by stained glass crafters for beginners are *How to Work in Stained Glass*, *Stained Glass Primer Vol. 1: The Basic Skills*, and *Stained Glass Primer Vol. 2: Advanced Skills and Annotated Bibliography*. See Appendix A for more information.

An excellent set of videos by the stained glass artist Vicki Payne can be extremely helpful as well. They are available in stained glass catalogs (see Appendix A) or you can check out her Web site at http://www.foryourhome.com.

Hot Glass

As a bead crafter, I have to confess I'm very intrigued by the hot techniques for working with glass, especially *lampwork*, which is used to make glass beads. To do hot-glass work, you need a torch and other special tools. This craft is not suitable for young children, but older children might enjoy it, along with adults.

In hot-glass work, rods of glass are heated and formed in the flame of a torch, and various tools are used to create patterns and textures. Another aspect of this craft is glass blowing, which is even more involved.

If you'd like to learn more about working with hot glass to make beads, check out *Making Glass Beads* or *More Than You Ever Wanted to Know About Glass Beadmaking*. See Appendix A for more resources.

Glass Mosaic

What to do with those broken glass pieces? How about making a *mosaic*?

Mosaics can be made of many materials, not just glass. A common material is tile, both broken pieces and fully formed geometric shapes. Broken pieces of mirror, tiles, china, and colored glass are also popular. You can even add glass marbles if you can find the kind with the flat backs sometimes called gems.

To get the idea of what it's like to fit small shapes together to make a pattern, you can even use paper. This would be a great side craft you could do with a younger child, while older children can work on more advanced glass techniques.

You can also use a number of materials on which to mount your mosaic. You can even apply mosaic to curved surfaces like glass bottles and jars, so it becomes another technique for decorating glass.

The basic mosaic technique is simple and the materials are relatively safe. Just apply the adhesive to the back of the tiles or glass pieces and adhere them to the surface you want to cover. You can fit pieces together in a pattern or just place them randomly. Then you fill in the spaces in between the pieces with *grout* (a thin, coarse mortar used for filling masonry joints and spaces between tiles or mosaic pieces), wipe away the excess, let it dry, and you have a mosaic!

If you'd like to start with a kit, try the one from Vicki Payne: Vic's Crafts Mosaic Glass Kit, from Vic's Crafts, Web site: http://www.foryourhome.com. Once you get the hang of it, you'll start hoping somebody drops the china!

Handiwords
A *mosaic* is a picture or decoration made of small pieces of inlaid stone, glass, etc.

Handiwords
A thin, coarse mortar called *grout* is used for filling masonry joints and spaces between tiles or pieces in a mosaic.

Bet You Didn't Know
Mosaics are believed to have originated in the Near East around 5,000 years ago, although they didn't become really popular until the 8th century B.C. They faded in popularity when stained glass windows replaced mosaics in churches at the end of the 12th century. They have enjoyed a revival in the 20th century.

For further reading about mosaic crafts and glass crafts in general, try these books and organizations. For more information, see Appendix A.

➤ *Making Mosaics: Designs, Techniques and Projects* by Leslie Dierks

➤ *The Mosaic Book: Ideas, Projects, and Techniques* by Peggy Vance and Celia Goodrich-Clarke

➤ The Art Glass Suppliers Association International (AGSA) P.O. Box 3388, Zanesville, OH 43702; (614) 452-2552; Web site: http://www.creative-industries.com/agsa

➤ The International Guild of Glass Artists at 54 Cherry Street, North Adams, MA 01247. The IGGA has a newsletter called "Common Ground: GLASS," and a Web site chock full of resources and information at http://www.bungi.com/glass/igga/.

Crafting with glass has lots of possibilities and we've only touched on a few. Start with crafts that don't involve cutting or using flame (painting on glass, mosaic) and then move on to the more complex techniques if you and your child have the interest and ability.

The Least You Need to Know

➤ Although some glass paints need to be fired, there are some paints that you can air-dry or harden in your oven.

➤ True glass etching is done by sandblasting, but there are etching cremes that are easy to use and give a similar effect.

➤ You can learn to cut glass effectively and safely by knowing a few simple tricks, such as holding your cutting tool perpendicular and breaking off cut pieces immediately.

➤ Stained glass is an advanced craft that can be done by older children. The fundamentals of stained glass are best learned in a class.

➤ Broken glass, tile, and china pieces can be used to make beautiful mosaic designs.

Part 3
Mixed Media

Now that you and your child are well versed in each of the major crafts areas, let's move on to some crafts that combine one or more of these skills and materials.

In this part, you and your child will get a chance to adapt your newfound skills in a different way. Enjoy working with clay? Whip up some bread dough in the kitchen and you'll give up "loafing" forever! Is working with wood your thing? Make your wood projects fly or sing by exploring toymaking and musical instrument construction. Did you like working with fiber and fabric, metal or glass? Learn how to transform natural materials or found objects into all sorts of usable and beautiful projects.

So, grab the kids, open up your eyes, roll up your sleeves, and let's do some more crafts!

Chapter 15

Now You're Cookin! Crafts in the Kitchen

> ## In This Chapter
>
> ➤ The kitchen as "crafts central"
>
> ➤ Important tips for safety in the kitchen
>
> ➤ Bread baking and bread dough crafts
>
> ➤ Basic candle making from start to finish
>
> ➤ Creating soaps, scents, creams, and cosmetics in the kitchen

If you think you spend too much time in the kitchen, think again! You and your kids will discover a whole new crafts room hidden in your kitchen. Think of your food preparation area as a laboratory, fully equipped with a heat source, the means to chill or freeze, running water, counter space to spread out and a variety of tools, and implements to challenge and enhance your creativity.

So, wash and dry the dishes, clear off the countertops, put on your aprons, and get ready to turn your everyday food preparation area into a crafts center *par excellence*!

Food, Fabulous Food

Never thought of cooking as a craft? Well, I think it is. Food preparation and presentation allow you to express your creativity in the way you combine colors, textures, and shapes. In addition, food preparation requires that you learn certain skills, just like any other craft. Finally, it offers lots of opportunities for experimentation and personalization. Sounds like a craft to me! And it's an activity that's extremely rewarding to share with kids.

Cooking is one of those survival skills that stays with us throughout our lives. Besides giving us pleasure (and making us popular!), cooking teaches us many other life skills. Through cooking we learn how to measure both liquids and solids, experience the magic in the chemical reactions of various substances, become familiar with the properties of extreme heat and cold, and learn how to use a variety of tools. We learn the methods of sifting, mixing, folding, kneading, boiling, simmering, baking, roasting, and grilling, to name just a few, and we learn to follow directions (and what happens when we don't). The kitchen is also the place where we create some of the most sensual experiences in life.

Bonding Experiences

Play the taste-testing game. Clean and cut up various food items. Include foods with different textures, as well as both fresh and dried ingredients. Blindfold your child and have her smell and taste each item, describe it in her own words, and then guess what it is. Then turn the tables—let her prepare the food, and you don the blindfold.

Safety Signals
Adults should always supervise the use of knives and should do all the cutting for younger children.

The kitchen is a good place to teach safety around sharp objects, heat, and electricity.

It helps if your kitchen has lots of counter space and is outfitted with materials that resist scratches and stains, but even if it's not ideal, there's a lot you can do to make it work as a crafts center. Put up a temporary table or cover the kitchen table with newspaper or plastic. Cover the kitchen floor with newspaper or a plastic painter's drop cloth. Be sure to protect your clothing and your child's clothing. Look over your kitchen area carefully with an eye to increasing efficiency, safety, and ease of cleanup. Use Chapters 3, 4, and 5 as your guide.

Start with the Staff of Life

I'm not going to cover the whole subject of cooking with kids here, since there are several good books that do the job very well (listed in Appendix A). But we are going to explore one cooking project that's good for even the youngest kitchen crafters and the basis for making a versatile craft material—bread dough.

Bonding Experiences

Get a good book on bread baking and learn about all the different forms bread can take. Research the history of bread making and its role in different cultures. One of the best basic bread books I've found is the *Tassajara Bread Book* by Edward Espe Brown. Not only are the recipes great and wholesome, but it has a reverence for bread that suits this noble food. Celebrate the "staff of life."

Project: Bread Baking

Level: Easy

Age: 5 and up

Materials needed:

Two bread pans

One package dry yeast

$^1/_4$ cup warm (105 to 115 degrees) water

$1^1/_2$ cups hot water

$^1/_3$ cup brown sugar

2 teaspoons salt

3 tablespoons shortening

2 cups stirred whole-wheat flour

3 to $3^1/_4$ cups bread flour or other high-gluten flour

big bowl

floured board

two hands (or more)

Directions:

1. Put $^1/_4$ cup of warm water in a warm mixing bowl and add yeast. Stir to dissolve and let stand three to five minutes.

2. Combine hot water, brown sugar, salt, and shortening; cool to luke-warm.

3. Stir in whole-wheat flour and one cup of the white flour; beat well. Stir in yeast mixture.

4. Add enough of the remaining flour to make a moderately stiff dough. Mix with your hands until you can knead the dough without having it stick to your fingers. To knead, fold the dough over toward you, then press away from you with the heel of your hand. Turn the dough and repeat until dough is springy, smooth, and satiny.

5. Clean your hands and move dough to a floured board. Knead it, dusting with small amounts of flour as needed, until it's firm, smooth, and springs back when poked with the finger, about 15 minutes. Shape into a ball and put into a lightly oiled mixing bowl. Turn once

continues

Project: Continued

to grease surface. Cover with a clean kitchen towel and let rise in a warm place until double in size (about one and a half to two hours).

6. Punch dough down gently. Divide into two equal parts and shape each into a smooth ball. Cover and let rest for 10 minutes.

7. Shape in loaves and put into bread pans ($8^1/_2 \times 4^1/_2 \times 2^1/_2$-inch size), then let rise again until the top of the loaf is rounded above the pan, about double in size, (this takes about one hour).

8. Bake at 375 degrees for approximately 45 minutes. If the bread browns too quickly, cover the pan loosely with foil for the last 20 minutes of baking. Remove the bread from the pan to a wire rack. Let cool at least 20 minutes before slicing.

Bread Dough as Craft Material

There are some differences between regular bread dough and that used for crafting, but the ingredients are pretty much the same. There are lots of recipes for bread-dough–like crafting clays, some edible, some not. If you're working with very young children, stick with an edible craft dough recipe. If you can be assured your child won't eat the dough (tempting though it may be), try some of the non-edible mixtures.

Here's a simple recipe for an edible salt dough: Add two cups of salt to two and a half cups of boiling water, then stir the liquid into four cups of flour in a big bowl. Knead on a floured board, shape, and bake for two to three hours in a 250-degree oven. Check often after two hours and bake until just slightly golden. Cool thoroughly, then paint with acrylic paints. Seal with an acrylic spray sealer.

One of the easiest and quickest ways to make non-edible bread "dough" for crafts is to use white bread and white craft glue. For each slice of bread, add one tablespoon of glue. Cut off all the crusts (you can use these to make homemade bread crumbs or feed them to the birds), break the bread into little pieces, and glue and mix with a spoon or popsicle stick. After the dough is mixed, knead it by hand. Break off pieces and shape and then let dry for a day or two. Paint the shapes with acrylic paints and then spray them with an acrylic sealer to preserve.

Crafty Clues

There are lots of sites on the Internet with recipes for everything from clays and glues to face paint and bubbles. One good one is among Jim Speirs' Scouting pages. Open www.geocities.com/Yosemite/5634/craftrec.htm and get busy in the kitchen.

These basic doughs can be used in any number of projects. Try making ornaments for the holidays (don't forget to make a hole at the top for the string!), refrigerator magnets (get the magnets at your local crafts store or through your favorite crafts catalog), or even beads (use a straw to make the holes). I'll bet you'll think of many more ways to use bread dough "clay."

Bread dough can be made into any number of craft items for decorating, wearing, or gifts.

Play with Your Food!

I know, I know. Adults always told you not to play with your food, but hey, this is craft time. What's great about playing with kids is that we adults have an excuse to do the fun things kids get to do. Here are some simple ideas.

Take out the fruits and vegetables from the fridge and look at them in a new way. Examine them from the top, the bottom, and sideways. What do they suggest? It's kind of like finding animals in the clouds. Add other vegetables, stems, dried beans, and nuts and create eyes, ears, legs, and antennae. Affix with toothpicks when necessary. For more ideas, pick up a copy of *Play With Your Food* by Joost Elffers.

Kids and adults can enjoy playing with food and making these and other whimsical figures.

177

Another fun food activity is learning to make garnishes. There are special tools for some of the more advanced techniques, but many garnishes can be made with tools you already have. Learn how to make radish roses, cucumber flowers, pimento stars, and anything else you can imagine.

Here are some other fun food garnish ideas:

➤ "Frost" fruits by brushing with slightly beaten egg white, dipping in finely granulated sugar, and letting dry on a wire rack. (This works great with bunches of grapes.)

➤ Make apple rings and add cherry or grape centers. Peel an apple and remove the center with a corer. Slice the apple crosswise into rings about $1/2$-inch thick. Dip the rings in lemon juice to prevent browning.

➤ Make carrot curls by resting the carrot on end on a cutting board and running a vegetable parer away from you along its length.

➤ Cut a watermelon in half and let your child scoop out the fruit with an ice cream scoop or melon baller. Let him make balls with other melons like cantaloupe and honeydew. Fill watermelon halves with different-colored melon balls and garnish with coconut.

Gingerbread Houses

Another fascinating cooking craft is the making of gingerbread houses. This can become a serious hobby all in itself. A traditional Christmas craft, there's no reason why you can't go into the construction business any time. How about a Valentine's Day cottage, decorated with heart candies? Or a "haunted" Halloween gingerbread house? Whatever style you choose, your gingerbread structures will improve with practice and experience, so any opportunity to increase your skills will mean even better results when Santa comes to call. Start with a basic recipe especially formulated for making houses. Here's a good one that makes about nine cups of dough:

Project: Gingerbread House

Level: Easy to medium

Age: 6 and up

Materials needed:

$1\frac{1}{2}$ cups whipping cream

1 teaspoon vanilla

$2\frac{1}{2}$ cups firmly packed brown sugar

2 tablespoons baking soda

1 tablespoon ground ginger

2 teaspoons ground cinnamon

$1\frac{1}{3}$ cups light or dark molasses

9 cups all-purpose flour

icing cement (see recipe below)

To make gingerbread:

1. Whip the cream and vanilla until the cream holds soft peaks.

2. In a large bowl, mix sugar, baking soda, ginger, and cinnamon. Stir in molasses and cream. Gradually add flour, mixing well.

3. On a lightly floured board, roll out a portion of dough until it's flat, but still thick enough to pick up easily without tearing. Place it on a greased and floured 12- × 15-inch rimless baking sheet. Finish rolling the dough on the pan, supporting the rolling pin on equally thick wooden strips placed along the opposite edges of the pan. Use about two cups of dough for each $\frac{1}{8}$-inch-thick slab, about four cups for each $\frac{1}{4}$-inch slab, and about six cups for each $\frac{3}{8}$-inch slab. If cookies are not of an even thickness, the thin areas will bake darker in color and be more brittle.

4. You can bake up to two pans of dough at a time in one oven. Bake the dough until it's fairly firm when pressed in the center. In a 300-degree oven, allow about one hour for $\frac{1}{8}$-inch-thick slabs; in a 275-degree oven, allow about $1\frac{3}{4}$ hours for $\frac{1}{4}$-inch slabs and about $2\frac{1}{4}$ hours for $\frac{3}{8}$-inch slabs. After 30 minutes, remove the pans from the oven and place the pattern pieces close together on the dough. With a sharp knife, cut around the pattern edges; lift off the pattern and scraps. (Later, bake the scraps to eat.) Return both pans to the oven, switching their positions, and finish baking.

continues

Project: Continued

5. When done, carefully loosen the cookies with a spatula and cool in the pan until firm, about five minutes. Transfer the cookies to a rack to cool completely. Decorate and assemble the structure with icing cement, or wrap pieces in plastic wrap and then store up to one month. (Cookies will keep crisp longer, but will not taste as fresh.)

6. Gingerbread should be very hard when it's cool. If it seems too soft, return it to the cookie sheet and bake for five or ten more minutes.

To make icing cement:

1. With an electric mixer, beat together two large egg whites, $1/8$ teaspoon of cream of tartar, and two teaspoons of water until frothy.

2. Mix in three cups of sifted powdered sugar; beat on high speed until icing is stiff, five to 10 minutes.

3. Use immediately or cover for up to eight hours. Makes about $1^1/2$ cups.

To assemble the house:

1. Make patterns on pasteboard, heavy paper, or cardboard, then cut them out. To test your design, fit the pieces together and secure them with tape. If the model wobbles, so will the gingerbread.

2. Use icing to assemble your house. Pipe it through a pastry bag with a plain or decorating tip. Hold the pieces together until they're set (extra hands help).

3. Fill in any gaps after the whole project is assembled.

4. Use icing to decorate as well, but before assembling the house. Let the decorated pieces dry for around 30 minutes before assembling the house.

5. Icing also becomes the "glue" used to attach candies. Some materials to try include jelly beans, gum drops, Starlight® mints, Lifesavers®, M&Ms®, Red Hots®, heart-shaped candies, wafer cookies (for doors and shutters), Necco® wafers for the roof, small candy canes, and red and black licorice.

If all this seems a bit daunting, you might want to start out just using whole graham crackers and working on a smaller scale. Make the icing cement recipe and assemble one unbroken cookie for each wall and one for each side of the roof. Decorate as you would a larger gingerbread house. These are simple enough that your kids can enjoy making a whole village.

Lighten Up: Candle Making

The kitchen is a good place for candle making, since you'll need a heat source for melting wax and a place to leave your candles to cool. If you and your child get more involved in candle making, you may want to find a portable burner, but to start, the kitchen stove will do nicely.

We can cover some of the basics here, but you'll want to do some more reading before you seriously get into candle making. This is one craft where you may find a kit is a good investment; it will give you all the things you need to make your first candle and see if it's something you and your child want to pursue. A good candle-making kit is available through the Lark Books catalog (see Appendix A).

Bet You Didn't Know

No one knows when the first candle was invented. Some historians believe candles were first used by the Egyptians around 3,000 B.C., and Tutankhamen had what may have been a bronze candleholder in his tomb.

Project: Candle Making

Level: Medium

Age: 7 and up

Materials needed: Candles you have around the house (for novice candle makers), cotton string, an old pot, a large, clean, empty can, old newspapers, an old pencil, the mold or container of your choice, a double boiler (you can create one using the can and the old pot)

Directions:

1. Fill the double boiler with just enough water that the can doesn't float around. Add water to the pot if it evaporates. Don't let it boil down. Melt the wax in the double boiler.

2. Cut a length of wick and dip it in the wax a few times to coat. Wrap the wick around the pencil and move it until it's the right length for the mold you choose.

3. When the wax is melted, use a potholder to pour it into the mold, holding it at an angle and pouring the wax down the side. Set aside some of the melted wax for later.

4. Put the wick in the exact middle of the mold. Let it cool about one hour. Reheat the leftover wax. Poke holes in the candle around the wick about halfway down the depth of the candle and pour wax up to the original fill line. Repeat two or three times.

continues

Project: Continued

When making candles, try to center the wick as perfectly as you can and position it so it reaches the bottom of the mold.

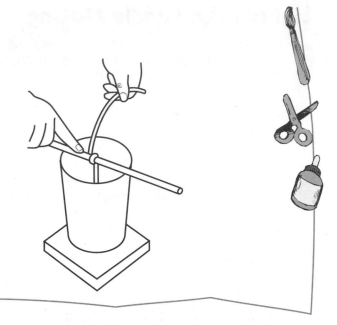

Crafty Clues

Some recommended books on candle making include *The Candlemaker's Companion* by Betty Oppenheimer and *The Complete Candlemaker: Techniques, Projects, Inspirations* by Norma Coney.

Safety Signals

When making candles, NEVER put wax directly on the stove burner. It will smoke and can pop and crackle, causing burns. Even when wax is in the double boiler, always watch it and never leave it unattended with a child.

Perhaps the easiest and least messy way to get kids involved in candle making is to use sheets of beeswax that can be rolled or layered together and cut into shapes. Add a wick and voilà, you've made a candle!

A mixture of three parts paraffin wax and one part block beeswax is a good formula for container or molded candles. Note that paraffin wax comes in different melting points, and the type of candle you're making will determine which melting point wax you'll need to get. There's container wax (130°F) for poured candles that will stay in their containers, mold wax (139–143°F) for candles that will set in a mold and be removed, and dipping wax (145°F) for making dipped tapers.

There are also various additives that harden candles, extend their burning time, or change them in some other way. You can experiment with stearic acid, lustre crystals, clear crystals, and other materials. You can also embellish the outside of your candle with items like coffee beans, cinnamon sticks, and dried flowers. Candles can be colored and scented, too.

Wicks come in different types and sizes. The types are flat braid, square braid, metal core, and paper core. The sizes are small, medium, and large diameter. The larger or longer-burning the candle, the larger diameter the wick.

There are a variety of molds available—from metal and plastic to soft rubber, hard rubber, and acrylic. You can also make molds from things you find around your kitchen, such as wax-coated fruit juice cans, milk cartons, canning jars, paper cups, and various empty food containers. Terra-cotta pots and small galvanized buckets also make good containers.

Mmmm...Smells Good! Scents and Potions From the Kitchen

Did you know you can make your own perfumes, soaps, body powders, after-shave lotions, hand creams, bath oils, and bath salts? It's easy, and they make super gifts for any occasion. All you need are a few easily obtainable ingredients and some essential oils, and you're in business.

A basic recipe for body powder is two parts arrowroot or cornstarch (or a blend of half and half) to one part baking soda. You can add other things to give it a nice scent or add to its deodorizing properties: To a blend of eight ounces of the cornstarch/arrowroot mixture and four ounces of baking soda, add one tablespoon each of ground clove, ground slippery elm, ground orange peel, and ground lemon peel. You can also add just a few drops (five to 10) of essential oil.

After-bath splash is another simple recipe. Take a pint of witch hazel and add a few drops of essential oil. (Different oils have different properties: Lavender is relaxing, and rosemary is a good choice for invigoration.)

Another recipe that's easy to make even for young children is bath salts. Combine $2^1/2$ pounds of Epsom salts (available at your local pharmacy), some food coloring, and a few drops of essential oil in a large bowl. Make sure you stir thoroughly so that the color and scent is evenly distributed. Put the mixture in small glass jars and close (jars with cork tops look nice) and let the bath salts "cure" for four to six weeks. This allows the scent to permeate the bath salts for best results. Tie a ribbon or some raffia around the neck of the jar and you have a pretty gift. Depending on the scent used, this could be for a man or a woman who enjoys a soothing bath.

Crafty Clues
Never pour wax down the drain—it will clog. Pour waste wax into a coffee can and either dispose of it or remelt it. Remove wax from countertops by letting it cool and then scraping it off with a spatula. Prevent messes by covering countertops and other work surfaces. Butcher's paper or wax paper works well and can be reused. Clean molds according to directions. Do not scratch metal molds, or every candle you make will have an imperfection.

Crafty Clues
When making scented gifts (perfumes or lotions), be sure you're working with essential oils. These are the most potent and long-lasting form of scent and are different from fragrant oils or perfumes. There are many sources for essential oils and herbs. One mail-order source is the San Francisco Herb Co., 1-800-227-4530. Visit their Web site at www.sfherb.com.

Safety Signals

Children need to know that no matter how delicious essential oils may smell, they're for external use only. Undiluted oils should not be used directly on the skin, since skin reactions could result. In addition, certain essential oils are dangerous to people with high blood pressure or epilepsy, and others are not recommended for use by pregnant women. Still others make the skin more sensitive to sunlight. Pay attention to all cautions, and when you're not crafting with your child, keep essential oils out of her reach.

The following recipe for bath oil is from Elaine White, author of *Super Formulas, Arts and Crafts: How to Make More Than 360 Useful Products That Contain Honey and Beeswax*:

Dispersing Bath Oil

1 whole egg

$^1/_2$ cup baby or mineral oil

2 teaspoons liquid soap or dishwashing liquid

$^1/_4$ cup vodka

2 tablespoons honey

$^1/_4$ cup whole fresh milk

Fragrant oil (about one teaspoon)

Mix all ingredients in a blender for 30 seconds. Use only one or two tablespoons of this oil in a bathtub of water.

These are just a few crafts you can enjoy with your kids in the kitchen. There are lots more. Try your hand at candy making, dehydrating and preserving fruits, vegetables and herbs, and just plain making good food together.

Bonding Experiences

Working with scents is a great time to broaden your child's vocabulary and talk about how the sense of smell affects our feelings. Buy a varied selection of essential oils and play a game in which you and your child take turns being blindfolded, identifying scents, and describing how they smell and how they make you feel. To broaden the experience, take a field trip to a store that sells herbs, health-food store, herb farm, or botanical garden.

The Least You Need to Know

➤ Think of your kitchen as a laboratory filled with possibilities for crafts.

➤ With a few precautions, you can make your kitchen safe for crafting with your kids and teach them some important safety lessons.

➤ Activities such as making garnishes and building gingerbread houses add a special dimension of creativity to working with food.

➤ Candle making and scent crafts are other fun crafts that make good use of the kitchen.

Chapter 16

Au Naturel: Crafts from the Outdoors

In This Chapter

➤ Crafty ways to get your kids outdoors

➤ Pressed flower crafts

➤ A potpourri primer

➤ Wreaths for every occasion

➤ Starting a window-sill garden

➤ Creating a living world: Making a terrarium

The great outdoors is not only a feast for the eyes and a boon to the spirits, it's also a veritable candy store when it comes to crafts materials. Why not get the family into the wild, get some exercise, and discover a whole new world of crafting as near as your yard or local recreation area?

In this chapter, you'll learn to use nature's bounty and grow your own, and we'll even explore ways to create a miniature natural world indoors.

Flowers and Other Pressing Matters

One way to make the green seasons last is with flower crafts. Flower pressing is easy enough for anyone to do, and it offers possibilities that can challenge even the most skilled craftsperson. Flower pressing is a great way to train the eye, to get the family outdoors, and to encourage design sense and creativity.

In the 19th century, children and adults made formal albums of pressed wildflowers and plants in order to learn their characteristics and names. Small portable flower presses were constructed to take along on a hike, or plants were placed in a container called a *vasculum* and pressed at home. Others used flowers from the garden and even grew particular flowers especially suitable for pressing. It always delights me when I buy an old book at an antique store or flea market and find some pressed blooms hidden between its pages. I can't help but wonder what the circumstances might have been…a gift from a favorite suitor, perhaps?

These days, a heavy book with blotting paper on either side of the pressed flower works just as well as those old albums. Another simple way to press flowers is to use newsprint and blotter paper layered between corrugated cardboard and secured by top and bottom wooden frames tightened with straps.

Crafty Clues
A professional-quality hardwood press is available from Smith & Hawken for about $80. To order, call 1-800-776-3336. This might be a worthwhile investment if your child becomes truly entranced with pressing flowers.

Place your flowers and plants so they don't overlap. Clamp down your press or close your book and add some more books on top. Check your flowers every few days to see if you need to replace the paper (it will be stained) and determine when they're completely dry and ready to use. Because they are fragile, avoid handling your dried flowers too much. (You may want to sketch out your project in advance, so you only have to pick the flowers up once.) Tweezers would be a helpful tool to have for positioning the flowers.

Crafty Clues
Don't be afraid to improvise with your flower materials. Take flowers apart and use individual pieces; mix different foliage and flowers together.

Some flowers especially suitable for pressing are alyssum, bleeding heart, columbine, cosmos, daisies, forget-me-nots, geranium, hydrangea, lavender, marigold, pansies, petunias, and zinnias. Experiment and you'll find lots more. Ferns, leaves, vines, and grasses add interest to colorful blooms. Don't forget herbs, which are suitable both while they're flowering and after.

A simple flower press you can build yourself, order from a catalog, or find at your local crafts store.

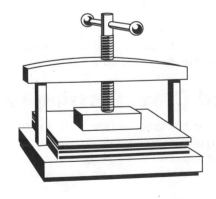

You can use your pressed flowers for a multitude of projects:

➤ They can be framed as nature art. Watercolor paper makes an especially nice background for framed flowers. Simply glue on flowers, mat, set with hairspray, and frame.

➤ You can add them to candles. Glue flowers on to a light-colored pillar candle, brush the entire surface with melted paraffin a little at a time (enough so that the flowers are covered yet visible), and let dry between coats.

➤ Pressed flowers can be used to decorate note cards, bookmarks, place cards, or lampshades, made into ornaments, and much, much more.

Project: Pressed Flower or Herb Ornament

Level: Medium

Age: 6 and up

Materials needed: Two microscope slides, clear-drying craft glue, ⅛-inch wide grosgrain or satin ribbon, dried flowers (you'll want tiny blossoms for this project, so herbs like thyme, sage, lavender, and marjoram work especially well)

Directions:

1. Arrange dried pressed plant materials on one slide and secure with tiny droplets of glue applied with the point of a pin.

2. When dry, cover with the other slide and secure at the corners with glue droplets. Press until dry.

3. Using ribbon in a color that blends well with the flowers and foliage, make a one-inch loop and glue it to the very edge at the center top of the slide.

4. When the loop is dry, make a border with the ribbon, covering the glass edges, and leaving four or five extra inches at each end for a final bow. Beginning at the top center, glue the ribbon in place.

5. When dry, tie the ends in a bow around the hanging loop and trim.

(This idea is from *Herbal Treasures: Inspiring Month-By-Month Projects For Gardening, Cooking, and Crafts* by Phyllis V. Shaudys.)

continues

Project: Continued

You might also try using metallic tape in silver, gold, or copper tones to secure the two slides together. Ask your local crafts supplier. You might want to use some thin metallic cord for the hanger in this version.

These lovely pressed-flower ornaments can be made inexpensively and make great gifts. They look beautiful suspended from a hook in front of a window, too.

Once Upon a Thyme—Herbs on Your Window Sill

Another activity that brings a touch of the outdoors into the house during the dark winter months is a window-sill garden. Herbs are ideal candidates to grow on the window sill and can be used for cooking as well. Indoor gardens show your kids how seeds germinate, and also teach kids to take responsibility for keeping their charges happy and healthy.

From a small window-sill herb garden, children can progress to other container garden plants (even vegetables or fruits) and may even develop an interest in outdoor gardening come spring. Be prepared to clear a small plot once the cold weather is just a memory!

To get started, find a window suitable for your herbs. You'll have greater success if you select a group of plants that all like similar conditions: all light-loving herbs for a sunny window, for instance, or shade-loving herbs for a low-light situation. (Consult an expert at your local nursery to find out which herbs will grow best in your particular location.) Some herbs that grow well indoors are parsley, sage, thyme, chives, and all the mints.

Choose planters for your herbs. You can purchase some terra-cotta pots or simply mix various containers you've found at yard sales or just hanging around the house.

Two important preparation steps are providing good drainage and good soil. Use broken pottery or small stones at the bottom of your pots and fill them with good-quality potting soil. You may want to consult your local nursery for the best soil mix for your particular plants.

You can either start with seeds or buy small plants. Sprouting seeds can be more satisfying, but sometimes children who've had little gardening experience haven't the patience and are more easily engaged with living plants. You'll need to judge your child's interest level and attention span.

If you do decide to start with seeds, why not make a seed viewer so you and your kids can watch the plants grow? Just take a tall glass or jar with straight sides, line with construction or blotting paper, crumple up some paper towels and fill the glass with them, then slip a few seeds between the glass and construction paper about an inch below the top edge of the glass. Pour water into the center of the paper towels until the blotting paper is thoroughly saturated. Make a cylinder with construction paper an inch taller than the glass and slip it loosely over the glass.

Set the seed viewer on a sunny window sill with the collar over it. Lift the collar each day to observe the seed's progress. Add water regularly to keep the paper towels moist. Once the seedlings have leaves on them, transplant some to a four-inch pot and fill with potting soil. Water well and put in a sunny window.

Continue to saturate the paper towels in the viewer. Observe the difference between the ones in the viewer and the ones in the window. Another interesting thing to do is to plant one seed upside down in the viewer and see what it does.

Water the plants regularly (you may want to add this job to your child's list of weekly chores so she doesn't forget) and fertilize as recommended. Once you've had success with your own herb garden, you may want to start others for gifts. What a lovely gift for a favorite Valentine, Mother's Day, a birthday, or Christmas. Other things to try: container tomatoes, plants grown from carrot tops, other sprouted vegetables, pits, and seeds. Pineapple tops make an interesting plant.

You can grow tasty herbs on almost any sunny window sill and kids can learn how things grow.

Bonding Experiences

Take a field trip to a garden center and spend some time browsing and reading the signs. Talk to the store manager about the different flowers and plants. Check out your area for junior garden clubs and 4-H groups.

Some great Web sites for gardening kids include Linda Mazar's Web page at www.geocities.com/Heartland/Hills/6160, which includes a monthly gardening with kids column; Michigan State University's 4-H Children's Garden site at commtechlab.msu.edu/sites/garden/contents.html, a virtual garden tour; and The Whole Herb Kid's Corner at www.wholeherbs.com/HKID.HTM. For young gardeners ages four to eight, a copy of *How a Seed Grows* by Helen Jordan will delight.

Potpourri Basics

Dried flowers, plants, and herbs combined with essential oils and spices equals that magical mixture known as *potpourri*. I think of it as the three-dimensional version of flower pressing!

Potpourri is a sensual experience—interesting to look at, fun to work with, and of course, it smells so good. It's also another great way to get the family out of doors looking for nature's bountiful materials to add to the mixture. Small pine cones, acorns, leaves, needles, seeds, and pods are all welcome additions to your potpourri, as are flowers and herbs from the garden or field.

The following is a list of some potpourri ingredients:

➤ small pine cones

➤ cinnamon sticks

➤ whole cloves

➤ dried flowers and buds

➤ leaves and other natural ingredients

➤ pine needles

➤ grasses

➤ nuts

➤ herbs and spices

Potpourri can be used in a variety of ways. Your child will undoubtedly like to place some of his homemade mixture in a bowl in his room. Together you can sew some up in small fabric pouches to be used as drawer sachets. These make great gifts, too. Another gift idea (remember, it's never too early to start thinking about holiday crafts) is hot mats filled with potpourri. A hot mat is like a pot holder, only you set hot things on it. As the hot pot or pan sits on the mat, its fragrance is released into the air. Potpourri can be simmered in a special electric pot or one heated with a tea-light candle.

Handiwords

Potpourri is a mixture of dried flowers, herbs and spices, dried fruit peels or slices, enhanced by scented oils used to freshen a room, closet, or drawer. It is sometimes left dry in an open container, simmered in water, or sewn into sachets or other items.

Crafty Clues

Where do you find ingredients for your potpourri? Essential oils and other botanicals can be purchased from crafts stores, floral supply stores, or mail-order catalogs. The San Francisco Herb Co. mentioned in Chapter 15 is a good source. You'll also find bulk supplies through the Appalachian Herb Co. on the World Wide Web at www.dezines.com/ herbs4u/potpourr1.htm (or call toll-free 1-888-300-3852).

  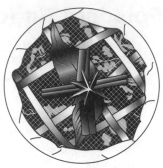

Versatile potpourri can be used in many projects.

Nature's Circles: Wreath-Making Fun

Wreaths are one of the oldest forms of decoration. They are extremely versatile and can be made from all kinds of ingredients, both natural and artificial.

Here is a list of ingredients that might go into a wreath:

➤ evergreen branches

➤ bay leaf clusters

➤ ornamental grasses

➤ wild flowers and ever weeds

➤ herb sprigs

➤ pods

➤ pine cones and nuts

➤ dried flowers

Safety Signals
Glue guns are great for wreath making and lots of other crafts, but they get very hot and are not suitable for use by most children. Stick to wiring, which is something even younger children can learn to do effectively.

Natural ingredients can be dried or preserved, or you can even make a living wreath from live plants and a planting medium. Decorations can include just about any natural material, from nuts and cinnamon sticks to dried apples and orange slices to garlic cloves and dried chili peppers. If you can attach a wire to it or glue it, you can add it to a wreath.

There are lots of forms you can use as a basis for a wreath. There are forms made of wire, straw, foam, grapevine, and moss, to name a few. Most of these wreath materials can be found in your local crafts or floral store.

Wreaths have many uses. Large wreaths, of course, make an inviting decoration for the front door at holiday time or any time. Children also enjoy making small wreaths to hang on their own doors or to lay on a table, or to surround a votive candle holder.

A Living World: Making a Terrarium

Creating a *terrarium*—a glass case with earth in it, where plants and flowers can grow—is a super activity to begin during the long winter months, when a bit of greenery perks up anyone's spirits.

Ideas for containers:

➤ Wine jugs

➤ Fish bowls

➤ Clear cookie jars

➤ Plastic cake domes

➤ Large plastic salad bowls

➤ Large mayonnaise or pickle jars

➤ Apothecary jars

➤ Candy jars

➤ Glass canisters

➤ Distilled-water jugs

If you plan a terrarium with a large-mouthed container or dome, smaller children can easily help. Narrow-necked bottles provide sufficient challenge for older children and adults. Most planters you can plant by hand, but those with smaller openings will require special tools. They take a little practice, but once you learn how to use them they become second nature.

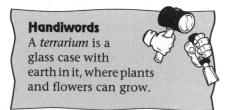

Handiwords
A *terrarium* is a glass case with earth in it, where plants and flowers can grow.

Look for miniature plants in nurseries and grocery-store plant departments. Pick plants that are compatible and that do well in the same environment.

You also need to consider temperature and moisture requirements. Some plants need a closed container with high humidity, some need a partially open one, and some an uncovered one. Generally, the narrower the neck of the container, the less likely the need for a cover.

Location of the terrarium will play a part, too. If it will be in a sunny place, *succulents* may work best. A succulent is a water retaining plant that does well in arid conditions (e.g., jade plant, Christmas cactus, sedum). If the terrarium will have a lot of shade and moisture, in a bathroom for instance, then ferns and mosses will most likely be a good choice.

It's easy to misjudge size, so take your container along when you go shopping for plants, if possible, to be sure they'll fit. Think about color and texture, too. Work toward creating some dramatic contrasts.

193

Here are some plants you may want to use:

Small plants:

- ➤ Ferns in the *Pteris* family
- ➤ Grape ivy
- ➤ Boxwood shoots

Medium plants:

- ➤ Chinese evergreen
- ➤ Fittonias
- ➤ Pileas
- ➤ Peperomia
- ➤ Small-leafed ivy

Ground covers:

- ➤ Baby's tears
- ➤ Crinkle leaf peperomia
- ➤ Selaginellas
- ➤ Mosses
- ➤ Wandering Jew
- ➤ Strawberry begonia

Flowering plants:

- ➤ African violets
- ➤ Miniature roses
- ➤ Miniature geraniums
- ➤ Begonias
- ➤ Miniature orchids
- ➤ Gloxinia
- ➤ Pilea
- ➤ Wintergreen

Desert plants (for a desertarium):

- ➤ Old man cactus
- ➤ Bishop's cap
- ➤ Bunny ear cactus
- ➤ Tiger jaw cactus
- ➤ Sand dollar cactus
- ➤ Opuntia
- ➤ Aloes
- ➤ Kalanchoes
- ➤ Crassulas
- ➤ Echeverias

Once you've got your container and your plants, you're ready to create a terrarium. Here's what you'll need:

- ➤ A wire hanger
- ➤ Pieces of rubber and sponge
- ➤ Horticultural charcoal (available from your local nursery)

➤ Potting soil

➤ Gravel

➤ A funnel

➤ A shovel (can be an iced-tea spoon)

➤ A placer (can be a wire puller from the hardware store)

➤ A tamper (can be a dowel with a cork on the end)

➤ Long-handled tweezers (find these at a aquarium supply store; some skilled people use chop sticks in a similar way)

➤ A small, soft-bristled brush

➤ Cotton swabs

➤ A sprayer bottle

➤ A kitchen baster

➤ Long scissors

Bet You Didn't Know

Oooo…

The first terrarium came about by accident in 1829. It was invented by Dr. Nathaniel Ward, an Englishman, who wanted to watch the adult sphinx moth emerge from its chrysalis. He took the soil where the chrysalis was resting and put it in a glass jar with a metal lid. He discovered plants grew well in this environment. (No one knows if he ever saw the sphinx moth, though.)

You'll also need a mixture of soil. Here's a recipe:

1 part sand

1 part topsoil

1 part leaf mold or peat moss

The soil you choose will depend somewhat on the plants you decide on…desert, tropical, or forest plants will all require different soils. Books on terrariums usually provide soil recipes or your local nursery might help with the right ingredient proportions. Some experimentation might be required.

Now you're ready to create a living landscape. First plant the larger plants, then the smaller ones. Next come the trailing plants and ground covers. Fill in with gravel or redwood chips and add any finishing touches.

Don't be afraid of making a mistake. It can easily be corrected. If a plant is in the wrong place, just move it. If it looks like it's going to outgrow the container, you can trim it back.

Watering will vary based on how much moisture you added when you first put the plants in, the types of plants in your terrarium, the temperature of the room, the size of the opening, and the humidity of the room (if your terrarium is even partially open).

You'll learn when to water your terrarium by observation. If there's no more condensation appearing, you need to water. If the terrarium feels particularly light when you pick it up, it probably needs water. If you can easily open the top of the terrarium, the best way to tell if it needs water is to feel the soil. After a while, you'll probably be able to tell just by looking at your terrarium when it's dry or you'll find that a watering schedule begins to emerge.

Crafty Clues

For advanced terrarium supplies, including those needed to keep reptiles, amphibians, and other creatures, the Black Jungle Terrarium Supply is a good source. Call 1-800-268-1813 or check out their Web site at www.blackjungle.com. The books *Terrariums* by Scott Russell Sanders and *Terrarium Habitats* by Kimi Hosoume and Jacqueline Barber should be helpful as well.

You'll need to air the terrarium every so often, even with plants that like a lot of humidity. If you find a lot of condensation, water standing at the bottom, or signs of fungus, mold, or mildew, open up the container and let in some drying air. Again, over time you'll probably see a fairly regular interval emerging: You may need to let in some air once a week or less.

Experiment with the amount of light you give your terrarium. You'll also have to trim and fertilize your plants from time to time. Generally, plants that need strong light do best in a window that faces west or south, while low-light plants favor a north or east-facing window. Use a houseplant fertilizer diluted twice as much as is recommended for regular houseplants. Use a baster or funnel to get the fertilizer into the soil—avoid getting it on the leaves of the plants.

The Least You Need to Know

➤ Nature offers a bounty of craft materials and ideas for families to explore.

➤ Nature crafts help get kids outdoors and make a closer connection with the natural world.

➤ Pressing flowers, creating window-sill gardens, and making wreaths, potpourri, and terrariums are just a few ways to experience nature crafts with your kids.

Chapter 17

Toyland: Handcrafted Toys for All Ages

In This Chapter

➤ Toys are always at your fingertips

➤ Making traditional toys: tops, dolls, and puppets

➤ Toys for the more advanced crafter

➤ Games and puzzles for everyone

Wondering why you'd want to make your own toys? I mean, there *are* a few toys on the market, right? Well, I can echo the same sentiment expressed by many parents. When my children were small, the most intriguing toys were the simplest, things like plastic containers and lids, pots and pans, wooden blocks, and the button box. The simple toys of our colonial ancestors still fascinate children today.

It's also true that sometimes you may find yourself in a situation when you have to make do. Maybe you suddenly have to entertain your children with few resources on hand. That's when knowing some easy toys and games to make from everyday materials might come in handy.

In this chapter, you'll learn how to make a host of simple toys, games, and puzzles, for both the very youngest child to the older, more advanced crafter.

Rockin' With the Classics

Bet You Didn't Know

Native American children made their own tops by pushing a stick through an acorn. Their parents made more elaborate tops out of wood, animal horn, stone, or clay.

Toys that now seem quaint in this age of computer games still have a following among the younger set: the stick horse, the top, the bean-bag, and the reliable "weapons" of childhood—the slingshot and the rubber-band gun. I see these in upscale crafts and collectibles shops and have watched children of all ages take delight in their simplicity.

Let's take the top, for instance. A small mass spinning on a shaft with a point at the bottom—what could be less complicated?

You and your child could spend hours just exploring this one toy, but here's a project that takes only a few minutes and can be made on the spot with practically no materials.

Project: On-the-Spot Top

Level: Easy

Age: 5 and up

Materials needed: Cardboard, a sharp pencil, a large nail, markers, paints, crayons, or colored pencils

Directions:

1. Using a glass, cup, jar lid, or anything else round, trace a circle onto cardboard and cut it out. Decorate it any way you want—the more colorful, the better.

2. Make a hole in the center of the cardboard circle with the nail and insert the pencil until it protrudes about two inches underneath, with the point facing down.

3. Spin the pencil from the top end and watch it go. Try making different sizes and see which spin best and longest.

Another easy top can be made from an empty wooden thread spool. Manufacturers are using plastic or Styrofoam for spools nowadays, but you can still find some that are solid wood (or you may have some hanging around in grandma's sewing basket). This can be hand-carved for the older wood worker. After finding a spool or carving the shape, the final step is to fit a dowel to the center hole of the spool and insert it after applying glue. One spool makes two tops.

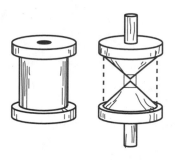

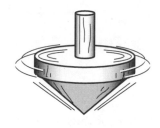

Tiny finger tops made from a wooden thread spool.

Another alternative is to find a pre-made wood-turning top at the local hardware store. These come in different sizes in the pointed dome shape you need. All you need to do is add a dowel into the pre-drilled hole and set with glue.

These small wooden tops can be painted or left plain.

A finger top made from a pre-milled wood-turning top and a dowel.

Dolls

Perhaps the oldest plaything is a toy made in human form—the doll. Both boys and girls enjoy playing with small replicas of themselves, and the doll has become a wildly popular adult collectible. Children from the most primitive societies have been known to fashion dolls out of sticks or clay, and the humble rag, yarn, or stuffed fabric doll is a perennial favorite of toddlers.

Some common dolls made during America's colonial period include those made out of corncobs, cornhusks, apples, rope, rags, and socks. We're going to make a cornhusk doll. You can easily make a whole doll family for next to nothing in cost and only a modest investment of time. These make beautiful Thanksgiving decorations (or year-round home accessories, for that matter).

Bet You Didn't Know

Part of an alabaster doll with moveable arms has been found in a Babylonian archeological site. In some Egyptian graves, dolls made of wood with hair of clay or wood beads have been found. These date back to 3000 to 2000 B.C. There are probably dolls even older that haven't survived because they were made of perishable materials like wood, fur, or cloth.

Project: Cornhusk Doll

Level: Medium

Age: 8 and up

Materials needed: Dried cornhusks (dry them yourself by laying them flat and letting them dry or purchase from a crafts store or mail-order supply company), corn silk (can be purchased or you can husk your own), pipe cleaners, household string, felt-tip pens, black and red, pins

Directions:

1. Soak cornhusks in lukewarm water for five minutes and rewet as needed. Husks should be kept moist as you work with them.

2. To make the head, tear the husk into $1/4$-inch wide strips and roll into a $3/4$-inch ball. Secure with a pin. Do the same for the body, only this time make the ball about one inch in diameter.

This is what a rolled head and body should look like when you're done.

3. To make arms, wrap a pipe cleaner inside a strip of husk that's about one inch wide and a little longer than the pipe cleaner. Roll lengthwise and tie at the ends with $1/8$-inch-wide strips of husk.

Arms being rolled and tied.

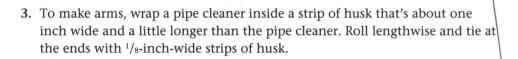

4. Using the clean inside part of a husk, center it smoothly over the front of the smaller ball, twist three times (to give the head more depth) and tie with a string around the neck. The excess should hang down about $3^1/2$ inches in front and back. Put the arms through under the neck, then insert the body form and tie underneath at the waist.

Project: Continued

The head, upper body, and arm assembly.

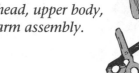

5. Take several husks and gather around the waist, using the narrow ends on top and making sure the husks at the bottom all turn under. Add more husks for the fullness you want and tie with two wraps of string at the waist. Trim so there's about 1/2 inch above the waist. Trim the bottom of the skirt evenly. (A male doll can be made by dividing the husks below the waist in half and tying the bottoms.)

Assembling the skirt.

6. Once you've made the basic doll, you can add various accessories as you wish. Try making a blouse, bodice, or shawl (using husks, fabric, felt, or burlap) and securing it with a cornhusk belt. How about a hat? Make a purse or satchel, a baby, or anything else you'd like to try. Bend the arms to the position you want and let dry.

continues

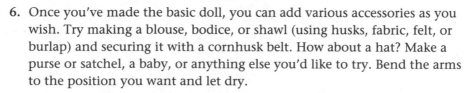

Project: Continued

More elaborate clothes and accessories can be made from scraps of fabric, chamois, and felt, although the classic cornhusk doll is made almost exclusively from the husks themselves.

7. Draw eyes and a nose with the black marker and a mouth with the red one. Or you can leave the face blank and imagine whatever features you'd like. Hair is corn silk (soak the silk for five minutes before working with it) sewn or glued to the head. You can leave it loose or make a braid or two.

If you'd like to explore working with cornhusks, you might try tracking down *Corn-Husk Crafts* by Margery Facklam. This book is out of print, but it can be found in some libraries or through used bookstores and search services.

Things That Go

Toys that roll, fly, or scoot are a mainstay of childhood as well. In an age when most every errand is accomplished in a car, is it any wonder toys with wheels or wings are favorites? Many children have flown on a plane before they can even remember the experience.

One of the simplest of all flying toys is the paper airplane, which I showed you in Chapter 6. Here's another flying toy that's almost as easy to make.

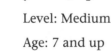

Project: Flying Machine

Level: Medium

Age: 7 and up

Materials needed: White pine or balsa wood about $5/16$ inch thick, $1/4$-inch dowel cut to about $7 1/2$ inches long, sandpaper, white glue

Directions:

1. Cut the wood to a width of one inch and a length of eight inches. Mark the exact center and drill a $1/4$-inch hole there. (See following diagram.)

Project: Continued

2. Carve the propeller blank a little at a time on either side of the hole. Round the ends and go over the whole thing with sandpaper to smooth it.

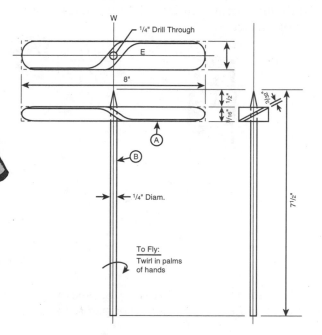

Flying machine cutting diagram.

W

¼" Drill Through

E

8"

½"

⁷⁄₁₆"

²⁹⁄₃₂"

A

B

¼" Diam.

7½"

To Fly:
Twirl in palms
of hands

3. Sharpen one end of the dowel in a pencil sharpener, apply some glue, and insert it into the hole. Let dry.

4. Test the toy's flight worthiness by rolling it along the edge of a table with the propeller hanging over the edge. Carve more wood from the side that appears to be heavy until it balances and rolls smoothly. To fly, twirl the shaft in the palms of your hands and release.

There are lots of other simple flying and rolling toys you can make. For some ideas, pick up a copy of *Easy-To-Make Articulated Wooden Toys: Patterns and Instructions for 18 Play-things That Move* by Ed Sibbet.

Puppets Put the World on a String (or Your Finger)!

Another toy with endless variations and possibilities is the puppet. Most of us grew up with the fabulous puppets of such masters as Jim Henson, but anyone can make a puppet. All you need is a Band-Aid or two! Okay, a Band-Aid puppet is the simplest, but it still works. Just take one Band-Aid and put it over your fingertip, then another across it. Use a permanent marker to put on a face, draw or glue on some hair, and you've got a finger puppet. You can remove the Band-Aids carefully, turn the bottom edges under and make several, so you have a whole cast of characters.

One of the simplest finger puppets, made from two Band-Aids.

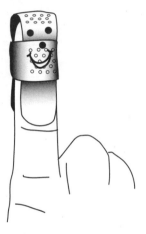

Other simple finger puppets can be made from peanut shells. Just break the shell in half, eat the peanut, and insert your finger in the shell. These can be painted and decorated with bits of paper, felt, or fabric scraps.

Still more finger puppets can be knitted or crocheted, but why go to the trouble when an old glove will do? That's right. Just cut the fingers off some old gloves and you have a whole puppet theater, right at the tips of your fingers. I suggest putting some non-ravel solution (available at sewing stores) at the bottom so the threads stay put, then start decorating your puppets. Try some other gloves for different textures, like rubber gloves (good for amphibians or aliens), garden gloves, or leather work gloves. (Make sure they're *retired* gloves, though! Your family members won't appreciate finding their gloves fingerless.)

> **Crafty Clues**
> Recycle the rest of a cloth glove whose fingers have been used for puppets as an accessory for a hobo costume for Halloween—or as actual winter handwarmers when you need the manual dexterity of exposed fingers.

You can use yarn or embroidery floss for hair, arms, and legs, sew on sequins for eyes, embroider features, and glue on felt clothes and accessories—whatever you can imagine. Try making both animal puppets and people puppets. Then put together a puppet theater using an old cardboard box. You can add a curtain by draping fabric over a cord held taut and secured to the front.

Another type of finger puppet that's great when you have a limited number of materials to work with is the flat-paper finger puppet. This is done by drawing and cutting out the upper body of the puppet and using the forefinger and middle finger for the legs. All you really need is some stiff paper (or lighter paper, which you can glue onto thin cardboard), scissors, and crayons or markers. The only tricky part is cutting out the leg holes, which an adult may need to do with very sharp, finer-pointed scissors.

A quick and easy puppet theater can be made out of a cardboard box, some fabric, and cord.

Flat paper and cardboard finger puppets are easy to make with few materials.

Hand puppets are easy to make, too. You can use a paper bag (as we do in Chapter 21) or old socks. Or you can make them from scratch using felt or other heavy fabric. Follow the basic pattern (shown in the following figure) and the rest is up to you. Once you get started making puppets, you'll be amazed at how many variations you can create.

Yet another simple, cheap, and easy puppet to make is the plastic-spoon puppet. All you need are white plastic spoons, craft foam or felt, trims and ribbons, wiggle eyes, and permanent markers or acrylic paint pens or craft paint. These are great rainy-day, spur-of-the-moment projects to make.

Crafty Clues
When making puppets from a pattern, make the pattern large enough so the finished puppet will fit many hands. It can even be a little large for a child, so that it can fit an adult hand. That way you'll all be able to use the same puppets and each family member will have a variety of puppets to choose from.

*A basic pattern for
an unlimited
variety of hand
puppets.*

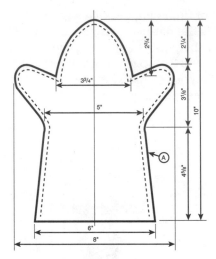

*Some spoon puppet
ideas.*

Crafty Clues
For rules to all
those backyard
games like marbles,
jacks, grapevine, and
Marco Polo, check out the
Games Kids Play Web site at
http://www.corpcomm.net/
~gnieboer/gamehome.htm.

For more homemade puppet ideas, check out *I Can Make Puppets/So Easy to Make!* by Mary Wallace or some of the many other books available on the subject. Also, keep your eyes open for puppet variations in crafts magazines and in stores. This just may become addictive!

Let the Games Begin!

Games are another type of toy that are easy to make, often require very few materials, and offer many hours of entertainment for kids of all ages.

One game you can make almost anywhere is the Memory Game. It's easy enough for a small child to play and still challenging for an adult.

Project: Memory Game

Level: Easy

Age: 5 and up

Materials needed: Cardboard (you can recycle old cereal or gift boxes), construction paper, scissors, glue, crayons or markers, straight edge or ruler

Directions:

1. Glue construction paper to the flat pieces of cardboard and let dry (or, if the cardboard is light-colored and clean enough, use as is).

2. Use the straight edge or ruler to make an even amount of rectangles of equal size. Have kids draw matched sets of pictures in the boxes, such as two hearts, two circles, two stars, two squares, etc. Cut out each card and you have a set of Memory Cards for the game.

3. Mix up the cards and turn them over face down. Each player gets to turn two cards over in a turn. If they make a match, the player keeps the cards and gets to go again. You play until all the cards are gone and the player with the most cards wins. This is the foundation of the classic TV game show *Concentration*.

Want an even easier game to make with your child? How about his very own set of jacks? If you think about the basic elements of a jacks set—a bunch of metal pieces and a ball—you'll find that can make jacks out of almost anything.

In Egypt, for example, children use seeds to play a version of jacks. All but one of the seeds is scattered, the held seed is tossed in the air, and the winner is the one who gets the most seeds before catching the falling seed. If you were wondering what to do with those pumpkin seeds at Halloween, now you know. Dry them, even decorate them if you like, and you have a set of "jacks."

Other possibilities include nuts or small screws, stones, or plastic pieces (perhaps from an old board game). All of these can be used with or without the ball. Make or find a small pouch and you now have a traveling game.

For more game ideas, find a copy of *The Big Book of Things to Make and Play With: Toys, Games, Puppets*. See Appendix A for more information.

Need an idea for a game to make that you can play in the dark? All you need is a flashlight, some paper cups, and a sharp pencil or other object to poke holes. Have kids make patterns in the bottoms of the cups and insert the flashlight into the cup. Then let them take turns projecting their creations on walls or wherever they like (tent ceilings and sides also work well).

Puzzles

Closely akin to the game is the puzzle. Puzzles are not only fun to make and to solve, they also make kids think, improve manual dexterity, and teach patience and tenacity. The following puzzle has probably the least number of materials of all—only two 60-penny nails.

Project: Nail Puzzle

Level: Easy

Age: 5 and up

Materials needed: Two 60-penny nails (about six inches long each)

Directions:

1. Bend both nails into a 270-degree twist (or ³/₄ way around), both exactly the same way (not opposite). You can bend the nails around a ¹/₂-inch pipe using a hammer while clamping the nail and the pipe in a vise. An adult may have to do this, but even a young child should be able to handle a hammer at least for part of the time. Make sure the gap created between the coils of the nail is too small for the other nail to pass through. File and sand off any burrs.

To create the Nail Puzzle, both nails should be bent like this.

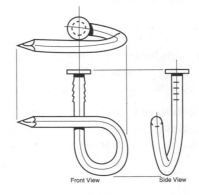

Front View   Side View

Project: Continued

2. Try solving the puzzle on your own by pulling the nails apart, but if you need the solution, it appears below.

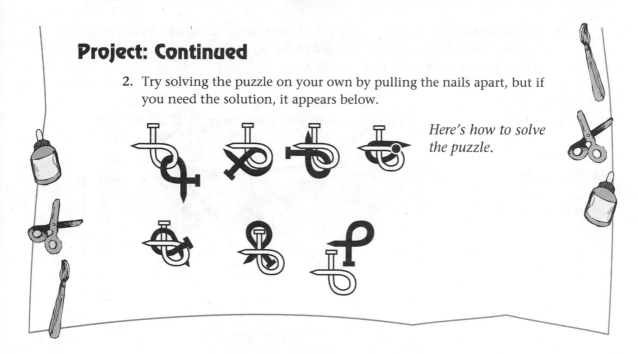

Here's how to solve the puzzle.

There are many more ideas for making toys, games, and puzzles out of everyday objects such as wood, yarn, fabric, or just about anything you can think of. Here's a list of quick ideas:

➤ Make a set of bean-bags out of fabric (felt works well) and beans. Make the bean-bags approximately the same weight and size. Use them for a bean-bag toss game, or learn to juggle with them.

➤ Make stuffed toys out of paper, newspaper, and a stapler. Cut two sheets of paper together in a shape. Decorate the back side of one piece and the front side of the other. Staple together with colored sides facing out, leaving a hole to stuff crumpled newspapers in. Fill and staple the rest up. (You can use paper towels or tissue instead of newspapers if that's what you have on hand.)

➤ Small yarn dolls make adorable Christmas tree or package ornaments. Use straw-colored yarn to make cute scarecrows for Thanksgiving or Halloween. Use white yarn, add a lace skirt and white lace gathered and tacked on the back, and you have an angel.

➤ Make a yarn doll. Wind yarn loosely around your hand. Tie at the top to secure the yarn bundle. Put a cotton ball or small Styrofoam ball at the top under the yarn. Tie under the neck. Cut open the bottom yarn and divide the yarn into legs and arms. Cut at the appropriate length or let the bottom hang loose for a skirt. You can glue on felt or fabric clothes, hats, or cutouts for features.

➤ Make a parachute out of a square piece of cloth, some string, and a clothespin "aviator." Attach the string to the head of the aviator with a screw eye. Weight the aviator by wrapping copper wire around her.

This is what your finished aviator should look like. All you need is a square piece of cloth, some string, and a clothespin.

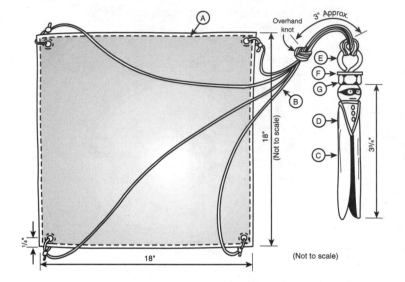

➤ Clothespins (the old-fashioned kind, without the spring) make great dolls. The top of the clothespin is a natural head, a pipe cleaner makes the arms, and you can use yarn for hair, fabric scraps for clothes, and decorate with ribbons and trims. Features can be applied with fine pens.

➤ Thimbles can be used as finger puppets. Just glue on felt for features.

➤ Whole peanuts can be made into marionettes. Use a large peanut for the body, a smaller one for the head, and longer-shaped ones for the arms and legs. Run a needle and thread (the needle must be longer than the longest peanut) through one leg, up through the body, and then through the head. Leave a string at the top of the head and clip. Do the same for the other leg. Do the arms from one arm to the other and through the body. Add felt hands and feet, and use felt-tip pens to make a face. Then make your marionette dance.

A sample marionette made of peanut shells, needle, and thread.

➤ Create a pinwheel out of a square piece of paper, markers, rubber stamps and/or stickers, a pencil (with eraser), scissors, a straight pin, a small piece of clay, and a ruler.

➤ Have your child draw, stamp and/or sticker one side of the paper. On the plain side, put a dot in the center and draw a line from each corner to $1/2$-inch from the dot. Cut along each line and fold each corner to the center without creasing, holding them in place at the center. Put the pencil's eraser behind the pinwheel and push the straight pin through. If it comes out the other side, cover it with clay. These can be decorated in different colors to match a particular holiday—red, white, and blue for the 4th of July, for example.

The Least You Need to Know

➤ The toys, games, and puzzles that delight children haven't changed much over the years.

➤ Many playthings are easy to make and require a minimum of materials, skill, and time.

➤ Knowing how to make simple toys can keep kids busy making them, as well as occupy them for hours once the toys are completed.

Mix and Beat Well: Music Making Crafts

Music soothes the savage beast, they say, and many a bored or overactive child, experience tells me. Music has been one of the mainstays of my existence from childhood. I've thanked my mother many times for making me practice and start taking music lessons when I was six. Music is one of the great pleasures in life and one of the great de-stressers. Sure, listening to music is great, but *making* music is even better, *and* making things that make music is better yet!

Don't worry if you can't tell a "ti" from a "la," this is your chance to get in touch with your musical self (I firmly believe that everyone has one) and learn along with your children how to bop to the beat, make beautiful (or, at least, unusual) sounds, and maybe even find a new voice.

Baby's Got a Beat

One of the earliest "instruments" most of us get a chance to play with is a rattle. Even a baby who can barely hold a rattle in his tiny hand can make noise and make everybody clap. (If we could just keep this attitude into adulthood, and forestall the development of performance anxiety, we'd be in great shape.) Simple shaking instruments can be made out of any variety of materials.

Project: Paper Plate Rattle

Level: Easy

Age: 5 and up

Materials needed: Two paper plates, some dried beans (about ¹/₂ cup), one paper towel tube, markers, crayons, rubber stamps and inks, paints, stickers, stapler, scissors

Directions:

1. Decorate the bottoms of both plates, the brighter, the better (makes the rattle sound better).

2. Put the plates on top of one another, tops together, and staple around, leaving about an inch between each staple. Before you completely close the circle, put the beans inside, then finish stapling.

3. Cut the paper towel tube to about six or seven inches, then make two 2-inch slits at one end opposite each other. Slide the plate rattle between the two slits and staple the handle to the rattle. You can decorate the handle, too, if you want.

4. Try using this rattle to add rhythm to music someone else is making (recorded or live) or just make rhythms with it alone. Try starting with the rhythm and adding a made-up song.

Bonding Experiences

Learn more about gourds and their uses in crafts. Gourds have been used by many ethnic groups throughout civilization for bowls, cups, drums, rattles, and lots of other useful things. Grow different kinds of gourds and experiment with them. Find out from your local nursery which ones grow best in your area and the things you need to do to grow them successfully.

Other rattles can be made using dried gourds. This summer, plant some gourds. Some may grow their own handles; others may need to have a stick pushed through and secured at the top and bottom for a handle. The dried seeds inside will make their own sound.

To make a rattle from papier-mâchè, blow up a balloon and tape it to the end of an empty toilet tissue tube. Tear up newspaper in 1 × 4-inch strips. Mix one cup of flour and one cup of water in a bowl to make a thin paste. Saturate the newspaper strips in the paste and layer over the balloon, smoothing them out as you go. Cover the tube, too, and don't forget to cover the end. Cover both balloon and tube with three to four layers of paste-saturated newspaper. Let the rattle dry and poke a hole through the rattle at one end. The balloon will pop and stay inside.

> **Crafty Clues**
> Make several rattles with different-size beans or other small objects inside. See how they sound. Try different weight and size paper plates, too. Use two aluminum pie plates to get a different sound.

Add some dried beans or pebbles until you like the sound and paste a few more strips over the opening to seal. Decorate with bright colors using tempera paints.

Other shakers or rattles can be made from plastic milk jugs (keep the jug intact and put beans, pebbles, marbles, screws, nuts, seeds, rice, or whatever you can think of inside, screw on the cap, and use the handle to shake), small plastic food containers, metal molds or tins, oatmeal boxes, and coffee cans.

By encouraging your children to create these simple rhythm-makers, you will begin to instill an uninhibited appreciation of music.

Little Drummer Boys (and Girls)

Drums can be made from almost anything. If you've ever known a professional drummer, you've probably watched him tap a spoon or knife or anything else that looks like a drumstick on anything within reach. A favorite pastime of my own children was to haul all the pots and pans out of the cupboard and beat on them with a wooden spoon, while "singing" some tune known only to them.

A drum is basically anything hollow that produces a tone when struck. You can make drums out of a hollowed-out tree trunk, the top of a metal garbage can, large pieces of plastic PVC pipe, or any manner of cans turned upside down.

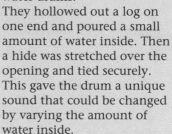

> **Bet You Didn't Know**
> *Ooooo...*
> Some native peoples made water drums. They hollowed out a log on one end and poured a small amount of water inside. Then a hide was stretched over the opening and tied securely. This gave the drum a unique sound that could be changed by varying the amount of water inside.

Project: Milk Container Drum

Level: Easy

Age: 5 and up

Materials needed: Three plastic milk jugs (all the same size and shape) heavy yarn, a single-hole punch, sticks or dowels, permanent markers, paper or fabric scraps, scissors, glue

Directions:

1. Cut away the top of one milk jug and the bottoms of the other two.
2. Punch holes along the sides of the bottom pieces, spaced about one inch apart.
3. Lace the two bottom sections over the first jug to form the top and bottom of the drum. Decorate.
4. Make drumsticks by rolling up a wad of cloth around the end of the stick or dowel. Wrap a piece of cloth around the wadded end and tie with string or yarn. Trim. This is your drumstick.

By cutting three milk cartons and finishing with some yarn, kids can create a simple drum from recycled materials.

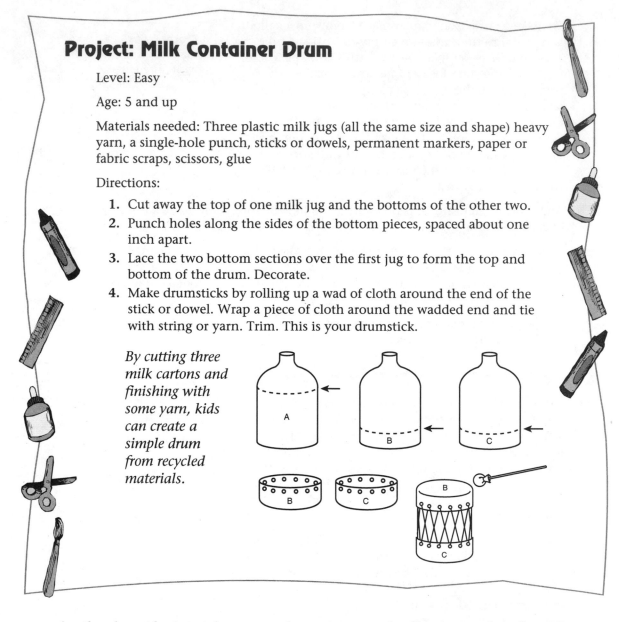

Another drum idea is to take any can, from a two-pound coffee tin to a clean five-gallon drum (the larger the can, the bigger the sound), and remove both ends. Paint it and decorate it. Pick up some *chamois* (a piece of soft, pliable leather) from a good auto supply store. You'll want the real thing, not the cotton kind.

Cut two circles from the chamois at least three inches larger than the diameter of the can. Lay the circles on an old board and punch holes around the edges, evenly spaced about an inch apart. Soak both chamois circles in ice water for about 20 minutes until they feel rubbery. While still wet, stretch the chamois over the ends of the can and lace using rawhide or strong string. When it dries, the chamois will shrink and make a nice, tight drumhead.

Handiwords
Chamois is soft, pliable leather from any of various animal skins dressed with oil. It also refers to cotton cloth finished to simulate this leather.

Bonding Experiences

Collect drum-making ideas and try them together. Start with simple drums and work up to more complicated designs. Begin a drum collection with the more successful drums you create. Take drum lessons together (it's never too late or early to start!).

The Gong Show

A related instrument, the gong, can be made from any object that makes a pleasing sound when suspended freely and struck with another object. Both the gong and the striker contribute to the sound. Most of us think of gongs as flat, and, indeed, the metal top from a large can (such as a paint can), makes a great gong, but other interesting sounds can be obtained from more unusually shaped objects.

Try going to a junkyard and appropriating some auto parts. Automobile coil springs and brake drums are some possibilities. Other parts might make good beaters. Cover with paint, drill some holes if necessary, and hang from some wire, chain, or heavy cord and you've got a gong like no one else's!

Crafty Clues
You might want to construct (or find) something to suspend a variety of gongs. An unoccupied garden arbor, a clothesline, a wooden rafter—almost anything will do as long as it will support what you plan to hang from it.

Another easy-to-make rhythm instrument is the tambourine. All you need is a small piece of wood (in a size that's easy to grasp), some bottle caps (the kind you have to take off with a bottle opener, not the twist-off kind), and a hammer and nails. Turn each bottle cap and hammer into the block of wood, but don't hammer the nail all the way in; leave a gap. Put about four or five bottle caps on, then shake. Kids can decorate however they like.

Handiwords

A *marimba* is a musical instrument consisting of a set of graduated wooden bars (often with resonators beneath to reinforce the sound) which is struck with mallets. A *xylophone* is a musical instrument consisting of a graduated series of wooden bars, usually sounded by striking with small wooden hammers.

The *marimba* (basically, a *xylophone*) is another instrument you can strike to make music. With the marimba, however, you can construct a series of notes by varying the length of the bars.

You can make a no-fuss marimba by finding wood that has a nice sound (hardwoods usually have the best tone), cutting it into pieces of different lengths, drilling holes through the top and bottom of each piece, running cords through each piece, and suspending both ends between two poles. A beater stick can be made from a wood dowel with a wood ball or large wooden bead on the end (these can be purchased already turned or milled at a factory and sold as finished pieces).

You can experiment by placing the bars in an approximate scale, or simply placing them at random in any pleasing tone arrangement. The placement of the drilled holes will alter the sound, so you'll need to experiment with that as well. Bars can also be attached to two cross pieces or risers, which are best made of a less-hard wood such as pine.

A marimba constructed with risers.

Another instrument to make that's struck, but in a much more delicate way, is a set of water-glass chimes. You can try using different glasses, or a set of the same glasses that are filled with different amounts of water. Use teaspoons to strike the glasses. Experiment until you have an eight-note scale, then play a melody.

Smaller children might have a problem being delicate enough with water-glass chimes, but older children are fascinated by them. You may end up collecting odd glasses at yard sales to let your kids make their own water-glass chimes when the spirit strikes them.

They may even want to form their own "bell" chorus, complete with harmony (produced by striking two or more glasses at once). Remember, the lighter and more gentle the tap, the clearer and more sparkling the sound.

Bonding Experiences

Take a field trip to a music store. Try out different drums and other percussion instruments. Notice their construction and talk about the differences in their sound and feel. Examine instruments from other cultures. You can also listen to recordings of music that feature unusual percussion instruments. Those of the Paul Winter Consort come to mind, but there are many others. Ask the clerk at your local music store for suggestions.

There's the Rub!

Besides instruments you shake and strike, there are an infinite number of sounds to be produced by rubbing two objects together or sliding one against the other. For example, a *rasp* is an instrument that produces a grating sound by rubbing one smooth piece of wood along another notched or scored piece of wood. You can easily make one from a paint stirrer and an unsharpened pencil or dowel. An adult will need to cut the notches out with a small handsaw (see the following illustration). To get the best sound, rest the notched stick on an overturned wooden or plastic bowl or a half of a coconut shell. Move the smooth stick back and forth over the notches.

Handiwords
A *rasp* is an instrument consisting of two sticks; one is notched and the other smooth. A sound is made by rubbing the sticks against each other.

A simple rubbing instrument can be made from sandpaper and two blocks of wood. Just cover two handsized wooden blocks with sandpaper. Affix the paper by stapling or gluing. Rub together rhythmically and you've got an instrument!

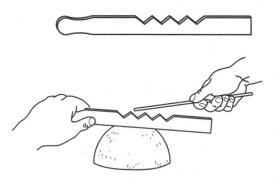

Pattern for notched stick.

How to use a rasp.

Make It Rain

An interesting sound to add to your band is that of the Indian rain stick. Native Americans used these sticks to call for rain; the sticks have a soft, dreamy sound. Lots of crafts and collectibles stores have them now, so you can hear some made by professional crafters. No two sound exactly alike.

Project: Indian Rain Sticks

Level: Easy

Age: 5 and up

Materials needed: A mailing tube made of heavy cardboard (hopefully with caps on the ends, otherwise you'll need some tape), some nails the same length as the diameter of the tube (a $1^1/_2$-inch nail for a $1^1/_2$-inch tube, and so on), a hammer, dried beans, rice, pasta (or other noisemaking material), materials to decorate your sticks with: paint, stickers, paper, glitter, and glue.

Directions:

1. Have the kids drive the nails straight in to the mailing tube (the nails shouldn't poke through) or help them with this if their hammering skills aren't up to it. The nails should be placed randomly perpendicular along the tube. Use lots of nails.

2. Seal up one end of the tube and experiment with pouring different things down the tube (a funnel might help). Try rice, dried pasta, lentils, beans, sand, unpopped and popped popcorn, and anything else you'd like to try. Once you've found a mixture that makes a pleasing sound, seal up the other end of the tube.

3. Decorate the tube. Then make some rain!

Get in the String

Make a guitar yourself? Bah, you say? Well, it may not be a vintage Gibson or Martin or one you can plug in, but it still makes music. Here's how to do it.

Project: Homemade Guitar

Level: Medium; smaller children will need adult help hammering nails

Age: 5 and up

Materials needed: A piece of wood about two feet long (a 2 × 4 or 1 × 4 scrap will do), six or more nails, a paint stirrer (about $1^1/_2$ inches wide), rubber bands (different sizes and weights), paint (optional)

Directions:

1. Sand the board until it's smooth and paint it if you like.

2. Hammer nails at one end, evenly spaced and a few inches from the edge. Line up nails at the other end to match and do the same.

3. Cut a bridge from the paint stirrer, about four inches long. Glue it in place (on end) across the guitar and nail it in place from the back.

4. Use different-weight rubber bands for strings (a different thickness will give you a different pitch). Also try stretching the rubber bands tighter (you can make a knot at one end to make it smaller if you need to) to give a different pitch (the tighter the rubber band, the higher the pitch). Try different variations until you get the sounds you want.

There are kits available for making all kinds of stringed instruments. Contact some of the following companies for information:

➤ Musicmaker's Kits, Inc., P.O. Box 2117, Stillwater, MN 55082, 1-800-432-5487, Web site: http://www.musikits.com/.

➤ Lark in the Morning, P.O. Box 1176, Mendocino, CA 95460, 707-964-5569, e-mail: larminam@larkinam.com, Web site: http://www.larkinam.com.

➤ The Early Music Shop, 38 Manningham Lane, Bradford, BD1 3EA, UK, Web site: htt://www.e-m-s.com/.

➤ For general information about folk music and links to all sorts of wondrous places, try the Folk Music Home Page at http://www.jg.or/folk/.

Toot Your Own Horn

Wind instruments are a little more difficult to make. The best way to start is with a one-note whistle and graduate to more complicated "flutes." If you can make a whistle, you can make a pan flute, which is simply a set of whistles of varying length tied together.

Here's how to make a basic whistle: Start with a piece of willow branch or bamboo. Hammer it lightly to bruise it and push the center bark out (a round file will help you make it hollow). You'll need to carve a notch to make it vibrate.

Another way is to cut the wood in half, hollow out the cavity, and put the split wood back together with rubber bands. A grass reed can be added before reassembling it.

A book that shows several ways to make flutes and gives instructions for how to play them *is Simple Flutes: Play Them, Make Them* by Mark Shepard. According to Mark, the easiest material to work with is plastic (PVC) plumbing pipe, since it's waterproof, split-proof, and nearly unbreakable. Mark offers complete instructions for free at his Web site at http://www.aaronshep.com/Mark/flute/, and gives permission for you to take the instructions and even make flutes and sell them. Mark also provides an online tutorial. What a deal!

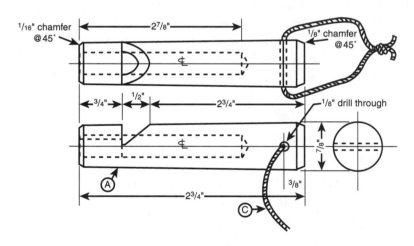

How to notch your whistle.

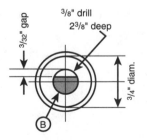

Also check out On Shambry's Pond at http://www.geocities.com/CapeCanaveral/35321. You'll find still more information on amateur flute building there.

For more ideas and musical instrument making projects, pick up a copy of *Kids Make Music! Clapping & Tapping from Bach to Rock!* by Avery Hart, Paul Mantell, and Loretta Trezzo Braren. This book has both projects and activities, including singing and dancing.

> **Bet You Didn't Know**
> *Oooo...*
> One of the easiest stringed instruments to make (and play) is the Appalachian Mountain dulcimer. This is a fretted instrument that is played on the lap, and most commonly comes in an hourglass or teardrop shape.

Sampling Sounds

In addition to traditional instruments, think about the sounds that are now "sampled" electronically and used as musical effects. In addition to making music with sound, kids get a kick out of experimenting with sound effects. A lot goes into creating creaks, screeches, roars, and more. In a recent documentary on the making of the movie *Jurassic Park*, for example, there was an interesting segment on how the dinosaur sounds were made. I mean, who has ever heard a dinosaur, right? This is a whole other area to explore.

Set your kids loose in the kitchen, the garage, or outdoors with a tape recorder. Ask them to tape a variety of sounds and keep track of where they got them from. Have them return and quiz each other on what the sounds are and where they came from. Consider whether they actually sound like what they are or sound more like something else. How could you use the sounds in a musical composition or a homemade movie?

The Least You Need to Know

➤ You don't need to know a lot about music to get started making instruments and learning to play them.

➤ Drums, rattles, shakers, and gongs can be made from a variety of materials.

➤ Stringed instruments can be made from the simplest of materials, and there are more involved kits available from several reputable companies.

➤ Children, with some adult help, can make simple wind instruments, starting with a whistle and working up to a flute. One of the best homemade flutes comes from plastic pipe.

➤ Music and instruments for making music are everywhere you look.

Chapter 19

The Second Time Around: Crafts from Recyclables

> **In This Chapter**
>
> ➤ The value of recycling
>
> ➤ What materials to save
>
> ➤ Tons of crafts ideas from castoffs

In just about every chapter so far (and in the ones to come), I've presented projects using materials you may generally throw away. We used tin cans for metal working, and paper plates and plastic jugs for making musical instruments. There are so many ways to use those materials that might otherwise become garbage, I decided to devote a whole chapter to it.

Before you toss anything in the garbage, think crafts. After you read this chapter, you'll have so many ideas for recycling your trash you may hardly have any!

Reduce, Reuse, Recycle, and Rethink

Reducing waste is part of a certain mind set. Experts who try to train people to cut back on disposables and recycle say that most of us fall into one of three categories. People in the first category have been recycling and thinking environmentally since they could walk. It's completely second nature to them. People of the second category would probably do something if they had more information or were reminded; they just don't think about it. And people of the third category won't do it no matter what. They're either resistant to change or they simply don't care. Hopefully, this last group will shrink in size as education and environmental consciousness grows.

If you are like most parents, you'd like your children to fall into the first group, and how you teach them, both by what you say and what you do, will have a huge impact. One way you can set an example is to focus on reducing waste at home in general, and when doing crafts in particular. You can start by teaching your kids the four Rs: *Reduce, Reuse, Recycle,* and *Rethink*. You can *reduce* the amount of trash you have each week by:

➤ Buying things with less packaging

➤ Buying in bulk to reduce packaging

➤ Making food (and crafts supplies like clays and paints) from scratch

➤ Growing your own fruits, herbs, and vegetables

➤ Cooking in large batches so you can buy in bulk

You can *reuse* many of the things you normally discard. That's what this chapter is about. But getting in the reuse habit involves changing how you think in many cases. Sometimes it means getting organized so you don't purchase what you already have. (How many times have you gone to look for an item and couldn't find it, then purchased a new one, only to find the old one a week or two later?)

This is particularly true in crafting. When you think crafts, think, "What do I have on hand?" Instead of going out to buy new materials. There are lots of great new products on the market and they have their place, but whenever possible, think of crafts as a way of using up what you already have.

Recycling is the next step in the chain. After you reduce the amount of products you buy, and reuse as many items as possible, you should only be recycling or finally throwing away a bare minimum. At least, that's the goal.

Crafty Clues

Around the house, fix items that are broken, or discard them and get new ones that work. Try to purchase appliances and tools that do several jobs, rather than buying a different tool for each job. A food processor is a good example.

Find out what your town's recycling program is—what is recycled and what isn't. If your town's recycling department won't take a particular item, some other organization might. Know what your options are. If your area doesn't recycle at all or if recycling is limited, work on getting that changed. Remember, it takes energy to recycle, so whenever you can reduce or reuse materials, you're ahead of the game.

Finally, *rethink* when it comes to your garbage. Look for items with reduced packaging. Buy products made from recycled materials. Don't throw away what can be reused or recycled.

What to Save

Here's a short list of household waste items that make good crafts materials. Following the list is a series of suggestions for ways to use them. I'll bet you and your family can think of a gazillion more!

If for some reason you don't produce enough of a particular item to do a project, enlist friends to save for you. You may even try contacting local businesses for supplies, particularly if you need a large quantity (if you're working on a project with a Brownie or Cub Scout troop, for example). Restaurants are often willing to oblige.

➤ Egg cartons

➤ Styrofoam trays, cups, and peanuts

➤ Film canisters

➤ Glass jars and bottles

➤ Baby-food jars

➤ Plastic jugs and cartons

➤ Milk or juice cartons

➤ Frozen juice cans and lids

➤ Coffee cans

➤ Margarine tubs with plastic lids

➤ Newpapers

➤ Magazines, catalogs, or color newspaper supplements

➤ Junk mail

➤ Used gift wrap

➤ Pieces of wallpaper

➤ Unused remnants of shelf or contact paper

➤ Ribbon and fabric scraps

➤ Old clothes

➤ Cardboard boxes

➤ Cardboard tubes from paper towels, toilet paper, and gift wrap; heavy cardboard mailing tubes

➤ Pieces of cardboard, such as those that come in shirts from dry cleaners

➤ Tin cans

➤ Cereal boxes

➤ Wire hangers

Now, I'm not suggesting you save these things just for saving's sake. It's better to recycle than to just accumulate clutter. (It's better still not to produce the waste at all.)

From Trash to Crafts

The following are suggestions to get you started thinking in the Trashy Crafts mode. I've given brief descriptions and, in some cases, illustrations to make the idea more clear. Keep your eyes open for ideas all around you. Look at craft fairs at what other people are doing with castaways. Magazines and books are full of project ideas using "found" materials.

Egg Cartons

Here are some crafts that use old egg cartons, either paper or Styrofoam (I like paper best, but either kind will do):

➤ Creatures and critters: Using one or more sections from an egg carton and some pipe cleaners, you can make a whole zoo. If you paint the sections black and suspend them from strings, these make great spiders for Halloween. Add cotton balls dyed yellow to a painted yellow carton section to make an adorable Easter chick.

Here are only a couple of the creatures you can create with used egg cartons.

➤ Similar to egg carton creatures, you can cut the sections apart and make egg carton flowers, using the carton pieces as the actual flower or the center of a larger flower and adding petals.

➤ Egg cartons make good holders for crafts in progress; for drying painted Easter eggs, for example.

➤ Egg cartons (or any other sectioned container) are great for sorting things like beads or any other small parts.

➤ Fill each well of an egg carton with different colored paints for small projects.

➤ Start seeds in each well. When they've sprouted, you can cut the sections apart and plant them (if they're the cardboard kind).

➤ Put flowers you want to dry in silica gel (one in each section) and cover with the gel.

➤ There are several strategy games that use sectioned game boards, which can be made out of egg cartons.

Styrofoam Trays, Cups, and Peanuts

Here are some crafts you can make out of Styrofoam:

➤ Use a tray as a paint palette. Cut out a hole for your fingers.

➤ An adult or older child can cut tray pieces out for stencils.

➤ Rubber stamps can be expensive, but you can make your own out of Styrofoam meat trays. Clean the tray, cut out the shape, and glue it to an empty film canister, cork, or the end of a large eraser. Press into an inked stamp pad and you're ready to stamp.

Simple shapes cut from Styrofam and attached to a "handle" make great stamps.

➤ Larger trays from bulk foods make good frames for artwork. You can also decorate them and use them as special trays.

➤ Cut pieces of Styrofoam into different shapes and decorate to make coasters.

➤ Decorate Styrofoam plates and use under plants to catch excess water.

➤ Use leftover Styrofoam cups to grow seedlings (after you've used an egg carton to start them).

Styrofoam cups also work well as paint containers (just rinse them first) and homes for seedlings. Peanuts can be painted and strung together as "beads" or glued on as decorations.

Empty Film Canisters

Here are some crafts that you can make with empty film canisters:

➤ Stamp bodies (see the earlier Styrofoam section).

➤ Film canisters make great containers for small things. (Just make sure to label them so you know what's inside without having to open each one.) I like them for holding tiny seed beads when I travel.

➤ Film canisters make nice, small salt and pepper shakers, perfect for a picnic. Paint and use an awl or nail to poke holes through the top.

So, next time you snap some pictures and send the rolls to be developed, remember to save the containers.

Glass Jars

Here are some fun uses of glass jars in all shapes and sizes:

➤ Baby-food jars make great snow globes. Larger jars make larger globes. I especially like the shape of the jar that marshmallow fluff comes in.

➤ Glass jars can be use to hold small candles. Use a baby-food jar to hold a tea light or a slightly larger jar to hold a votive candle. You can also use heavier glass jars for container candles. Place them inside your luminaria (see Chapter 21). This increases safety and ensures that the flame won't blow out.

➤ Make a windproof candle lantern. Turn the jar so the opening is right side up and insert a candle into the jar. Attach a wire or cords around the neck, and hang.

➤ Use glass jars to store kitchen crafts, like dried herbs, spice mixtures, scented potions, and bath salts. You can also place these crafts in decorated glass jars to give as gifts.

➤ Make decorative powdered-sugar or talcum-powder shakers by perforating the tops of the jars and decorating the glass. Use the glass painting or decoupage techniques you learned in Chapter 14.

Using the glass painting techniques you learned in Chapter 14, you'll be able to decorate these to make items even more attractive.

Glass Bottles

Like glass jars, glass bottles of all sizes can be used in crafts. Here are some ideas:

➤ Use them for terrariums (discussed in Chapter 16).

➤ Using the techniques you learned in Chapter 14, you can decorate nicely shaped discarded glass bottles and use them as vases or rooting jars, or as containers for homemade oils, vinegars, bath oils, and many other items.

Using a bottle cut you can expand the possibilities still further. An overturned bottle with the top cut off makes a minigreenhouse for tender spring seedlings.

Plastic Jugs and Cartons

Here are some creative ideas that make use of clean plastic containers:

➤ Use them as musical rhythm shakers (see Chapter 18).

➤ Use plastic milk cartons to make a dulcimer pick, which are much like a guitar picker only lighter. They're just the right weight and you can cut them in any shape you want. Margarine-tin tops cut into wedges make another good stringed-instrument pick.

➤ Cut the bottom off a clear plastic jug, unscrew the top, and use as a mini-greenhouse to protect plants outside when it's still cold and plants are tender. (Be sure to remove the jug if it gets really hot and sunny, or the plant will burn.)

➤ Milk cartons and large plastic containers make excellent planters. A half-gallon milk or juice container can even be cut in half lengthwise and used as a tray to start seeds. Decorate with adhesive-backed paper and be sure to put pebbles in the bottom for drainage.

➤ Use a clean plastic bleach bottle as a bird feeder. On each side, two inches from the bottom, cut two feeding holes about three inches square. Put small drainage holes in the bottom of the bottle. Hang from a wire threaded through two holes in the bottle's neck. The birds will never know.

Newspapers and Other Scrap Paper

Newspapers and other scrap papers are among the most commonly recycled items. Before you throw paper into the recycling bin, think about the crafts you can create with it:

➤ Make paper hats.

➤ Make papier-mâchè.

➤ Use for drawing.

➤ Use for making patterns.

➤ Use newspaper to cover special surfaces (floors, countertops) while you do crafts or household projects for easy cleanup.

➤ Newspaper makes great gift wrap. The comics pages work especially well; or use the regular printed pages and stamp or stencil them with bright colors.

➤ Save greeting cards from any occasion. These can be used in decoupage or cut-and-paste projects. Decoupage is the traditional art of decorating with cutout paper.

Usually, a product is used to both adhere the paper to the object and to coat the paper and provide a hard finish. Several finishing coats are applied.

➤ Seed packets often have beautiful illustrations of vegetables, herbs, and flowers. Save them and use for decoupage projects for the kitchen.

➤ Leftover paper bags make luminaria (see Chapter 21), masks, and puppets.

Instead of always asking which paper to buy for a project, ask yourself which paper you can reuse.

Old Clothes

Before you give old clothes to a local church or Goodwill, think about these crafts ideas:

➤ Remake into other clothes. A full skirt, for instance, can become a straight skirt or a shell blouse.

➤ Make doll and teddy-bear clothes.

➤ Make into rag rugs.

➤ Make a scrap quilt.

➤ Make pillows. You can either use one piece of fabric or make patchwork pillows out of many different pieces.

➤ Take the two back pockets off an old pair of jeans, glue Velcro across the tops with fabric glue, and sew both sides together to make a coin purse.

This trendy coin purse is sure to be a hit with the younger set.

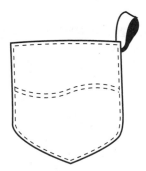

➤ Denim is strong, and can be patched together and decorated to make aprons, jackets, vests, and tote bags.

➤ Cloth diapers can be used for cleanup and polishing. Retired T-shirts can, too.

Carton Boxes

Empty carton boxes have many uses in crafts:

➤ Boxes in different sizes make great building materials for forts and castles.

➤ Use boxes for dioramas.

➤ Make individual settings for miniatures.

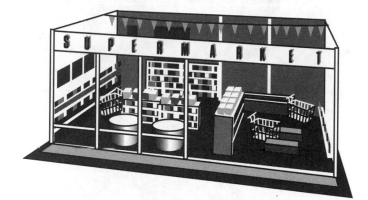

Who needs a dollhouse? Boxes turned on their sides make a great setting for miniatures.

➤ Attach several boxes together to make a dollhouse.

➤ A large appliance box becomes a playhouse. Cut windows and doors and decorate.

➤ Make play furniture from sturdy cartons.

➤ One box makes a puppet theater. Cut out the bottom and suspend a curtain from a cord (see Chapter 17).

➤ Use cut-out corrugated cardboard as a base for ornaments.

➤ Heavy cardboard can be used as wreath forms. Materials can be glued to the cardboard or it can be covered with moss.

Tin Cans

Don't throw away old tin cans! They make wonderful organizers and crafts materials:

➤ Turn a coffee can with a plastic lid into a bank by decorating the can and making a slot in the lid for coins.

➤ Create desk accessories. Use two or three cans the same or different sizes. They can be separate or you can attach them. Decorate one for pencils, one for pens, and one for markers.

➤ Coffee cans in different sizes can be used for a canister set. There are infinite ways to decorate them. One of the most interesting decorative ideas I've seen uses belt leather, sisal cord or string, and bridle rings.

This rustic-looking canister set is made from coffee cans, belt leather, sisal cord, and bridle rings.

➤ Groups of cans in different sizes can be spray-painted and glued together, then mounted on the wall with a nail through the cans into the wall stud (or a toggle bolt if there's no stud). Use for storage.

You can use different size cans to make a great storage space.

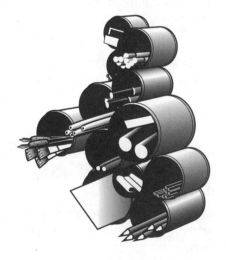

➤ Cans from hams have an interesting shape. With both sides removed and a hanger added (the following illustration uses a wooden bead and a wooden drapery ring), they make graceful lanterns, bird feeders, or whatever else you can think of.

This candleholder is just one example of the uses of a ham can.

➤ Coffee cans make excellent planters. Cover the cans with any durable material, then punch six evenly positioned holes at the top along the rim. Knot the end of some heavy cord (rawhide strips or whatever else you have on hand) and make them long enough to hang as planters.

Miscellaneous Materials

Not enough ideas for you? Here are a few more, all using recycled materials:

➤ Use the cardboard from a shirt box to make place mats. Decorate and laminate them.

➤ Large pieces of broken glass can be cut with a glass cutter and made to fit a smaller frame. You can also sandwich two pieces of the same size together to make a floating frame or dried-flower ornament (as we did with two medical slides in Chapter 16).

➤ Milk or juice cartons (with plastic or wax coating) or cream cartons can be used as molds for candles (see Chapter 15). Just peel them away when the candle has hardened.

➤ Many objects, such as discarded watering cans or flower pots, can be made into clocks. Decorate and drill a hole for the clockworks and insert the turning mechanism inside the hole. You can put the clock face on the outside and attach the hands.

➤ Interesting works of art can be made of assemblages sprayed all one color. These can be from any odds and ends.

➤ Decorate and paint six juice or soup cans, then attach them in a six-pack. This can hold paint brushes, tools, or even silverware for a buffet. Or you can plant a mini-herb garden in it.

➤ Use a cereal box or other box as a magazine holder. Cut off the top at an angle, then cover the box with adhesive-backed paper.

➤ Cigar boxes can hold anything. They can be decorated in a variety of ways, including wood burning (burning designs into wood using a special tool with various tips), decoupage, or painting.

➤ A discarded lampshade can be recovered with wallpaper and a pin-pricked design, or covered with ribbon suspended closely together between the top and bottom wire rings.

➤ Brown paper bags make puppets, sacks for Halloween, and luminaria (see Chapter 21).

➤ Scratched holiday ornaments can be reused. Remove the metal neck, then remove the metallic finish by dipping in a solution of bleach and water. Rinse and dry and fill the ornament with confetti, potpourri, sand, shells, or whatever. Replace the metal neck and hanger. Add some ribbon and tiny dried flowers with glue.

➤ Wire hangers can be covered in various ways (ribbon, batting and fabric, string) to make decorative hangers that are kind to your clothes and pretty to look at. Or hangers can be cut and the wire itself reused in other crafts.

➤ Lamps can be made out of almost anything. Take an interesting tin, vase, or teapot and fit it with a lamp assembly, available at any hardware store. (Be sure that you use the proper drill to make any holes for your lamp assembly.)

➤ Wood turnings, finials (an ornament at the top of a piece of furniture, lamp, or other decorative trim), and other small parts from furniture, lamps, etc. can be used for all sorts of things, from miniatures to decorative trims. I've even seen wood turnings, cabinet knobs, and empty thread spools turned into an imaginative chess set and toy soldiers. Another chess set was made out of discarded Tinkertoys and wooden beads, then painted.

➤ Cardboard mailing tubes can be cut into short sections and made into ornaments.

These elegant ornaments are just one idea for recycling cardboard mailing tubes.

➤ Broken china pieces can be applied in an interesting mosaic pattern to a flowerpot or recycled table. You'll need tile mastic, which is an adhesive especially for tile, to hold the pieces, and after it's dry you'll grout in between.

There's something very satisfying about using discarded items and making them beautiful or useful again. Not only are you doing your part to help the environment, but there's the secret pleasure of knowing how clever and thrifty you've been.

Crafty Clues
Clean and collect a week's worth of items that you'd normally throw away and challenge your children to think of ways you could use the items in crafting.

The Least You Need to Know

➤ Teach your children (and yourself) to observe the four Rs of waste reduction and control—Reduce, Reuse, Recycle, and Rethink.

➤ There are many basic materials—including glass bottles and jars, plastic containers, scrap paper, and cardboard boxes—that can be useful in a great variety of crafts projects.

➤ Not only is reusing discarded items good for the environment, it's good for the pocketbook.

Part 4
Holidays Are for Crafty Kids of All Ages!

There's no other time like holidays to get kids and adults alike thinking, "What can I make this year?" This part will show you how to make crafts for every occasion, whether it's a special card for that first Valentine sweetheart, an ornament for the Christmas tree, or any one of hundreds of other reasons to get crafting.

Tight schedules can add pressure, but relax and read how you can whip up quick and simple decorations, cards, wrappings, and gifts for just about any occasion—using the techniques you've already learned in Part 2, plus a few new ones.

We'll take Valentine's Day to heart, boo-gey through Halloween, and X-cel at Xmas, plus explore lots of other holidays that are an easy excuse for getting out the scissors and glue (and whatever other materials you and your charges like to work with). Some craft ideas presented here are as old as the hills others use exciting new materials that make traditional crafts easier than ever to create.

Love Is the Answer: Crafts for Valentine's Day

Valentine's Day is hyped as a day of adult romance, what with the exchange of candy and flowers, poetry, and sexy come-ons, but Heart-Day is equally for kids. (One major greeting-card maker says it sells twice as many valentines for children as for adults.) Valentine's Day is a super time for thinking about the meaning of love and telling our loved ones what we appreciate most about them.

When seen in this broader context, we can find thousands of crafts and activities to help us celebrate the day. One couple I know skips mailing out Christmas cards and sends valentines instead. Another friend sends both, considering Heart-Day just as important as Christmas. How about declaring February "Warm and Fuzzy Month" and celebrating Valentine's Day all 28 (or 29!) days? What a great way to make the long, sometimes dreary days of February bright and cozy.

If you've followed my suggestions in Chapter 3, you've got all your Valentine's Day crafting supplies and ideas stored in a box and folder just waiting for you. The time to get out the crafting supplies for Valentine's Day isn't in February, either. As soon as the New Year's party hats and confetti are a thing of the past, start thinking *hearts* and *flowers*!

Was There a St. Valentine?

Where did all these romantic, lovey-dovey notions come from, anyway? And who (or what) was Valentine?

Actually, there was at least one St. Valentine (some say there were as many as seven!). The credit is generally given to Valentinus, a priest who suffered a grim death in the 3rd century and was martyred. Not the stuff of our modern celebration, for sure. The date of February 14 was probably chosen because it coincides with the Roman mid-February Feast of Lupercalia, a holiday to honor Juno, the Queen of Roman gods and goddesses, and a celebration of spring.

Bonding Experiences

Before you get out the paper lace and red construction paper, do a little research with your children about the history of St. Valentine's Day and the superstitions and customs surrounding it. To get you started, check out *Tokens of Love* by Roberta B. Etter (Abbeville Press, 1990) and point your browser to http://www.bconnex.net/~mbuchana/realms/valentine/facts.html on the Internet.

Bet You Didn't Know

In the 18th century, the custom was for young men to draw names of eligible maidens and pin them on their sleeve. This is where the expression "wearing his heart on his sleeve" comes from.

The exchanging of love letters on February 14th began in the Middle Ages. The first commercially manufactured valentines in America appeared in the mid-1830s. The "Golden Age" of the valentine is generally considered to be the Victorian era, especially the years between 1830 and 1860, and, more particularly, the 1840s.

Valentine messages weren't always sweet and sentimental. In the 19th century, many insulting cards were sent. Called "penny dreadfuls," "vinegar valentines," and "rudes and crudes," these cheap, ugly cards were often sent anonymously and with postage due!

P.S. I Love You!

Perhaps more than any other holiday, Valentine's Day is the day of The Card, and cards are one of the easiest crafts to do with kids. What could be simpler than folding a sheet of paper in half, decorating it, and writing a message inside?

Victorian valentines showcased the printer's art and included moving parts, three-dimensional effects, feathers, real lace and fringe, spun glass, and even pearls. Valentines were sent between friends, not just to objects of romantic affection.

Bonding Experiences

There's a fun and visually eye-catching site on the World Wide Web devoted to Victorian valentines and other Victoriana. Visit The St. Valentine's Messenger at http://ourworld.compuserve.com/ homepages/Malcolm_Warrington/ stvalent.htm and enjoy an elegant virtual tour of this bygone era. It should give you and your children lots of ideas for your own valentines!

One simple way to decorate a card is to make a design on white or light-colored paper using a traditional pin-pricking or piercing technique. The result can be as simple or complex as you choose.

Project: Pin-Pricked Paper Heart Card

Level: Medium

Age: 7 and up

Materials needed: Fairly stiff white paper (lampshade paper works well; get it white on one side, colored on the other), red construction paper (or other kind of paper), a sharp needle or piercer (like a small skewer), baby's breath (or other small dried flowers) scissors, utility knife, glue (optional)

Directions:

1. Draw or make a template first and trace around a heart for your basic outside shape.

2. Create a simple pattern. Embroidery books can give you some ideas. You can draw this freehand or create one pattern and trace it at even intervals.

3. Use the utility knife to make straight and curved cuts (this should be done by an adult); use the needle or skewer to pierce holes. Make sure to go all one way from back to front of the surface you want to show.

4. On straight lines that have been cut, use the needle to raise one edge of each line open to a slit. On curved lines, use the needle to roll the curve to the inside and open it up so the card color will show through.

continues

Project: Continued

5. Glue baby's breath, other dried flowers, or small silk flowers to the back of your heart, so they extend out the top.

6. Glue the pierced heart to a card of contrasting color (white on red is nice), putting glue on the outer edges only. Glue a small bow to the top.

7. Write a message on the front and inside.

8. Do not flatten. Deliver your card in a small box.

Here are some more card ideas:

➤ Cut a heart out of removable sticker paper (available from rubber stamping stores and catalogs or crafts stores) and type, rubber-stamp, or print a message over it. The words can be terms of endearment or "I Love You" in different languages (check out the list at the "I love you" web page at http://www. tu-chemnitz.de/~lpo/ lovep.html). Experiment with different typefaces or colors. Remove the sticker paper and you'll have a clear heart suspended in a sea of type.

Crafty Clues
Use a corrugated cardboard square with hard plastic taped to the back so your child can't pierce through and hurt himself or mar the work surface.

➤ Pop-up cards are easier to make than they may seem. The following illustration shows the basic pattern. Create a design on the cut center part. Experiment first with some prototypes.

➤ Mirror cards can use an actual mirror, or better yet, some mylar (available from crafts or art supply stores). Cut out a heart shape and then cut the center out in a heart shape. Cut the mylar just a tad smaller than the outer edge of the heart. Glue the paper heart "frame" to the front of your card, with the mylar sandwiched in between.

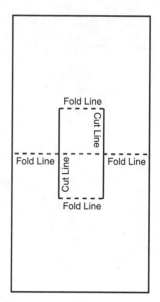

Fold Line

Cut Line

Fold Line | Cut Line | Fold Line

Fold Line

A pop-up card adds interest and is really quite simple to make.

Look into this mirror clear

And my truelove will appear

This mirror card is a clever way to tell the recipient who your valentine is!

➤ A birdcage or spiral card was popular in the 19th century. These featured an image hidden beneath a piece of paper cut in a spiral, which, when lifted, revealed the image underneath. One popular idea was a bird under a birdcage. Cut paper in a spiral as shown in the following illustration and tack the outside edge to the card. Make a tab in the center of the spiral by inserting a piece of ribbon through a slit and taping it flat on the underside.

Cut a spiral using this pattern to create an interesting "cage" card design.

➤ Cards don't have to be simple bi-folds. Try using a tri-fold or multi-fold and making a big, bold greeting inside.

Multiple folds allow still more creative card-making possibilities.

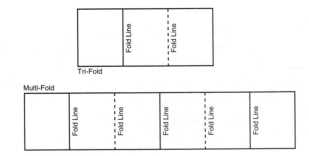

➤ Make a simple pinwheel card. For these you'll need some extra-stiff paper, about the stiffness of a manila folder. Adapt the basic pattern shown in the following illustration.

A pinwheel used as a card is a novel idea.

➤ Cards that unfold when you open them add some interest. See the following illustration for a simple pattern you can experiment with.

Cards that fold are a little more complex to create, but well worth the effort.

Crafty Clues

A great source for sentimental and old-fashioned stickers is Dover Publications (see Appendix A). These are reproduced from vintage printed images and come in a wide variety of themes, including cats, birds, butterflies, angels, valentines, romantic images, and animals.

Crafty Clues

If you're looking for ways to use your computer as a card-making machine, check out these programs: Microsoft Publisher 97, Hallmark Connections Card Studio, Printmaster Gold CD Publishing Suite, and Print Artist CD Edition (all for Windows CD-ROM); Print Shop Deluxe Ensemble and CardShop Plus Deluxe (both available for Macintosh and Windows CD-ROM); and Microsoft Great Greetings (Windows disk).

➤ Throw in something extra. Add heart-shaped confetti, glitter, flower petals, potpourri, or some other surprise to your card.

➤ Experiment! Try using fabric instead of paper for your glue-on decorations, play with rubber stamps, use cut out images from magazines and old calendars, and look around at card and craft stores for ideas.

You don't have to stick with hearts and flowers, either, when it comes to images to use on Valentine's Day cards or gifts. Other symbols include rings, lovebirds and doves, roses, and cupids. Love knots and gloves were Victorian symbols. Animals can also make for all kinds of variations. Put your imagination to work and come up with phrases for any animal that appeals to you: "Hog wild for you!" "Don't monkey around! Be mine!" "I can't bear it...Be my valentine!" The cornier, the better.

And just one more note...make sure your kids have valentines for everyone in the class, not just their favorites. It's also a lovely gesture to send a valentine to someone you know probably won't be receiving one. You can sign it "from Your Secret Admirer" or your own name and wish the person a happy day.

You might also want to make a valentine mailbox with your child. I recommend making two—one for home and one for school. These are easily made from shoe boxes. Make a good-sized slit in the top of the box, cover the box with appropriate wrapping paper or fabric, and decorate. All the valentines that come in the mail can go into the home box, along with the ones you've made for each other. The school box can be used to carry valentines to and from school.

Think of special places to hide valentines where the receiver can discover them: in a lunch box, under a pillow, in a cabinet, or in a briefcase or purse.

Wear Your Heart on Your Sleeve (or Anywhere Else)

Decorating clothing for Valentine's Day (or any holiday or occasion) is another fun way to celebrate. Kids love special hats, T-shirts, vests, sweatshirts, and sneakers, and there are many ways to do these projects with even the youngest children. The new *fusible webs* (a fabric that when heated creates a bond) and iron-on transfers mean no sewing, although an adult will need to handle the hot iron.

Add some fabric paint, buttons, ribbons, charms, and trims and you can turn even thrift-store finds into special-occasion wear.

If you'd rather not make something permanent, why not try a simple removable pin (or a bunch of pins) instead? They can go on shirts, jackets, hats…anywhere!

Project: Felt Heart Pins

Level: Easy

Age: 5 and up

Materials needed: Felt squares in red and white, scissors, a permanent marker, glue, a safety pin, embellishments, such as glitter, small bows, tiny gems or charms

Directions:

1. Cut out two hearts, one red and a smaller one in white.
2. Write a cute phrase such as "#1 Valentine," "Dr. Love," or "You're Special" in the center on the white heart. Glue the white heart to the larger red one.
3. Glue a safety pin on back.
4. The pin can be trimmed with blanket stitching around the edge, zig-zagged or serged, or you can add glitter, trim, small bows, or glue on gems.

Felt heart pins make great accessories on Valentine's Day.

Let's Have a Party!

Families need to find more excuses for parties. They don't need to be elaborate occasions, just small festivities that make for a special day. On Valentine's Day, you can turn any meal into a party:

➤ Make pancakes ahead of time. Keep them in the refrigerator overnight. In the morning, allow some extra time for breakfast and let the kids cut them out into heart shapes with cookie cutters (start collecting these in all sizes right away, if you don't have them already).

➤ Make heart-shaped sandwiches for lunch or for an after-school tea party.

➤ Create a doll and teddy-bear tea party together. Make heart-shaped peanut-butter-and-jelly sandwiches for everyone. Bake sugar cookies ahead of time and use the afternoon to decorate them. Make a pot of tea and add milk or lemon and honey. Decorate everything you can find with paper hearts, including the table. If your child has a small table and chairs and miniature tea set, use that, or if he or she prefers, use the "grown-up" table and dishes and let the dolls and animals sit there. Play and sing songs that have "love" in the title.

> **Crafty Clues**
> Remember to refill food and water frequently. It's important to maintain food and water once you start because the animals will become dependent on it, especially in winter. Have kids make this part of their daily or weekly chores to further teach responsibility.

Another idea is to make a Valentine party for wildlife. This is a great way to get kids thinking about the living world right outside their door. Pick a tree and decorate it for the birds, squirrels, raccoons, and other creatures. There are lots of books with ideas for what's best to feed birds, complete with recipes. One is Dick E. Bird's Birdfeeding 101: A Tongue-In-Beak Guide to Suet, Seed, and Squirrelly Neighbors by Richard E. Mallery (Main St. Books. 1997).

Simple ideas are usually the best. Here are a few ideas for throwing a "wild" Valentine party.

Project: Wild Animal Valentine Party Favors

Level: Easy

Age: 5 and up

Materials needed: Pine cones, peanut butter, nuts and dried fruits, bird-seed, oranges, peanuts, suet, string, wire, ribbon, a plastic-covered wire soap dish, plastic containers

Project: Continued

Directions:

➤ Spread pine cones liberally with peanut butter and roll in birdseed. Hang them on a tree with wire or string.

➤ Make peanut-butter balls by combining peanut butter, birdseed, raisins, and chopped nuts. Chill in the freezer and put in plastic mesh produce bags (I like the ones that oranges come in). Tie the bag at the top with a red ribbon and hang.

➤ Cut fresh oranges into quarters and tie the pieces to the tree branches.

➤ Buy suet at the supermarket and spoon it into a wire soap dish. Tie the dish around the trunk of the tree.

An ingenious suet holder is made from a wire soap dish.

➤ String peanuts on a long string and hang. Watch the squirrels do acrobatics to get them.

➤ Take a plastic margarine container or an old wooden salad bowl and poke or drill four holes. Draw string through each hole and knot at one end. Pull strings together and hang. Fill with seeds.

continues

Project: Continued

No need to spend money on a bird feeder. An old wooden bowl or used margarine container will do nicely.

➤ Put suet in a plastic mesh produce bag and hang it on a tree branch. This gives suet to both small and large birds and gives them something to cling to.

➤ Make sure to provide some water for your friends, too. You can purchase a birdbath, but the top to a plastic garbage can that's not in use works well, too. Just nestle it in the dirt so it won't tip and fill it with water. Birds and ground animals will enjoy a drink.

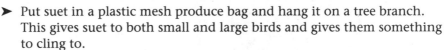

Gifts of Love

Valentine's Day gifts need not be expensive. The homemade kind show more about the heart of the giver than the kind you buy in a store. If you start early, you and your family will have plenty of time to make gifts for everyone.

Boxes make great gifts. Heart-shaped papier-mâché boxes of all sizes are available from crafts stores and are quite inexpensive. The possibilities for decorating them are endless. They can be painted, découpaged, covered in fabric, and embellished.

Paper valentine baskets are fun to make. They can be hung from a seasonal celebration tree (who says you can only have a decorated tree for Christmas?) and filled with candy hearts.

Project: Woven Paper Heart-Shaped Basket

Level: Easy

Age: 5 and up

Materials needed: paper, pencil, ruler, and scissors

Directions:

1. Make a pattern (see the following illustration) in the size you want. Make one on white paper and one on a paper of contrasting color.

2. Cut out the oval patterns, then fold each in half with the ends meeting. Cut along each of the three lines. Refold the opposite way so your pattern lines don't show.

3. Weave the two pieces together by following the diagram below.

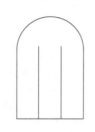

Use this diagram to weave your heart.

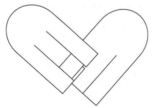

Basic pattern for a woven heart basket.

A finished woven paper heart basket.

Woven Paper Cards

Woven paper can be used for cards, too. In this case, you cut strips of different colors and attach them to a frame. The following illustration shows how this might be done with a heart shape, which can then be attached to the front of your card or on a wrapped gift.

A woven paper heart makes for a unique decoration for a Valentine card.

Celebrate With Scrapbooks

Another great gift idea is an "Ode to You" scrapbook. Each member of the family can do one for the others. Make a small booklet, fill it with pictures, and decorate it with scrap, stamping and other decorations, using them to illustrate what you love about the other person. A photo where the recipient is boasting an especially big grin, for example, could have the caption "I love your smile." Encourage children to look for photos and messages that celebrate talents, character, and personal qualities as well as physical attributes.

Fancy Paper Hearts

> **Bet You Didn't Know**
> As early as 1723 in America, there were "valentine writers." People could buy these volumes and consult them for the right words to put on their hand-made greetings or gifts.

Explore further the paper-cutting technique of *scherenschnitte* produced by the Pennsylvania Dutch and their European counterparts. (I mentioned it in Chapter 6.)

You can make a paper love token out of white paper and paint it with watercolors or tinted inks, using essentially the same technique discussed in Chapter 6 for making snow-flakes. Add a heartfelt inscription, the more sentimental the better, and frame it with a dark background behind the white lace cutout to make it stand out. Smaller versions can be used for Valentine's Day cards for that extra-special someone. This intricate work is done using a small, sharp scissors, but a pared-down version would work well for younger hands.

Older children can handle fairly elaborate patterns. Just fold white paper in half and draw or trace the pattern, using a heart as the center motif. When unfolded they'll have a lacy confection to frame and give.

Fancy paper cutwork or scherenschnitte makes a lacy decoration to frame or attach to a gift or card.

The Greatest Gift of All: YOU!

Valentine's Day presents a great opportunity to teach children ways to give of themselves. Unfortunately, the simplest and most meaningful gifts are often overlooked in favor of material things. But the gift of oneself, whether a performance, poem, song, task, or pampering a loved one doesn't cost a thing.

My family used to make what we called Rain Checks. These would be filled out for a favor or service and could be cashed in any time the recipient wanted. For Valentine's Day, these could be called Love Coupons. Some ideas that a child might be able to give include fixing a simple breakfast in bed (perhaps with some adult help), a foot massage or back rub, drawing a bubble bath, or washing the car (again, with a little adult supervision).

Let your children help you make a list and have family members share things they'd enjoy having done for them. Keep this in your family craft ideas folder (see Chapter 3).

Giving of yourself doesn't have to stop with family and friends, either. Consider it a family project to visit those in the community who might not see anyone for Valentine's Day. Bake a cake and take it to the local convalescent home. Older people love to see small children. Call first and see what would work best. Visit the children's ward at the local hospital. Ask what you can do that would most be of cheer. Have the children make valentines to hand out and dress up for the occasion, if only to wear something bright red.

The Least You Need to Know

➤ Valentine's Day is the perfect time for families to express their love.

➤ Handmade cards can be simple or complex, depending on the techniques used.

➤ Valentine parties don't have to be just for people. Dolls, teddies, and even wild animals can share in the fun.

➤ Gifts for your valentine don't have to be expensive. In fact, they don't have to cost anything if the gift is of yourself.

➤ The Day of Love is a great time to show kids how they can share themselves with those less fortunate.

Chapter 21

Happy Haunting: A Handmade Halloween

In This Chapter

➤ Jack-o'-lanterns in many forms

➤ No-fuss costumes for all ages

➤ Theatrics add another dimension

➤ Halloween parties to delight any child

➤ Luminaria to light the way

Many parents have misgivings about Halloween. Some see it as too materialistic and commercial or as glorifying the wrong things. Some feel it's just downright unsafe. To me, Halloween can and should be a magical holiday. There's nothing wrong with goosebumps, if they're all in good fun and nobody gets hurt. Halloween can be fun and safe with some imagination—and a lot of craftiness!

This chapter will take you through all the aspects of a happy and appropriately spooky Halloween. You'll learn how to take advantage of the opportunities Halloween offers for fantasy and make-believe, whether it be taking on a new persona in costume or creating theatricals and puppet shows. There are ideas aplenty you can use to substitute for trick-or-treating altogether or simply add even more excitement.

Halloween Harvest

Halloween celebrates All Hallows' Eve, also once called Samhain. This occasion marked the end of the harvest and the grazing of animals. In times past, this was actually viewed as the new year, when the remnants of the crops died, debts were paid and accounts settled, and the dead were put to rest before the coming winter.

It was believed that on All Hallows' Eve the veil between our world and the spirit world is at its thinnest and the dead may return to walk among the living. This was not thought of as something to fear, but a time to honor the dead. It was considered the best night of the year to gain insight into the other world and the future.

Halloween is a transition from autumn to winter. It's a time for moving inward; a time to think of our ancestors and our roots. It's also a good time to take some of the scarier images of Halloween and familiarize ourselves with them. Things that children might find frightening, such as bats, black cats, owls, night creatures, wolves, witches, and even death might seem far less scary if children knew something about them.

Perhaps our relatives in the last century had the right idea. Victorian Halloween celebrations were dominated by play acting, costumes, and parlor games that centered around fortune telling and slight of hand. It was magical, mystical, and mysterious. And all in good fun!

Bonding Experiences

Find out more about witches. These were often wise women with special knowledge of herbs and healing. At one time they were revered; later they were persecuted and killed. If you're nearby, visit the witches' museum in Salem, Massachusetts. Next best: Read about the Salem witch trials.

Another suggestion: Visit a graveyard, an old one, in broad daylight. Read the headstones. Make a gravestone rubbing. A gravestone rubbing is made by placing thin paper (like pellon or rice paper) on a gravestone and rubbing the paper with a large fat crayon or rubbing wax. Talk about death and what it means in our society. Compare different beliefs. Discuss your beliefs.

Carving Pumpkins

Pumpkins are a major symbol of Halloween. There are lots of ways to make jack-o'-lanterns, but the most common is the traditional carving of the pumpkin.

Have a pumpkin-carving party. Make it a family affair and invite other families over. Let kids design the faces; parents can do the carving. Pumpkin carving is indeed a craft, and in the hands of some, even an art.

Here are some tips for carving a perfect pumpkin:

➤ Either decide on a design first and find a pumpkin that fits that shape or look at some oddly shaped pumpkins and see if you can imagine a good design for that shape. Get the kids in on this!

➤ Pumpkins aren't the only things you can carve. Don't overlook the many interesting squashes available this time of year. These make interesting carved lanterns and faces, too.

➤ Not all pumpkins have to have faces. Consider different designs that suggest autumn or just decorative cuts that let the light shine through.

➤ Look for a pumpkin or squash that's as smooth and as blemish-free as possible.

➤ Let kids participate according to their ability. Older kids can help carve. Younger kids can draw designs for older kids to cut out. Very small kids can help by removing seeds and getting them ready to toast.

➤ Draw your design on paper first. Wet the paper and position on the part of the pumpkin you want to carve. Spread out the paper so it conforms to the surface. Thumbtack the edges so it won't move. Prick an outline of your design with a skewer. Remove the paper.

➤ Rub flour into the holes to make them easier to see.

➤ Consider hanging your pumpkins in plant hangers. This will make them more visible and keep them out of harm's way.

➤ Use the right tools. There are special tools around just for carving pumpkins, although wood-carving tools work well, too. Just make sure to clean them and store them in a safe place.

➤ Coat the carved edges with petroleum jelly to keep the pumpkin from drying out.

➤ Put your carved pumpkin in a cool, dry place when you're not displaying it. An unheated garage or basement works well. Your refrigerator would be ideal, if you have room.

Safety Signals
Use a flashlight or lightstick instead of a candle in jack-o'-lanterns. If you'd like to use a candle, votive candles or tea lights are less likely to tip over. Be very careful where you put your lighted pumpkin, and keep it away from anything flammable. Don't forget that pumpkins placed outside might get brushed with visiting children's costumes and catch their clothes on fire.

➤ Limit the time you light your pumpkins and squashes. The more heat they are exposed to, the quicker they will spoil. If they do begin to shrivel up, try soaking them in water overnight to add back lost moisture.

➤ For a great smell, make some scores in the pumpkin lid and rub with cinnamon and nutmeg. As the candle in the pumpkin burns, the luscious odor will fill the air.

Cooking with Pumpkins

Make sure you buy some pumpkins for cooking and making breads, muffins, and pies.

When you're hollowing out your pumpkin before you carve it or cook it, don't wash the seeds. Just take as much of the stringy stuff off as you can and put the seeds in a single layer on a cookie sheet that's been sprayed with cooking oil. Salt the seeds lightly and bake them at 300 degrees until they're toasted, stirring occasionally.

You can use your jack-o'-lantern for cooking, too. Just cut it into sections and scrape away the outer layer, being sure to remove any candle wax and smoky areas. Spray a baking sheet with cooking spray and bake at 375 degrees for an hour to an hour and a half, depending on the size of the pumpkin. Scoop the flesh out and mash or purée in a food processor. Then get out the cookbooks or check out your favorite Internet site and start collecting pumpkin recipes!

Decorating Pumpkins

Since the sharp implements used for carving limit how much smaller children can participate in pumpkin carving, why not have them make some safer jack-o'-lantern alternatives? Kids can simply cut a pumpkin shape out of construction paper and draw or paint on the features. These are great for decorating windows or mirrors, too.

Another safe idea is to have kids draw and cut out eyes, a nose, and a mouth on black construction paper and stick them onto the pumpkin with a brass paper fastener or thumbtack. Or they could paint their pumpkins instead. Use washable acrylic paints, available in crafts and art supply stores, and fairly large paint brushes. (Make sure to cover your work surface with newspapers and cover your child with a smock or old clothes.)

Paper pumpkins can also be made out of brown paper bags, stuffed with old newspapers that have been crumpled up. Fill to about $^3/_4$ full and gather the top edges together and twist tightly for the stem, wrapping it with masking tape to hold it together. Paint the pumpkin orange and the stem green. Use a washable black marker to draw on the face. These can be made in various sizes and used as decorations wherever kids would like.

Bonding Experiences

Find out more about the legend of the jack-o'-lantern. The Web site at http://www.jack-o-lantern.com/history/ is a good start. This isn't a sweet fairy tale, but a good way to talk about heaven, hell, the devil, the soul, and even the evils of drinking. Bet you've forgotten this one (or never knew the story in the first place)!

Quick, Creative Costumes

Oops! No costume? Or just stumped this year? Here are some great costume ideas to whip up in minutes! They're so simple, kids can do many of them with just a little of your help.

Start with a sweatsuit. Sweatsuits make great costume "bases." (Plus, when Halloween's over, they still "have a life"!) Collect them in different colors so you'll have lots to choose from whenever a costume's needed. Use hooded sweatshirts for costumes that need headgear. Pick them up on sale and you'll have a costume base that's safe, warm, and loaded with possibilities.

Here are some costume ideas:

➤ *Skeleton* (black sweatsuit and gloves): Cut "bones" out of white contact paper and stick them on the sweatsuit. Use a skeleton illustration as a guide. Paint the child's face with black and white face paint like a skull.

➤ *Burglar* (black sweatsuit, black stocking cap, and black gloves): Paint on a black eye mask. Have the child carry a pillowcase for a goodie sack, and a flashlight so he's sure to be seen.

➤ *Flower* (pink sweatshirt and green sweatpants): Sew or make out of construction paper a flower petal "necklace" that extends over the shoulders. The cap could be brown and yellow for the center of the flower and you could add a bumblebee on top.

➤ *Tree* (brown sweatpants and green sweatshirt): Sew or pin leaves all over the top, including arms, and make a pointed cap and cover it with leaves. Add a bird and nest on one shoulder.

➤ *Grapes* (green or purple sweatsuit): Blow up green or purple balloons and attach them with safety pins all over the suit. Be sure to stay away from sharp objects!

➤ *Carrot* (orange sweatsuit): Put green mousse in hair or have child wear a green cap. Paint the child's face with green face paint. Add green pipe cleaners to the cap for carrot top.

➤ *Bunny* (pink sweatsuit with hood): Add ears you've sewn or made from construction paper and cardboard. They'll need to be stiff enough to stand up. Attach a cotton tail. Use white face makeup and draw on whiskers and use pink makeup for the nose. To make this into the Energizer Bunny, add black sunglasses and an old

Crafty Clues
Start a costume-making box. Collect items that would make good costume materials, such as old sweats, caps, interesting pieces of fabric, felt scraps, and leftover Christmas decorations. On a rainy day, get out the costume-making file and your costume books and have a ball with the kids. Make sure you get in on the fun, too.

hat box for the drum, which is attached to the shoulders with rope or nylon webbing. Make a drumstick out of a stick or dowel with cotton batting on the end or a carved sponge.

➤ *Mouse* (gray sweatsuit): Similar to the bunny, except make mouse ears and tail. If your child has two siblings or two friends who'd all like to go together, dress them as the three blind mice by adding sunglasses and canes. Make sure sunglasses are light enough so they can see.

➤ *Black-eyed pea* (black sweatsuit): Put black makeup under the eyes and sew or pin a big letter "P" to the shirt. See if you can think of other word-play costumes.

➤ *Traffic light* (black sweatsuit): Cut out red, yellow, and green circles and tape or sew them to the shirt, back and front. Felt would work well for this.

➤ *Night sky* (black or dark navy blue sweatsuit): Cover with silver or gold glittered stars and a big white moon.

A leotard and tights also make a good costume base. Most any of these costumes can be made using similarly colored tights. You can also make a great spider. Take three pairs of black pantyhose and stuff with old nylons to make six spider legs. Tie them to the waist of the leotard. Use a stocking for a cap and black pipe cleaners sewn on for antennae.

Here are some more simple ideas:

➤ *Mummy.* Use gel or hair dressing to slick hair straight back away from face. Cover face with white makeup. Tear strips or muslin and wrap around the entire body or use gauze. In a pinch, use toilet paper. Use adhesive tape to hold strips in place. After you're all done, take a dirty dust cloth or mop and gently pat all over. Then dust with baby powder. Be careful not to wrap too tightly around nose and mouth and make sure it's easy to see. Wrap the head last.

➤ *Pippi Longstocking.* Braid hair and run wire through the braids. Bend so they stick out. Dress the child in bright crazy clothes that don't match and baggy, funny socks (red and white striped would be good). Put on lots of freckles with face paint or eyeliner and black out a big space between top front teeth with black wax (available from costume or party stores at Halloween).

➤ *Lumberjack.* Have child wear bright plaid flannel shirt, overalls, boots, and work gloves. Make an ax out of cardboard and tin foil. Add a knit cap.

➤ *Coat of arms.* This one's in the silly department, but it tickled my funny bone: Get an old coat from Goodwill or other thrift store. Using old shirts, also from the thrift store, cut off the sleeves and attach gloves to the ends with safety pins. Attach arms to the coat. Ask people to guess what it is. This is fun for the medieval buff in the family or those who just enjoy a goofy play on words.

As you can see, the ideas are endless. Let the kids be a part of the design. Look for variations each year in magazines, clip them out, and add them to your Halloween costume file. This is a great file to have, since costume making is an any-time-of-year activity.

An extremely helpful book, if you can find it, is Gail E. Haley's *Costumes for Plays and Playing*. This book covers everything from making patterns and sewing costumes from scratch to adapting existing clothing to making costumes from paper, cardboard, and other craft materials. See Appendix A for more information.

Paper or cloth sacks for carrying goodies are part of the costume. Make them coordinate if you can. If you're having a Halloween party before Halloween itself, the kids can take their party goodies home and then re-use the sacks on Halloween. Paints, paper, rubber stamps, stencils, fabric...put all your new crafting skills to work as you decorate these.

One important thing to take note of when you're making Halloween costumes is that chances are your materials aren't even remotely flame-resistant. Even flame-resistant fabrics can still catch fire. Avoid costumes with big baggy sleeves or billowy skirts. Make sure they're short enough so your child won't trip. To add to their visibility, decorate costumes with reflective tape (available from hardware, bicycle, or sporting goods stores). Have children carry flashlights. Make sure shoes fit well (no high heels). It's better to use face paint or makeup than masks, since you want your child to be able to see clearly. Swords, canes, knives, or any other accessories should be soft and flexible.

Special Effects and Finishing Touches

Kids, especially older boys, seem to love being gross. Let this be the time of year they get to indulge this natural impulse. Together you can whip up some inexpensive concoctions that make the difference between an O.K. costume and one that really rocks.

Here are some recipes for fake blood and other disgusting makeup. You, too, can turn your kitchen into a Hollywood special effects laboratory!

Fake Blood

One pint of clear corn syrup

1 ounce red food coloring

1 or 2 teaspoons of yellow food coloring

Mix the corn syrup and red food coloring. Add the yellow a little at a time until you get the color you want. Dilute with a little water to get the right consistency. This recipe makes a large quantity of fake blood.

Safety Signals
This corn-syrup mixture is safe if ingested, but don't let your child get it in his eyes, as red dyes may cause eye infections.

Blood Bombs

Fill small balloons with a few tablespoons of fake blood (not too full, though). Wipe the outside clean. Pin the balloons to a shirt worn underneath outside clothing, but make sure the opening of the balloon is not completely closed (you could try taping as an alternative). Make sure the neck of the balloon is pointing up. Hit your chest as if you've been hit by a monster (or whatever), slapping where the balloon is attached. Fake blood will be forced out and the wearer can act out an appropriately melodramatic death in front of his audience. (Make sure whatever clothes you use aren't good ones. Food coloring can stain.)

Rotting Flesh

Mix $1^1/_2$ cups of dry oatmeal with $^1/_4$ cup of water and stir into a thick paste. Spread onto skin with a rubber spatula. Or put a small amount in a circular or oval pattern. Add a few drops of red food coloring or fake blood to the middle of the "wound." This is good for a while, but when the mixture dries out it'll flake off and have to be reapplied.

Face Makeup

Cold cream

Food coloring

Use cold cream by itself for white makeup. Add one or two drops of the desired color to about two teaspoons of cold cream. A paper cup and popsicle stick works well for mixing each color. Keep this stuff away from eyes.

Face Paint

2 tablespoons white shortening

5 tablespoons cornstarch

1 tablespoon flour

3 or 4 drops of glycerin (available in drug stores)

A few drops of food coloring in desired color

Blend the first three ingredients to make a smooth paste. Add enough glycerin to make a creamy consistency. Divide into paper cups and add color to each as needed. Cocoa can be used for dark brown to make mustaches and other facial hair. Remove with soap and water. Avoid eyes.

Scars and Wounds

> 1 teaspoon or one packet of unflavored gelatin
>
> 1 tablespoon hot water
>
> 1 small plastic container (a 35mm film canister works well)
>
> A plastic knife or popsicle stick

Mix gelatin and water in a container until it's about the consistency of honey. Spread it on skin to form scars or burns. You can apply makeup color with theatrical makeup or cheap lipstick. Dab on baby powder with a cotton ball to set the colors.

Some things you might want to buy from the theatrical supply store that add even more to your repertoire are spirit gum, nose wax (also called putty), and liquid latex. You can apply spirit gum to any spot you want to put a scar, lump, wart, or whatever. Let it dry enough to get sticky. Shape the wax to fit your purpose and press it into the spirit gum. Make an incision in the wax to simulate a cut. Brush latex over the whole thing and allow it to dry. Cover with base makeup that matches skin color and blend. Apply fake blood using a Q-tip or blue/purple/black color to get a bruise. Old eye makeup and lipstick works great for making bruises, scrapes, and cuts.

How to Host a Horror-ble Party

Many parents throw parties for their kids as an alternative to trick-or-treating. Others just make it an addition to the festivities. Make your party one in which crafts play an integral part.

Picking a specific theme, not just "Halloween," pulls everything together. Just one Halloween symbol can do it. Put bats in your belfry or spiders in your web. Whatever you and your child choose, take it to the hilt. Make decorations, costumes, favors, food—everything—follow your theme.

Here are three suggestions.

Pumpkin Party

Serve foods made with pumpkin and carve or otherwise decorate your Halloween pumpkins (if the party is held in advance of Halloween).

You can make lots of little decorative styrofoam pumpkins. Use them to decorate wreaths or even add a pin to the back of one and wear it.

Here are the directions:

1. Take a styrofoam ball and cut it in half.
2. Make grooves with a serrated knife that simulate the lines on a pumpkin.

3. Brush with craft glue and cover with orange twist paper.

4. Work the paper into the grooves.

5. Glue on brown twist paper stems and green paper leaves.

Ghostly Gathering

For this party theme, everyone could come as a ghost. It would be interesting to see everyone's variations on such a simple idea.

There are lots of ways to make craft ghosts: Take a Styrofoam ball, dab it with white glue, and drape white fabric over it. Make two eyes with a black marker. Or take white wrapping tissue and drape it over a Tootsie-Roll pop, twist at the stick, add eyes, and it becomes a pint-sized spirit.

Project: Starchy Ghosts

Level: Easy

Age: 5 and up

Materials needed: A selection of different-sized plastic jugs and bottles, aluminum foil, white gauze or cheesecloth, laundry starch

Directions:

1. Take aluminum foil and crumple over the top of each jug and bottle until it forms a ball.

2. Cut white gauze or cheesecloth into 18-inch squares, one for each ghost.

3. Dip squares into a bowl filled with laundry starch.

4. Take each square and squeeze out excess moisture. Drape one over each bottle.

5. Use crumpled aluminum foil at different heights under each ghost to shape shoulders and arms, draping gauze appropriately.

6. Spread out the lower edges of the gauze and let dry for several hours. Once dry, lift carefully and place on any flat surface.

Going Bats

Bats make another good theme. Make bats and suspend them from the ceiling with string. Kids could come to the party as bats (or Batman, for that matter) and could make and decorate bat cookies. Read a short story or book about real bats and discover their unique abilities. Make bat puppets.

Project: Bat Puppet

Level: Easy

Age: 5 and up

Materials needed: One piece of black construction paper for each puppet, a pencil, scissors, light-colored crayon

Dircctions:

1. Draw a bat on the black paper. (You may want to make a cardboard template first that the kids can trace.) Make it as wide as a child's hand.

2. Cut out the bat and fold along the lines, as shown in the following illustration.

3. Fold the center lines up and the outside lines down. Fold the head down.

4. Hold the bat in your hand and squeeze it to make the wings move.

Follow the diagram to make your bat puppet.

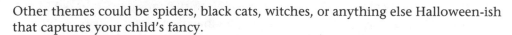

Other themes could be spiders, black cats, witches, or anything else Halloween-ish that captures your child's fancy.

Fearsome Food

One traditional food associated with Halloween is popcorn balls. Kids love making them because they can get their hands all sticky and they offer lots of possibilities for decorating. Find some orange cellophane you can use for wrapping. Tie with orange and black curling ribbon.

Try this recipe for popcorn balls.

> $1/2$ cup margarine
>
> 2 10-oz packages white marshmallows, large
>
> 20 cups popped popcorn

Stir in the popcorn until it's covered well with melted marshmallow and the mixture starts to get stringy. Let stand for five minutes. For ease of handling, smear butter on your hands and form the mixture into balls. Let cool and wrap.

Here's another recipe for popcorn balls:

One quart of popped corn ($1/2$ cup unpopped kernels), kept warm in the oven

> $1/2$ cup sugar
>
> $1/2$ cup water
>
> $1/8$ teaspoon salt
>
> $1/3$ teaspoon vinegar

Combine the sugar, water, salt, and vinegar in a saucepan and bring to a boil, stirring constantly. Cover and cook over medium heat for about three minutes. Uncover and cook until it forms a soft ball when dropped in very cold water. Pour over warm popped corn, mixing with a wooden spoon. Raisins, nuts, chocolate chips, dried fruit, or candy corn can be added to the mixture if you like. When it's cool enough to handle, but still warm, butter hands and shape into balls.

Make a paste of powdered sugar and water and use as "glue" to attach candy pieces, nuts, or raisins for adding faces. Let cool completely, wrap with cellophane and tie with a ribbon.

Look for ways of taking "normal" foods and making them spooky foods by adding or dipping in food coloring. Peeled apple slices with the ends dipped in red food coloring become "bloody claws." Whatever drink you make, be sure it's green! Kool-Aid works well or you can add green food coloring to clear soda. Add peeled grapes (you know… eyeballs!) to the punch bowl. Use your imagination.

How about a brain salad? You can buy a jello mold from various catalogs for this or you can make your own version. Cook elbow macaroni and add food coloring to the water to make it a pinkish gray. Drain and put into a dome-shaped bowl (a stainless steel mixing bowl works well) that's been sprayed with cooking spray. Push it down well so the elbows stick together. Refrigerate and unmold just before serving. Slice it and cover with red sauce.

Instead of sugary party favors, do some "make and take" kitchen crafts. Make up sugar cookie dough and let it chill in the refrigerator. You can either have kids slice the cookies, bake, then decorate them with icings and toppings, or you could roll them out and let kids cut them out with cookie cutters. Look for cookie cutters in Halloween shapes and make enough so kids can have some for refreshments and still have goodies to take home.

Lighting the Way

Lighting sets the mood for so many occasions and Halloween is no exception. For lighting the way for their friends and neighbors, children can make *luminaria*, light sources that shine through paper bags.

If you live near a party store, drop by and pick up coated, colored paper bags. If you can't find colored bags, plain brown-paper lunch bags will also work just fine. These can be decorated with markers or small cutouts.

Handiwords
Luminaria are light sources that shine through paper bags.

Here's a more elaborate version, using your home computer.

Project: Halloween Luminaria

Level: Medium

Age: 7 and up

Materials needed: Spooky clip art or rubber stamps of spiders, bugs, etc., transparency plastic for your printer (either laser- or inkjet-compatible; available at office supply stores), paper bags (small lunch bags work well), lightsticks, votive candles, or a string of (Christmas-style) lights, sand

Directions:

1. Locate spooky clip art or let your kids draw their own images. Images with dark colors (red, black, brown, deep orange) work best.
2. Print onto transparency plastic and cut out in a simple shape (such as an oval).
3. Make a cutout in the side of the bag that's slightly smaller than the plastic shape. Center and tape the transparency into place. Weight the bottom of the bag with sand so it won't blow away and place the candle inside.

For super-safe luminaria, lightsticks provide an eerie green glow, although they don't provide enough light for a truly dramatic effect. Christmas-tree lights strung through or a small votive candle placed carefully in each bag works better.

Creepy Curtains

Halloween is the perfect time for "acting out," and I don't mean having a temper tantrum! Amateur theatrics are fun party activities you can do at home in the days leading up to Halloween. Kids can put on puppet shows and plays using their own stories, classic tales, or stories especially written for the occasion that can be found at your local library.

Kids not only get a chance to exercise their imaginations, but can perhaps vocalize their fears and burn off excess energy to boot. A fun idea is to ask kids to work out a short skit using all the characters (costumes) that have come to the party. Or they can make inexpensive paper-bag puppets and put on their own puppet show.

Project: Paper Bag Puppets

Level: Easy

Age: 5 and up

Materials needed: Lunch-size paper bags, construction paper in various colors, yarn, ribbons, lace, buttons, and trims, scissors, crayons, craft glue

Directions:

The fold in the bag is the mouth. The hand goes inside the bag with the fingers working the upper part of the face. The child's arm becomes the neck.

1. Cut a piece of construction paper the same size as the bottom of the bag and glue it in place. This is the "face."
2. Place the bag flat on the table with the folded bottom facing up.
3. Slightly above the fold centered horizontally, make the puppet's nose. You can glue on a pompom or a button for the nose or draw it on with crayons. Add eyes above and on either side of the nose.
4. Under the fold, draw the inside of the mouth in a large oval from the edge of the fold down to the crease. Teeth can be drawn in or cut individually out of paper. Glue a piece of red construction paper cut to look like a tongue in the center of the mouth.
5. Use glued-on yarn to make hair.

The Least You Need to Know

Now you're all set to have a safe and spooky Halloween that you've crafted yourself.

➤ Halloween can be slightly spooky, lots of fun, and super safe.

➤ Crafts add a whole other dimension to celebrating Halloween.

➤ Using sweatsuits and simple materials, kids can make an unlimited variety of costumes.

➤ Parties can be used in place of trick-or-treating and crafts can make the party.

➤ Plays and puppet shows provide opportunities for acting out and using creative craft skills.

Chapter 22

Christmas, Chanukah, and Kwanzaa: Celebrate with Crafts

In This Chapter

➤ Old-fashioned crafts to cheer the season

➤ Easy ornaments that sparkle

➤ Wreaths, garlands, and other decorations

➤ Gifts from the kitchen and the craft bin

➤ Making your own traditions

Every year, reams are written about the sorry state of the December holidays. We've all heard it. But what to do about it? Why not give it back to the children? Instead of the frenzy, why not make it a time of family? Instead of expensive gifts and exhausting shopping trips, why not give of yourself and teach your child to do the same? Give of your time, attention, patience, creativity, and love by crafting your holiday by hand. What could be more precious?

Through the ideas presented in this chapter, you can select activities that would most delight you and your little ones. They won't have to think about "being good" 'til Christmas or Chanukah; they'll have so many opportunities to celebrate and fun activities to keep them busy. Working with your hands will relax you, too, and when you're done your home will say "holiday greetings," and you'll have handmade gifts for your loved ones.

Don't Wait for the Holidays!

One reason we're always so rushed during the holidays is we don't start thinking about it until Thanksgiving, when there's only a month left to do it all. Kids feel the pressure, too. Why not begin celebrating the holidays in July? Yes, July!

This is actually an old-fashioned custom, and one that, in my opinion, should be revived. In the lazy days of summer, have a family meeting to discuss holiday activities for the year. You plan your garden in the winter, right? Why not plan your holidays in the summer? Haul out the books and magazines. Select the projects you'd like to do and make a list of materials you'll need. Kids and adults can keep their eyes open for bargains at discount stores, thrift shops, and yard sales. If you need to save materials like tin cans, jars, or whatever, you've got time to accumulate what you'll need.

Discuss what activities you each can't possibly do without and make these a priority. Agree that if time gets tight, you'll skip anything not on the High Priority list.

Here's one way to answer the common cries of "I'm bored!" or "There's nothing to do" during summer vacation: Just whip out your holiday list, file folder, and materials box and get started.

Deck the Halls

Make an exploratory trip around the house and go through each room. What ways could that room be decorated for the holidays? Do you have something already or is something needed? Add to your list things like "garland for the mantel" or "decoration for kitchen window." You'll find specific ideas later. Let the kids suggest ways to decorate their own rooms, and don't forget the bathrooms! This year you're going to have happy holidays "all through the house."

Trimming Your Tree

Every year, pick a new ornament to make. Each year you can use a different type of craft or stick with the ones you and your children most enjoy. There are lots of ideas in books and magazines every year. I pick up every holiday magazine on the stands, plus I watch all the craft shows. I take out the ideas that really appeal to me and put them in my file.

There are ornaments that use each of the new craft skills you've explored with this book—paper, clay, wood, glass, metal, fabric, beads, recycled materials, natural materials, and kitchen ingredients. You name it, you can adapt it to an ornament.

One advantage of picking only one or two types of ornaments each year is that you and your child can master it through repetition, plus you can really explore different variations.

You can also join with other crafty members of your extended family or circle of friends and have an ornament swap, much as some folks combine the results of their cookie baking.

Looking for some simple and quick ideas? Well, I'm here to help!

➤ Styrofoam balls can be used in endless ways. They can be covered with fabric and trim, studded with beads and sequins attached with straight pins, or covered with yarn.

➤ Clear plastic balls make another good base. Glue on lace appliqués for frosted confections (make sure you use a clear-drying glue) or wrap in a tulle square, gather at the top and tie with ribbon. Glue on some silk or dried flowers.

➤ Corrugated cardboard makes another base material with unlimited possibilities. Cut the cardboard in a square. Cut quilt batting about a $1/4$-inch larger than the card-board, then glue it around the back of the cardboard. Next, cut a fabric square (satin looks good for a Victorian feel) slightly larger than the batting and glue that around the back. Decorate this padded base with trims, beads, bits of Victorian scrap, lace, fringe, or a small tassel. Cut felt to cover the back and finish the ornament.

➤ Or glue yarn to corrugated cardboard as in the following illustration. Use a clear-drying glue and change colors as desired.

Colorful ornaments can be made from corrugated card-board, yarn, and glue by even a very young child.

➤ Recycle old Christmas cards. Cards with circular images work best. Cut out two circles the same size. Put the "wrong" sides together (the sides without images) and make small holes around the edges with a paper punch. Finish the edge using a needle threaded with yarn, or if you and your child have learned how to crochet, a single crochet edge.

Recycle old holiday cards into new ornaments for the tree.

➤ Use the bread dough clay recipe in Chapter 15 to make ornaments that you can paint after they dry. Don't forget to make a hole for a hanger.

➤ Using a compass, make a circle on corrugated cardboard. Make a smaller circle in the center and cut out, making a wreath shape. Paint the front and edges gold. Glue on old white buttons so they overlap to cover the cardboard completely. Add a few gold small gold buttons or small pieces of gold trim at random for accents. Trim with a gold bow and hang with gold cord.

Bet You Didn't Know

Many of the icons of Christmas have ancient symbolic meaning. Holly was believed to have sprung from Jesus' footsteps as he walked the earth preaching the gospels and was called "holy." The red berries symbolized Jesus' blood; the leaf his crown of thorns. Ivy was thought to bring fruitfulness. The Druids worshipped mistletoe and the Greeks used it as a charm against evil.

➤ Roll out polymer clay (see Chapter 12) on waxed paper using a marble rolling pin or a large drinking glass (don't use wood; it will stick). Using cookie cutters in Christmas shapes, cut out ornaments. Decorate with smaller pieces of clay in different colors. Make a hole for hanging. Bake according to manufacturer's directions (usually about 30 minutes).

➤ Use laminating film (available in crafts stores) or use a laminating machine if you have access to one, to turn any kind of paper design into a durable ornament. Cut out shapes from old Christmas cards, use rubber stamp designs that you embellish, or even cut out photographs using Christmas-themed templates.

➤ Make plastic canvas ornaments using existing designs or your own. See Chapter 7 to learn how.

➤ Almost any figure that can be done in origami can be hung and used as a Christmas ornament. To learn more about origami, see Chapter 6.

➤ Make pleated paper fans like an accordion. This can also be done with wide lace. To make a pleated circle, bring two corners of one long side together and glue. Use a clothespin to hold together until it dries. To make a pleated bow, tie in the center. Add trim.

➤ Use cut paper techniques you learned in Chapter 6 to make small snowflakes. Cover with glitter and hang.

These are just a few ideas. You'll be sure to find scads of your own as the seasons pass. Look for ways to decorate window sills, mantels, and over your doorways. Don't neglect the chandelier, either. Gather greens (evergreens like a mild pruning) and look for ways to use them throughout the house. For instructions on how to make a basic wreath or garland, refer to Chapter 16. There are also many good books on the subject.

You might want to pick a theme and do everything in that theme—snowflakes one year, Santas another. Kids really enjoy themes and it helps define the activities for any given event. If you decide early enough (remember, Christmas in July!), you can be looking for months for ideas and materials to execute your theme. One year we did teddy bears— you'd be amazed at the many different incarnations our bears took.

Beyond Sugarplums: Christmas in the Kitchen

What's a sugarplum, anyway? If you don't know, this is the year to find out. Learn what the traditional holiday foods are and how they originated. Try your hand at making them or buy some to taste and see if you and your children like them. If you do, make plans to add them to your holiday food traditions. There's figgy pudding, plum pudding, sugarplums, Christmas pudding, gingerbread, and lots of international favorites.

Try other recipes throughout the year to add new traditions. Start a holiday foods file. I have a loose-leaf binder just for Christmas. In the food section, I add foods I've tried that would make exciting holiday fare or yummy gifts. I add notes about what I actually make each year, and about what worked and what didn't. Some traditional holiday foods, such as Christmas pudding or fruitcake, need "curing," (time to age and increase the flavor) so make sure you allow plenty of time for these to be made ahead.

Create your own holiday food traditions. At our house there are three or four different kinds of cookies that must be made each year or everybody squawks. Fudge is another must, along with candied citrus peels. Experiment and find your own annual food traditions. Even when the kids come home for Christmas as adults, they'll want to make their holiday favorites.

Ever want to try making one of those elaborate gingerbread houses, but thought it was beyond you? Or are you looking for a simpler way that the kids can join in? Well, here's the perfect solution:

Project: Graham-Cracker Houses

Level: Easy

Age: 5 and up

Materials needed: Graham crackers and chocolate graham crackers, royal icing (recipe can be found in most any general cookbook), pastry bag and tips (or large plastic bag with corner cut out), an assortment of candies for trims (including dots, wafer shapes, licorice strings…use your imagination).

Directions:

1. Put the house together using whole (unbroken) graham crackers for the side walls, half crackers for the end walls, and whole ones for the roof. Use generous amounts of icing for the "glue."
2. Using a small tip, outline the doors and windows with icing.
3. Attach decorations with icing.

You can make a whole village of these houses. Try making two-story houses as well, using a whole graham cracker as the floor of the second story. Have fun!

A simple, delicious graham-cracker house.

Bonding Experiences

Pick a country each year and make the traditional holiday foods of that country. Read about the country you've chosen and look for picture books and videos to give even more of a flavor. If you know someone from that part of the world, have the children "interview" that person about his or her holiday traditions. You'll even get some new recipes!

Make sure you include the children in your holiday dinner preparations. They can wash, peel, and chop vegetables; set the oven timer; or help set the table. Making place cards and table decorations together makes them feel a part of the celebration.

The Joy Is in the Giving

Just as you and your children can use all your crafting skills for making ornaments, you can make truly beautiful and useful gifts that are always one of a kind. With your gift lists beside you, review the earlier chapters in this book together and make notations about what projects you'd like to do. Look for ways to vary the same project, since it's usually less expensive and time-consuming to repeat the same project for several people.

Kitchen and nature crafts present many inexpensive and fast projects that make excellent gifts. Foods are nice for the person who has everything, since they are consumed and you can simply make more next year!

There are certainly more ideas for gifts than we can even begin to describe in this chapter—even in this book—but here are a few to get you started:

➤ Force spring bulbs in a pretty container in time for Christmas. Many nurseries and garden supply centers have jars and other containers made especially for this, plus they can give you lots of hints about which bulbs to choose and how to time their growing so they open in time for the holidays. Amaryllis, paper-whites, and hyacinths are good ones to try.

➤ Mix up your own potpourris using the directions in Chapter 16. Put in decorated jars or into handsewn or tied sachets.

➤ Do a scrapbook page using pictures from a special event that happened in the past year. Frame it.

➤ Find glass votive holders or other plain glass objects at flea markets, yard sales, or discount stores. Using the glass-etching techniques you learned in Chapter 14, transform the plain glass object into a one-of-a-kind gift.

➤ Make up kits and baskets using the homemade mixtures you learned to concoct in Chapter 15. Try a basket with hot cocoa mix and two mugs. Throw in a little bag of tiny marshmallows. Put a bottle of homemade vinegar and oil in a container with two salad bowls. Decorate the container.

➤ Make a flowerpot candle. Insert a wick and fill a small clay flowerpot (after you've decorated it in one of many possible ways) with candle wax or use wax crystals according to directions. What could be simpler?

➤ Wrap ordinary hangers any number of ways to make pretty gifts for the closet that also have a practical purpose: Clothes are protected and don't slip off. Use yarn, ribbon, or string and weave, using two bundles of your material and holding the hanger between your knees with the hook facing you. Hold one bundle taut to the left and create a loop by crossing it over the hanger with your right hand. Take the same bundle and thread it under the hanger, through the loop you've created. Pull the string, ribbon, or yarn tightly to create a knot. Repeat in the opposite direction with the second bundle. Alternating bundles, continue until the hanger is covered. Knot the ends together and cut, tucking it under the neck where the wire meets.

➤ Give a stocking that follows a theme. Buy a pair of warm socks; take one and put the mate rolled up inside. Fill it with a small jar of homemade flavored honey, a mesh tea ball, some loose tea, and a wooden honey spoon. There are lots of variations on this one.

➤ Make pomander balls. These are fruits that have been studded with cloves, scented, dried, and preserved. They can be hung on the tree as ornaments and later hung in a closet or laid in a drawer as a sachet.

Project: Pomander Balls

Level: Easy

Age: 5 and up

Materials needed: Firm apples, oranges, pears, lemons, or limes, a skewer, whole cloves, orris root (This is a power made from a root commonly used as a perservative or fixture in potpourris and pomandes. It is available from crafts or health-food stores or by mail order. See Appendix A.), ground cinnamon, cloves, nutmeg, and/or allspice

1. If you're using an apple, wipe it with a greased cloth before inserting the cloves.

2. Insert whole cloves into the fruit skin so they touch each other, with no skin showing. Use the skewer to make a hole first in tougher skins.

3. Combine two teaspoons of orris root and two teaspoons of ground cinnamon or other spices. Roll the completely studded fruit into the mixture of cinnamon and orris root, patting the powder into the fruit.

4. Put the fruit in a paper bag and leave it in a cool dry place to shrink and dry. Rotate the fruit every three days or so.

5. After several weeks, look at the fruit and see if it's dried. Shake off the excess mixture, decorate it with ribbon, and pop it into a gift box. If you made an apple, tie a ribbon to its stem. Refresh with scented oil when the scent fades.

Project: Candle Luminaries

Level: Easy

Age: 5 and up

Materials needed: Colored tissue paper, empty, clean 2-liter plastic pop bottles (clear), craft glue, large artist's paint brush, small plastic container, small glass jar (a baby food jar works well), votive candle, scissors or knife

1. Take off the bottle label.

2. An adult can cut the top and bottom off the bottle. This will leave a clear cylinder.

3. Tear tissue paper into small pieces.

4. Mix one part glue to one part water in the plastic container. Brush glue onto the cylinder and press on tissue paper pieces, overlapping the edges. Work around the top half of the cylinder, then turn it over and finish the bottom half.

5. When the bottle is covered, brush on a little more glue and smooth everything down. Trim away any paper that extends beyond the edges after the glue dries.

6. Put the candle in the glass jar and slide the finished cylinder over it.

New Traditions and Old

It's fun to read about Christmas in times past and learn about old-fashioned traditions. The thought of a tree lighted exclusively with real candles sounds dreamy, even if it's more than a little impractical and even downright dangerous. The nice thing is that today we can pick and choose which traditions fit into our lifestyle. We can make them a priority and gear our crafting accordingly.

One thing I'd like to bring back in our own family is the celebration of the many other days that were once associated with Christmas and are now rarely even mentioned. I'd like to add Advent (Dec. 1), St. Nicholas Day (Dec. 6), St. Lucia's Day (Dec. 13), Twelfth Night (January 6), and Candlemas (February 2).

This seems so much better to me than trying to cram all of Christmas into one or two days. Christmas is not one day, but a season. Making the holidays a series of smaller celebrations and de-emphasizing the shopping and the self-indulgence helps children enjoy all the many moments of the season. It helps soothe parents' jangled nerves, because it takes much of the pressure off "the big day." Gift-giving can even be spread out, offering small handmade tokens rather than an orgy of shopping and spending.

Here's a project for Advent.

Project: Personal Advent Calendars

Level: Easy

Age: 5 and up

Materials needed: Colored posterboard, gold foil, scissors, a sharp pencil, utility knife, drawing paper, ribbon, clip-type clothespins

Having a calendar for each child means there's no fighting over who gets to open the windows on these lovely calendars. Make an extra one for yourself.

1. Sandwich two pieces of colored posterboard with a piece of gold foil between.

2. Lay them on a flat surface and cut through all three to make an outer shape. A Christmas tree works well.

3. On the top piece, have children draw a Christmas scene or decorate. Draw 24 small square windows on the top sheet with a sharp pencil, pressing hard enough to make an impression on the gold foil. Number the windows and keep them all the same size, except for number 24, which should be larger and in the center.

4. Draw pictures you want to show through the windows, ending with a picture of the Christ child in a crib. Cut them out and glue them to the foil-covered bottom sheet.

5. Place the top sheet on a cutting board and cut three sides to each window with a razor or utility knife (the adult does this), leaving the left side as a hinge.

6. Loop the ribbon through the top to stick out and glue cardboard together around the edges. Hold layers together with clothespins or clips until glue dries. Hang and open one door a day.

Here are a few other old crafting traditions that are back in style:

➤ Cigar boxes are back, and not just the cardboard kind, either. There are neat wooden boxes in a variety of shapes and sizes. Check with your local tobacconist and see if he'll save the empty boxes for you. Cover them with fabric or decorative paper and decorate. Give as a jewelry or treasure box or an extra-special gift box.

➤ Another great recycled gift is giving a yard-sale frame new life. Repaint or refinish it and have a glass company cut a mirror to size. Ask them to drill two holes through the mirror and use screws and a rubber washer to hold it or use clips to hold the mirror in the frame.

Of course, we could go on forever, but these projects should get you started. What's nice is that they don't have to just be for Christmas. Make these gifts year-round with your children and you'll always have something on hand to give away.

Sharing Celebrations: Chanukah and Kwanzaa

Although Christmas is our main focus here, there are crafts associated with both the Jewish Festival of Lights Chanukah (or Hanukkah, as some people spell it) and the African-American festival of Kwanzaa.

Chanukah usually occurs sometime in mid-December, according to the Jewish calendar, and lasts for eight days. Symbols representing Chanukah are the nine-branched menorah, the dreidel, Chanukah gelt (chocolate coins), and the eternal flame.

You don't have to be Jewish to enjoy learning about this holiday celebration and making a menorah or dreidel. I've seen some beautiful menorah made out of polymer clay and others made from wood. You'll find many ideas for crafts that celebrate Chanukah in the book *Crafts for Hanukkah* by Kathy Ross (see Appendix A).

Kwanzaa is not a religious holiday, but more of a cultural one. It honors the history of the black people and celebrates seven principles using seven symbols and three colors: red, green, and black. Kwanzaa is celebrated on seven consecutive nights beginning December 26 and ending January 1. The symbols of Kwanzaa include a place mat, a candle holder, a big cup, and candles, as well as gifts. These all provide numerous opportunities for crafty kids and their parents.

For more information on the African-American celebration of Kwanzaa and Kwanzaa crafts, check out *The Children's Book of Kwanzaa: A Guide to Celebrating the Holiday* by Delores Johnson; *Celebrating Kwanzaa* by Diane Holt-Goldsmith and Lawrence Migdale; and *Crafts for Kwanzaa* by Kathy Ross and Sharon Lane Holm. (See Appendix A for more information.) Or point your Internet browser to the Kwanzaa Information Center at http://www.melnet.com/kwanzaa/.

The Least You Need to Know

➤ The holidays can be less hectic and more enjoyable if you and your children get an early start on handcrafted gifts and decorations.

➤ Planning well ahead of time allows you to find materials all through the year so you can use your family crafting time efficiently.

➤ Tree ornaments, decorations, and gifts can be made using all the skills you've acquired in this book.

➤ Rediscovering old traditions and creating new ones through crafts will add meaning to your holiday celebrations.

Any Excuse to Celebrate!

You celebrate all the major holidays, right? I covered a few of them in Chapters 20–22. But what about some of the minor ones? I'm talking about small projects and touches that will help your family mark the seasons, note and learn about important events in history, and remember significant people.

There are enough holidays or special occasions to fill every week of the year. Now, I'm not suggesting you remember them all (although you can if you want to), but you and your children can pick and choose those you want to highlight in any given year. So, read on and discover new ways to bring joy and ritual into your life!

Birthdays That Take the Cake

Let's take birthdays, for starters. I think of a birthday as a personal holiday. Make it your child's special day, and let him call the shots (as much as possible): where to go, what to eat, how to celebrate.

You can also work with your children to make a spouse's birthday "the ultimate"—and you don't have to spend big money on gifts, either. Feeling special has to do with getting attention. Here are some creative ways to celebrate:

➤ With younger children, invent a Birthday Fairy (a relative of the Tooth Fairy). You and your birthday child can draw a picture of the Birthday Fairy and leave it as a gift for her under a pillow. In return, the Birthday Fairy leaves a present at the foot of the bed or under the pillow of the birthday boy or girl.

➤ Rather than splurging on one big gift, try giving out little gifts throughout the day— one at breakfast, one in the lunch box, and perhaps the main gift at dinner.

➤ Make a special breakfast, even if it *is* a school or work day. If your child's favorite food is pancakes, make them the night before, put waxed paper in between, and reheat them the next morning in the microwave.

➤ Decorate the birthday boy or girl's chair with ribbons and balloons or drape it with fabric and gather with ribbon. Decorate the table, too. Make a special gold or silver crown (foil works well) to be worn by the birthday boy or girl at family meals on the special day. Glue on fake gems and trims. This can become a family "heirloom"— that is, reused for each family member.

➤ Pack a birthday cupcake in the birthday boy or girl's lunch box.

➤ Make handmade gifts from the many ideas you've read about in this book and others. Remember, a gift doesn't have to be an object. A gift can be a poem, an essay, a song, a musical piece, or even a skit or presentation. Get the rest of the family involved; kids love planning surprises!

➤ If you're planning to have a party for your child, think crafts! Add a craft project as part of the festivities. Put together (or purchase) crafts kits for each party-goer. Invite a crafts instructor to come to the party, rather than a clown or magician. Or, if you have an entertainer, make it someone who teaches the kids how to do magic tricks or create clown makeup. Drag out the pretend box and have the kids dress up and create a skit or short play or act out their favorite fantasy. Provide materials for them to make appropriate accessories. As much as possible, let the kids themselves be the entertainment.

Getting Creative Helps Kids Get Well!

Don't believe me? Try it sometime. Of course, if your child's really sick, she's not going to feel like doing much of anything, but if she's just down with a cold or a minor illness or injury, turn off the TV and bring out the arts and crafts supplies. Maybe I'm stretching it a bit to call a sick day a "holiday," but the more special you make it, the sooner your child will get well.

Keep a "sick-day box" filled with special treasures only for sick days. (You might even want to make one of these for yourself!) Fill it with craft supplies that don't make a mess and that your child can use while propped up in bed with a bed tray. Here are some goodies that can go in the box:

➤ Stickers

➤ Crayons and coloring books

➤ Puzzles, word games, and puzzle books

➤ Construction paper

➤ Blunt scissors

➤ Lifesavers or Jolly Ranchers candies

➤ A bell to ring for Mom or Dad

➤ A special pillow

➤ Some dried or silk flowers

➤ A small bedside table to place supplies. (a snack tray works well for this)

➤ A bed tray or lap desk to work on

I guarantee your little one will begin to feel better sooner rather than later.

A Calendar of Holidays

What follows is a calendar of holidays, month by month, for you and your family to use to celebrate and find themes (and an excuse, if you really need one) for crafts. Some of the special days listed here may be obvious and familiar, but you may never have heard of some others. More adventures to embark on with your children!

New Year's: December 31–January 1

New Year's as it's celebrated today tends to be a distinctly adult holiday, but it needn't be. You can certainly include children in the symbolism of ringing out the old year and ringing in the new. In fact, you may have become weary of the shallow way many people celebrate the changing of the calendar. Here are a few ways to meaningfully welcome the New Year:

➤ Shift the emphasis from New Year's Eve to New Year's Day and host a dinner or brunch with other families. You might want to make the traditional New Year's food called Hoppin' John, a mix of black-eyed peas (symbolizing luck), rice (health), and collard greens (prosperity). Everyone's required to have at least a taste.

➤ Make it a day to reflect on the year passed and the one ahead. Kids can write their New Year's

Bet You Didn't Know

In early Victorian times, this was the day of the Open House, when everyone went from house to house "making calls." Open House was usually held from noon to 6 p.m. Ladies and children stayed at home and gentlemen went calling, leaving their calling cards in a special holder near the front door of every home. This practice was eventually limited to family calls and receptions for invited guests only.

resolutions out on paper and tuck them away to read the following year. They can roll them up into little scrolls, tie them with a ribbon, and decorate with small flowers or charms.

➤ New Year's can also become a celebration of winter: When the Christmas decorations come down, decorate for a Winter Festival. This is the time for sledding, ice skating, making snowmen, sipping hot cocoa, and creating paper snowflakes (see Chapter 6).

➤ This is also a good time to start window-sill gardens or small pots of herbs, force bulbs, pour through seed catalogs, and plan a spring garden. Turn to Chapter 16 for some ideas for garden projects to do now.

➤ Make calendars for each member of the family using family photographs, paper scraps, stickers, and other crafts materials.

➤ If you and your children are into miniatures, celebrate the changes in season in miniature. You can do this with a dollhouse, but even a simple box turned on its side (which can become a room), can be furnished and decorated with images of the passing holidays and seasons. The furniture and accessories need not be expensive (although you may want to begin collecting some special ones). Many can be made from small found objects. A lamp, for example, can be a small round bead with a toothpaste cap on top for a shade. The possibilities are endless.

➤ Instead of just a Christmas tree, make a seasonal tree.

Project: Seasonal Tree

Level: Medium

Age: 5 and up with adult help

Materials needed: Small tree limb with lots of branches, spray paint (any color), heavy decorative pot, sand, stones, moss

Directions:

1. Spray paint the limb (or you can leave it natural, if you prefer) and let dry.
2. Block off the hole in the bottom of the pot (if there is one) and fill with a mixture of sand and stones. Make sure the limb is firmly planted and won't fall over. Making the sand damp might help.
3. Cover the top of the sand with stones or moss.
4. Decorate. Change decorations with each season, holiday, or special occasion.

Twelfth Night (Epiphany): January 6

Traditionally, this is the day the Three Kings from the Orient came to Bethlehem bearing gifts for baby Jesus. It's called Twelfth Night because it's the twelfth night after Christ's birth.

Get some incense made from frankincense and myrrh. Check in religious shops, health food stores with larger herb departments, and herb specialty shops (or see Appendix A). Learn what frankincense and myrrh look and smell like. Find out where they come from and how they were used.

Another nice idea is to make a treasure cake, which is a cake with charms, coins, or small rings hidden inside. A plum cake is traditional, but a pound cake works just as well. You can even use a store-bought cake and insert the objects, then cover the cake with icing. This is a fun holiday to counteract the letdown of Christmas past and prolong the Christmas spirit.

> **Bet You Didn't Know**
> Candlemas was for many the traditional ending of the holiday season. All vestiges of Christmas were removed on this day and any greens were burned in the fireplace. The lady of the house made an inventory of the supply of candles and candle making was traditionally done at this time.

Candlemas or Groundhog Day: February 2

On Candlemas, churches all over the world bless the candles that they will use throughout the coming year.

Celebrate Candlemas by gathering lots of candles and lighting them all. That night, do everything by candlelight, including eating dinner and reading your child's bedtime story. Put burning candles in front of mirrors for even more reflective light.

Look for tiny white flowers called snowdrops—also known as Candlemas Bells or Mary's tapers—peeking up through the snow. (Plant some bulbs next fall if you don't have any.)

Americans also celebrate February 2 as Groundhog Day. In times past, it was believed that hibernating animals (such as groundhogs) wake up on Candlemas Day and check to see if it's still winter. If it's a sunny day and the groundhog sees his shadow, he gets frightened and goes back to hibernate for 40 more days. It it's cloudy and he doesn't see his shadow, he stays above ground. So, if it's cloudy on February 2, that means an early spring.

> **Safety Signals**
> Of course, no candles should be left burning unattended. Instruct your children to be especially aware of safety around burning candles. Watch fabric and any combustible materials. Always burn candles on something fireproof and keep them away from small children or pets.

Lincoln and Washington's Birthdays: February

I know, we're supposed to celebrate both Lincoln's and Washington's birthday on President's Day (February 19). Well, hogwash, I say! Instead, celebrate these events on their actual dates and give each president his due.

Bet You Didn't Know
Lincoln Logs were created by John Lloyd Wright, son of Frank Lloyd Wright, the famous architect.

Make Lincoln's birthday, February 12, the day you and your children learn about Lincoln and his place in history. Bring out the Lincoln Logs building toys and make a log cabin. You can also make a Lincoln Log with your children for dessert. This is essentially the same as a Yule Log or Bûche de Noël, a traditional European holiday cake made to look like a log.

Consult your favorite cookbook or use the recipe below:

Lincoln Log Cake

Cake:

4 eggs

$^3/_4$ cup sugar

$^3/_4$ cup sifted all-purpose flour

$^3/_4$ teaspoon baking powder

$^1/_4$ teaspoon salt

1 teaspoon vanilla

Frosting:

$1^1/_2$ cups heavy cream or two ($2^1/_8$-ounce) packages whipped topping mix

$^1/_4$ cup instant powdered chocolate drink

$^1/_4$ cup sifted unsweetened cocoa

Preheat oven to 350 degrees.

1. Grease a $15^1/_2 \times 10^1/_2 \times 1$-inch jelly roll pan and line it with waxed paper. Grease the paper and set aside the pan.

2. In a large bowl, beat the four eggs until foamy. Gradually add $^3/_4$ cup sugar and continue beating five minutes more. Sift together the all-purpose flour, baking powder, and salt. Add to the egg mixture and blend at low speed until well mixed. Stir in the vanilla and pour the batter into the jelly roll pan.

Project: Continued

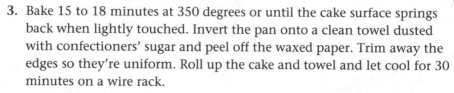

3. Bake 15 to 18 minutes at 350 degrees or until the cake surface springs back when lightly touched. Invert the pan onto a clean towel dusted with confectioners' sugar and peel off the waxed paper. Trim away the edges so they're uniform. Roll up the cake and towel and let cool for 30 minutes on a wire rack.

4. Unroll the cake and remove the towel. Press the cake gently to flatten it. Spread a thin layer of jelly, fruit filling, softened cream cheese, chocolate or vanilla pudding, or any other desired filling over the cake. Re-roll, using the towel to coax it along. Place the cake seam-side down on a serving plate and chill for at least 2 hours.

5. Make the frosting by beating the heavy cream until it's stiff and folding in the instant chocolate drink and unsweetened cocoa. Frost the chilled cake and use the tines of a fork to give it the look of bark.

Celebrate Washington's real birthday on February 22. Make a cherry pie and read why it's associated with Washington's birthday. What is all that stuff about Washington crossing the Delaware, anyway? Couldn't explain it to your kids? Don't know why he's called The Father of Our Country? Then you have some boning up to do. Why not do it together?

St. Patrick's Day: March 17

This is the day to learn about Ireland, Irish music, and Irish culture. Here are several ways:

➤ Go out to hear Irish music played live, or listen to it on a tape or CD (see Appendix A for information on Irish music recordings).

➤ Rent the video "Riverdance." Learn to do the Irish reel or jig (there are videos, honest!).

➤ Find out about the legend of the shamrock and make one out of any medium you choose.

➤ Make crafts with rainbows, fairies, and elves as themes.

➤ Make flower fairies, which are flowers with human faces. Read the books of Cicely Mary Barker, such as *A Treasury of Flower Fairies* and *A World of Flower Fairies*.

➤ Let your children dress as fairies. Make wings out of cardboard and decorate. Read *Peter Pan*.

➤ Dress in green and make a leprechaun hat out of felt.

Bet You Didn't Know
St. Patrick's Day isn't really a holiday originating in Ireland, but one that began in America; it's celebrated by people of Irish descent—and anyone else who wants to join in.

Bet You Didn't Know
Do you know how the date of Easter is determined and why it falls anywhere from late March to late April? Some people know it as the first Sunday after the full moon on or after the March Equinox, but most of us still would have trouble figuring that out. You can find a clear explanation on the Internet at http://www. ips.oz.au/papers/ richard/easter.html. It should spark an interesting discussion about calendars and dates.

Handiwords
Pysanky refers to the highly decorated Easter eggs from the Ukraine.

This is also a good time to celebrate the arrival of spring:

➤ Take a walk and look for signs of spring in the garden, if weather permits.

➤ Read *The Secret Garden* by Frances Hodgson Burnett (or watch the movie).

➤ Begin growing a living Easter basket by putting a small layer of pebbles in the bottom of a tightly woven basket, then filling it with a few inches of potting soil. Scatter some fast-sprouting rye grass seed on top, keep the soil moist, and put the basket in a sunny spot with a plastic tray or dish underneath. In about a week, you'll have some real grass growing in your Easter basket. Let it grow tall and decorate the basket for Easter.

➤ Feed the birds. and thank them for their songs. Check in Chapter 20 for treats you can make to tempt your backyard wildlife.

Easter: March or April

The word "Easter" means "new beginning," and actually coincides with a pagan celebration honoring the goddess of light. It's a true "good-bye to winter, hello spring" kind of holiday, as well as a religious observance for many. Whatever your beliefs, you can incorporate them into this festival of returning life.

This is the time, of course, for egg crafts. You can go from simple hard-boiled eggs and store-bought coloring kits all the way to highly detailed and beautiful Ukrainian eggs, called *pysanky*.

Pysanky is a craft that is thousands of years old. The method used to create designs is similar to batik. Designs are drawn on the egg with wax, which keeps the color from dyeing the area that is protected by the wax. By repeating the process and drawing with wax in different places, then dipping in different colors of dye each time, a multicolored design is created. When the wax is removed, the design is revealed.

The symbols and colors used on the eggs pre-date Christianity, although, Christian interpretations have been added.

For crafted eggs that last, try using wooden eggs, or making blown decorated eggs.

Project: Blown Decorated Eggs

Level: Easy to medium

Age: 5 and up, with this caveat: Some kids at age 5 just don't have a gentle enough touch to do this. You know your child.

Materials needed: Fresh eggs, a carpet needle, bowl, a beading needle, embroidery floss, egg dyes (either purchased or homemade), a white wax crayon, markers, paints (or whatever else you want to use for decorating), acrylic fixative

Directions:

1. Make a hole on each end of the egg using the carpet needle. Make one hole larger than the other.

2. Use the needle to break the yolk.

3. Blow the yolk out from the smaller hole end. If you're having trouble getting the insides to come out, make the holes larger.

4. Decorate the egg by dyeing and/or painting it. When done, "set" your child's work with acrylic fixative. Use the white wax crayon to keep the dye from adhering to a particular area and to "write" on an egg.

5. Cover the larger hole with ribbon and a little silk flower or little chenille chick.

Another neat thing to do with an empty egg is to fill it with chocolate. Just make one fairly large hole instead of two. Rinse the egg out with hot water. Use a small funnel and pour melted chocolate into each egg. Let the eggs cool and harden (use the egg carton to hold them in the refrigerator). Cover the hole with a decoration and watch your child's surprise when she cracks the egg and finds a chocolate one inside!

Make eggs or other Easter symbols out of *marzipan* (you can find recipes in most comprehensive cookbooks for this luscious almond paste confection). They can be colored or painted with special food dyes and paints.

Bet You Didn't Know
There are hidden codes in some software applications that require special keystrokes to see. They're called "Easter Eggs." To find out why and where to find some, go to http://www.cnet.com/Content/Features/Howto/Eggs/ss26.html. This would be a fun activity for older kids to do on their own once you point them in the right direction.

Use your seasonal tree (from earlier in this chapter) to display your decorated eggs. Put a bunny at the top and hang eggs with bright ribbon loops. You can make little baskets from large pieces of shell (your kids are bound to break a few eggs while blowing them out). For a handle, glue on fine ribbon or fine wire.

You can also take a branch from a flowering tree or shrub and keep it in water indoors. This can serve as a tree for displaying your eggs, and will display some pretty blossoms when your branch is "forced" to bloom. Flowering cherry, dogwood, or pussy willow work well. (If you don't have some in your own garden, they can sometimes be purchased at a florist or nursery.)

Make Easter bonnets. You can get plain straw hats at crafts stores, or look for plain hats in thrift shops and at yard sales. Use silk flowers, ribbons, dried flowers, fake birds and animals, or anything that suits you and your child's fancy. Make it really something! Then dress up and have a fashion show.

Bonding Experiences

If you and your child enjoy making and wearing Easter bonnets, you may want to dive deeper into the subject of hats. Take a book out of the library on millinery. Investigate the story of the hat in fashion history. Take a field trip to a department store and try on different hats. Decide which ones look best on each other. Take along a camera to photograph the results!

April Fool's Day: April 1

April Fool's Day is a good time to talk about practical jokes and about what kind of humor is appropriate. Whatever events you plan for the day, be sure to put the emphasis on comic surprises, not hurtful jokes at another's expense.

Here are other ways to add laughter to April Fool's:

➤ Collect riddles and jokes and make them into a book.

➤ Play role-switching games with your children. You be the child, while your children play at being the parents. Kids adore doing this and you may get some surprise insights into how you really sound to your kids (oops!).

➤ Make an April Fool's supper and let your child help plan it. Get creative and funny with food: Try mock-turtle soup or French-fried string potatoes made into birds' nests (with tiny potato "eggs"). Make foods into shapes that disguise what they are.

➤ Make a list of rainy day activities. Check your crafts box (see Chapter 3) and make sure you've got plenty of materials for the rainy weather ahead.

Arbor Day: April 22

Arbor Day originated in 1872 by J. Sterling Morton, a pioneer who moved into the Nebraska territory and became concerned with the lack of trees. He began planting immediately upon arriving and, in his role as a journalist and newspaper editor, spread his enthusiasm and agricultural knowledge. Visiting Nebraska today, you'd be hard-pressed to see how it could have once been a treeless plain.

Crafty Clues
If your child will help you garden, make sure she has scaled-down tools that really work, not toys.

Make this a gardening day:

➤ Clean your tools and take an inventory.

➤ Plant a tree for each family member and give each a garden patch. Let your child decide what he wants to grow in his plot. (It helps to start small and try different things each year.)

➤ Take care of your trees on Arbor Day. Clean up around them. Decorate one with a bow and put out treats for the animals (see Chapter 20). Make a birdhouse (see Chapter 10).

➤ Plan your first picnic on Arbor Day, if weather permits. If not, pack for a picnic anyway and have it on a blanket on the living room floor. You can even make fake ants out of clay or paper.

Contact the National Arbor Day Foundation for more ways to celebrate: 100 Arbor Avenue, Nebraska City, NE 68410; phone (402) 474-5655 or visit them at www.arborday.org to learn more.

Mother's Day: May

In Europe, Mother's Day began during the middle ages as "Mothering Sunday." Young people of the proper age would leave their homes to learn their trades and begin their apprenticeships, but shortly before Easter they would return to see their families. The Sunday following their return was know as Mothering Sunday. The family would attend church and the young person would give gifts to both the church and his mother.

Dads and kids should work together to make mom "Queen for a Day" on this day. Pamper her and do any work around the house that needs doing, such as washing the dishes. Prepare her breakfast in bed.

Encourage your children give a gift of nature or something they've made themselves: Many projects in this book are easily adaptable to Mother's Day. Make homemade cards. Take this time to tell and show her how much you appreciate what she does for the family the whole year through. Tell her you love her.

Decoration Day or Memorial Day: May

Memorial Day marks the beginning of the summer holidays, but for many, its original meaning is lost. Established in 1868 to commemorate those who lost their lives in the Civil War, it is now a time to remember all those who have sacrificed their lives in wartime.

Visit the war memorials in your town, if there are any, and explore the your local military history. Watch movies about the Civil war, such as *Gettysburg*, or attend living-history events in your area. Check into any programs at historic sites near you.

Father's Day: June

For some reason, mothers get quite a bit of attention on their day, but fathers seem to get short shrift. Moms, make sure that doesn't happen this year. Turn the tables on dad and make him "King for a Day." Have the kids help you and do all the little things that will make him feel special. Serve *him* breakfast in bed. Make it his favorite breakfast, even if you and the kids need to make some preparations the night before. Give him a small gift (some handmade aftershave would be nice...see Chapter 15). Reinstitute the custom of wearing a red rose throughout the day to honor a living father, and a white rose to honor a father who's passed away.

Ask dad about something special he'd like to do on his day, or surprise him with a special event. My family has made it an annual ritual to plan an outing for Father's Day. Dad has no idea where we're going and just surrenders to our devices. In times past we've done a jeep tour and a picnic, and future plans include a river rafting trip in the Grand Canyon.

Independence Day: July 4

Despite all the parades and the hoopla, do you and your children really know the details surrounding Independence Day? How long has it been since you've read the Declaration of Independence? Do you even have a copy? Get a copy of *The Fourth of July Story* by Alice Dalgliesh and read it with your kids. Get a copy of the Declaration of Independence and frame it.

Start off the day with a red, white, and blue breakfast. Fresh blueberries, strawberries, and a little cream would fit the bill. Have a family picnic or a neighborly potluck. If you decide to attend a parade, make it an event. Pack some old-fashioned lemonade and healthy snacks (a mix of dried fruits and nuts works well). Bring a flag for waving and some kazoos or small horns to blow. Have a blanket or chairs for sitting down and some wipes for dirty hands and faces. These accouterments would be helpful at the evening fireworks, as well.

Christmas in July

We talked about this in Chapter 22, but it's worth repeating. Pick a day at the end of July, when kids are just beginning to get the "I'm bored" summer blues, to plan your December holiday festivities and gifts in advance. Play some holiday music. Start assembling the materials you'll need for holiday crafts and get started. Nobody will have time to be bored!

Labor Day: September

This can be a bittersweet holiday. The summer is winding down and kids are back at school, or soon will be. The true focus of Labor Day, however, is the world of work. Here are ways you and your family could bring back that focus:

➤ Do your children really understand what you do for a living? Have they ever come to your place of work for a day? Perhaps you could arrange a visit. Talk to your older kids about their futures, as well. What kind of thought have they given to their chosen path?

➤ Think about the various people who produce the goods and services you use every day. Take one product—bread for instance—and research all the people who contribute to that loaf of bread.

➤ Talk about the household chores and whether everyone is doing his or her share. This may be the time to review your chore delegation and reminder system to see how it's working.

➤ Visit some local businesses or factories that you and your children might not know that much about. Call and ask for a tour before you go. When you arrive back home, children can illustrate what they've seen or express their reactions in various ways.

Michaelmas: September 29

Dating back to the 6th century, Michaelmas, or the Feast of St. Michael the Archangel, is still celebrated in the Celtic provinces in England and France. According to the Bible, Michael was the angel who threw Lucifer out of heaven. St. George, the Archangel's earthly representative, slew dragons.

St. George is the patron Saint of England. The story goes that in a village in a far distant country, there was a fearsome dragon that terrorized the community. Unless the villagers appeased him, the dragon would destroy crops and homes (and people) with the flames and smoke that poured from this nostrils. To keep him happy, they fed him sheep and other animals every day. When they ran out of livestock, they drew lots and began offering people from the community. When the lot fell to the King's daughter, she was prepared to be sacrificed and tied to the tower. St. George appeared as a valiant knight who slew the dragon with this magic sword, Ascalon. The people were so grateful, they all were baptized and became Christians.

This is a good time to learn about dragons in myth and legend. Make costumes and play knights and damsels. Watch a movie such as *Ivanhoe*, *First Knight*, *Dragonslayer*, or *Dragonheart*. Find your local chapter of the Society for Creative Anachronism, a medieval recreational society (see Appendix A), and attend one of their public events. Learn about the different ways dragons have been represented in different cultures. Make one out of papier-mâchè or clay or make a dragon costume.

Thanksgiving: November

What is the true meaning of Thanksgiving? Do you really know its history? Who made Thanksgiving a national holiday and where do the foods and customs we have today originate?

You may believe the way we celebrate Thanksgiving is the way the Pilgrims did—but you're wrong. Our celebration actually dates back to Victorian times. The modern observance of Thanksgiving was the result of a campaign initiated by Sarah Josepha Hale, the editor of *Godey's Lady's Book*, a popular Victorian women's magazine. Mrs. Hale almost single-handedly created the Thanksgiving we celebrate today. Before her efforts, Thanksgiving was an irregularly celebrated occasion that differed from state to state.

Often, with so much attention focused on Christmas, Chanukah, and Kwanzaa, Thanksgiving is given only cursory attention. Don't let this happen in your family!

Have each member of the family create a gratitude journal they can keep all year long, perhaps even daily. Each day, write down five things you are thankful for. It may be difficult to think of five things at first, but as you start looking more closely at the little things, you'll have difficulty sticking with only five (so don't!).

At Thanksgiving dinner, have each person write five things they're grateful for on a slip of paper, roll it up, and secure with a piece of raffia or some other natural material. Collect the scrolls, mix them up, and then redistribute. Have each member of your celebration read their scroll aloud.

Make sure you invite people for dinner who have nowhere to go on Thanksgiving. It's really not much trouble to set the table for one or two more people. Prepare a box of food with your children and take it to someone who is less fortunate or perhaps can't get out to celebrate.

Other Holidays to Investigate

I don't have room to cover all the possibilities when it comes to holidays and special occasions throughout the year and the crafts and foods associated with them, but I believe I've got you well on your way. Here are few more holidays to investigate:

➤ Martin Luther King day: Third Monday in January

➤ Chinese New Year: Date changes year to year on Western calendar

➤ Cinco de Mayo: May 5

➤ Flag Day: June 14

➤ Midsummer's Night's Eve: June 23 in most countries

➤ Bastille Day: July 14

➤ Grandparents' Day: Second Sunday in September

➤ All Soul's Day: November 2

➤ Martinmas: November 11

➤ Jewish Holy Days and festivals throughout the year

Another holiday we celebrate in our family is Appreciation Day. This can be held at any time and celebrated in any way. It simply focuses on one individual who's gone above and beyond in some way or who's simply been neglected during the year. It can even be Doggy or Kitty Appreciation Day, when we give recognition and attention to our favorite animal companions.

The Least You Need to Know

➤ There are enough holidays to keep a family busy and happy celebrating every month of the year.

➤ Crafts and activities can enhance any occasion, and any occasion can be an excuse for pulling out the crafts basket.

➤ Holidays provide abundant opportunities for learning and strengthening family ties.

Part 5
Presenting "Handmade by You!"

Among the most fun aspects of making things by hand is displaying your creations proudly and giving them away. This is where you get to enjoy the fruits of your labor and share them with the rest of the world (or at least your friends and family). There's an important lesson to impart here, too. The road to building self-esteem and finding happiness in life is paved with learning how to express pride, accept praise, and give to others. This part of the book is filled with ideas for doing just that.

There's also a brief economics lesson, should your child actually want to sell his or her crafts. There's much you can teach here, since seeing your kids grow into independent adults who understand the value of money and the importance of satisfying work is one of the major objectives of good parenting. These next chapters should give you plenty of ways to "show and tell" for fun and (perhaps) profit.

Chapter 24

Wrap It Up!

In This Chapter

➤ Wrapping basics for your handcrafted gifts

➤ How to wrap gifts of any size

➤ Making your own gift wrap

➤ Adding handmade trims and gift tags

➤ Do-it-yourself boxes and other containers

One of the great pleasures of engaging in crafts is giving the results away. Indeed, all of the crafts in this book should suggest plenty of gift-giving possibilities. But why wrap your lovingly handcrafted creation in just any gift wrap? Why not make the presentation a craft in itself?

The focus of this chapter is gift presentation in all its forms. Your children will enjoy trying some of these ideas and coming up with their own.

It's a Wrap

In its most basic terms, gift wrapping is a means of hiding or disguising a gift. It's supposed to add to the presentation, as well as to the suspense and enjoyment of getting a gift. Most of us have undoubtedly exclaimed at one time or another, "It's too pretty to open!"

Beautiful, intriguing, interesting, or whimsical—gift wrap can be all of these, and it certainly doesn't ever have to be boring or mundane, especially not in the hands of an experienced crafter like you. The first thing you need to become a master gift-wrapper is to know and understand the basic tools of the trade.

Boxing Basics

First, there's the box. Now, not all gifts need to be contained in a box. A CD, audiotape, videotape, or book, for example, can be wrapped "as is." But perhaps you don't want the recipient to pick up your gift and immediately have the look that says "I know what *this* is." Part of the fun is to confuse or mislead. So, open your mind to odd shapes and sizes when wrapping familiar gifts. Put that CD or tape in a round box or one twice (or even 100 times) its size. Or wrap it in a series of ever-larger boxes.

It's also fun to play tricks with the package's weight. You can wrap a small gift in a shoe box with loads of tissue paper, then add a heavy book at the bottom of the box so the person getting the gift is completely thrown off course.

Another trick is to break a gift into parts and wrap each one. So, for instance, a potpourri simmer pot becomes four separate packages: one for the potpourri itself, one for the pot, one for the candle holder, and one for the candle or tea light. It's fun to create a series of directions on each gift leading the giftee to the next one, detailing which to open first and why. Try a poem or series of riddles to make it even more interesting.

Usually, once you've packaged a gift, you can wrap the entire thing with a sheet of gift wrap or tissue. Another variation is to wrap the box in sections; try covering just the top in gift wrap, or covering the top and bottom in different coordinating papers.

Another idea is to make the box part of the gift. How nice to receive a lovely beaded ornament in a handcrafted wooden box. Or a necklace that's cradled in velvet inside a cigar box you've decoupaged to become a new jewelry box. Boxes for gifts don't have to be boxes at all. Think of your gift box as an attractive container and all sorts of possibilities come to mind—either ready-made or out of the craft basket. Here are some all-in-one gift and wrapping ideas to try:

➤ Place cookies in a cookie jar you decorated yourself with the glass painting or etching techniques you learned in Chapter 14. A bow or ribbon and a gift tag is all you need to complete the gift.

➤ A handmade candle in a punched and snipped tin holder adds to the gift—and also solves a problem for the recipient. No need to find a candle holder!

➤ Metal mini-loaf pans with homebaked bread in them can be wrapped in cellophane once they're cooled. Gather the wrap together at the top and tie with a ribbon or raffia. Add a rubber-stamped and embossed gift card.

Mini loaf pans with homemade cookies baked inside and attractively wrapped.

➤ Spray-paint a coffee can gold or silver. Fill it with cookies or other goodies. Replace the plastic lid and attach a gold or silver mylar bow. The can becomes a canister when it's empty.

➤ Homemade potpourri given in a handcrafted clay bowl, simply wrapped in tulle (netting) and tied with a ribbon, is another completely handmade gift.

➤ An empty oatmeal carton can be covered with paper or painted and used as both a gift box and a container to keep.

➤ A clay flowerpot can be used as a gift container. Decorate the pot or leave it plain.

➤ Give edibles in a lunch box or bread box.

➤ Use all or part of an egg carton to hold several small, delicate gifts. Decorate or paint the outside.

➤ Decorate a pail or bucket with paint or some other method. Fill with tissue and your gift.

Crafty Clues

A computer program (PC only) for creating boxes is available from Aunt Annie's Crafts. Called Boxes and Bags, it prints out patterns and includes unusual shapes such as the diamond collapsing bag, tube, oval, and novelty shapes. Call (937) 898-8221 or order from Aunt Annie's Web site at http://auntannie.com/software.html.

There are lots of resources to teach you how to make your own boxes. Here are a few useful ones (see Appendix A for more information):

➤ *Joyful Origami Boxes* by Tomoko Fuse and Tamoko Fuse

➤ *Making Your Own Decorative Boxes With Easy-To-Use Patterns* by Karen Kjaeldgard-Larsen

➤ *The New Book of Boxes/A Stunning Collection of Elegant Gift Boxes* by Kunio Ekiguchi

➤ Mr. Ekiguchi has also written a highly recommended book on general gift wrapping called *Gift Wrappings: Creative Ideas From Japan.*

When you start using objects as gift containers that weren't originally intended for that purpose, suddenly you begin to see possibilities all around you. Yard sales and flea markets are full of inexpensive containers that can be adapted for gifts. Keep your eyes open when you read magazines or watch homestyle shows on TV, since they often show innovative gift-wrapping ideas. You might want to start a folder in your crafts filing cabinet just for gift-wrapping!

Bag It

For some gifts, a bag works better than a box. Gift bags can be made from paper, or you can recycle paper bags by adding clever decorations. Bags can be made from fabric, as well. Here are some great gift-bag ideas to get you started "bagging it:"

➤ Use burlap to make a narrow sack for a bottle of homemade herbed vinegar or oil or a bottle of wine or sparkling cider.

➤ A larger burlap bag could hold a metal crafted tray. Include a package of mixed cookie dough. The dough could then be tied with a ribbon and a cookie cutter used as an outer decoration. Fray the top edges of the burlap.

➤ Brown paper bags can be used as gift bags after being stamped with rubber stamps or homemade stamps made from Styrofoam, a clean, new sponge, or cut potatoes. (See Chapter 6 for more on stamping.) Citrus fruit sliced in half and then dipped in acrylic paint make another interesting decoration. Use acrylic or tempera paints for this (thin with water if necessary). Leave the top of the bag open and fill with colored tissue (or ivory tissue for a more natural look).

➤ A fabric sack is an excellent way to disguise an odd-shaped gift. Part of the fun is trying to figure out what the heck made that shape! Just use a string to measure around the object so you know how big to make the sack.

➤ Want a ready-made fabric sack? Recycle an old pillowcase. If the pillowcase is printed, just add a matching wide ribbon at the top. If it's plain, stamp or stencil it with fabric paint.

➤ Sew up a lace bag to hold potpourri. Tulle works well for this, too.

➤ Cut the leg off a worn pair of jeans. Cut a tube the length needed and sew across the bottom. This works great for a long narrow gift, such as a piece of sports equipment or an umbrella.

Crafty Clues
Wrap a piece of string around an item to measure how much paper you'll need to wrap it.

➤ Use a long, warm winter sock for a Christmas stocking. Roll up the mate and put it inside. A glove can be used the same way for a different gift. Use one glove as the "wrapping" for a small gift. Place the other glove inside as well and tie the opening with a colorful ribbon.

➤ Make a fabric or canvas tote bag and put your gift inside, along with some tissue.

➤ A velvet bag with a drawstring makes an elegant gift wrap, then becomes a travel bag for jewelry.

➤ A fabric bag is a good way to wrap and later store a quilt or fabric throw.

➤ Make a crocheted doily into a bag by lacing ribbon through the openings around the edge.

Bags are great when you're in a hurry, since they don't require precise folding and taping—just pop in the gift and go. Keep some ready-made ones around and consider sewing up a few fabric bags out of scraps so you have them available "just in case."

Paper Tigers

Wrapping paper doesn't have to be humdrum, either. Here are some inventive ideas for either creating your own wrapping papers or using paper materials you have on hand in new ways:

➤ Use colorful but outdated maps as wrapping paper. This is especially appropriate for a man's gift or a gift related to travel. Topographical maps that are no longer accurate can sometimes be obtained for free from local community agencies and are quite colorful and interesting.

➤ Plain brown paper becomes an excellent base for any number of homemade paper techniques. For example, use a hot glue gun (adults should do this) to glue pennies onto a brown-paper-wrapped package in either a pleasingly spaced pattern or a specific design.

➤ Plain white paper (butcher's wrap works well) is also a nice "field" for decoration. Cut out colorful magazine pictures and glue them on with white craft glue, or make snowflakes out of silver or gold paper and glue them on. Stamp the paper with silver or gold ink or draw squiggles with a gold or silver paint pen for another variation.

➤ Use fabric as you would paper and wrap your gift in pretty fabric scraps. This is especially appreciated by other crafters, who can use the fabric for their own projects.

➤ Scarves, tea towels, napkins, or handkerchiefs also make wonderful fabric wraps. The wrap becomes a gift, too!

➤ Tulle makes a lovely wrapping for bottles or baskets. If you don't want the contents to show through, double the tulle or wrap the object loosely in tissue first.

➤ Wrap a gift in a poster or full-page magazine photo. Choose an image that will clue the recipient into the gift (or completely mislead him or her!).

➤ Antique photographs photocopied onto paper make beautiful gift wrap paper. Or go to a copy shop and make color photocopies of snapshots of the giftee. Glue them onto plain paper.

➤ Use some of the handmade papers you learned how to make in Chapter 6.

Bet You Didn't Know
The technique of marbling or marbleizing paper and fabric has been practiced at least since the 12th century. Some scholars believe it began even earlier in China, but this has not been verified. The earliest known evidence places the art in Japan. The method most like that used by western marblers today originated in 15th-century Turkey and Persia.

➤ Wallpaper makes great gift wrap. Some embossed wallpapers are especially elegant.

➤ Use computer clip art to create unique gift wrap for smaller gifts. Color clip art (printed with a color printer) is one alternative, but even black-and-white printouts can be jazzed up with colored paints, markers, or crayons (or left alone). Kids can "paint" or draw in a software graphics program and create their very own designs.

➤ Use old sheet music or old calendar pages as wrapping paper. You can also cut up old calendars and use them as decorative scrap.

➤ Use kids' drawings or coloring book pages to wrap smaller gifts.

➤ Make your own marbleized papers. These are easy to do, and since I didn't show you how in Chapter 6, I'll give you easy instructions here.

Project: Marbleized Paper

Level: Easy

Age: 5 and up (with adult supervision)

Materials needed: One disposable foil roasting pan, sheets of plain white paper, enamel oil paints in assorted colors, water, paint thinner or turpentine, a comb, pencil, and/or stick, squeeze bottles or eyedroppers for each color (optional), old newspapers

Project: Continued

Directions:

1. Cover your work area with newspapers. Leave some room to lay your finished paper.

2. Fill the disposable roasting pan with water. Drop a small blob of each color into the water in different places or try some short strips of color. (Use your squeeze bottle or eyedropper if necessary.) If the paint is too heavy and sinks, thin it a little in a glass jar with a little paint thinner or turpentine.

3. Using your stylus (comb, pencil, stick, or other household object), swirl the colors in the solution.

4. Lay the paper on the surface of the water immediately. The best way is to hold opposite corners and touch the surface of the water with the center first, then let go of the corners.

5. Wait three to five seconds, then gently pick up the paper by the corners, allowing the excess water to drip off. Hang the paper to dry (spring-type clothespins work well) or lay it on newspaper face up.

6. When the paper is completely dry, you can lightly press the back with a warm iron, then use it to wrap your gifts.

Note: Start with fresh paint after two or three pieces of paper have been painted. To remove the old paint before adding the new, drag some newspaper over the top of the water.

Try experimenting with different papers, different paints, different colors, and making different patterns.

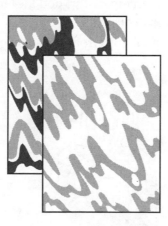

The patterns you can make with the marbelizing process are infinite.

Marbleizing paper and fabric can be much more involved than the simple process I've given you, with exciting results. There are several good books you might want to consult to get into this beautiful craft further (see Appendix A for details):

➤ *Techniques for Marbleizing Paper* by Gabriele Grunebaum

➤ *Marbling Techniques: How to Create Traditional and Contemporary Designs on Paper and Fabric* by Wendy Addison Medeiros

➤ *Marbling Paper and Fabric* by Carol Taylor, Patty Schleicher, Mimi Schleicher, and Laura Sims

For paper and cloth marbling supplies, (and lots of other neat stuff), contact Educational Innovations at 151 River Road, Cos Cob, CT 06807, (203) 629-6049; Web site: http://lmg.com/edinnov/marbling.htm.

Other suppliers are Talas, 218 W. 35th Street, New York, NY 10001-1996, (212) 736-7744; and Colophon Book Arts Supply, 3-46 Hogum Bay Road SE, Olympia, WA 98506, (206) 459-2940.

All Tied Up

Ribbons are what most of us think of when we consider ways to trim or close up a package. There are so many beautiful ribbons available today. But there are many other ways out there to tie up gifts, and they don't all involve ribbon. Here are some ideas for tying things up:

➤ Raffia adds a warm, rustic touch. It can be used around the neck of a bottle of homemade bubble bath and goes well with simple brown paper wrappings.

➤ Wired ribbon allows you to give a bow or other formation that "frozen in time" look. It's a great invention.

➤ Use yarn instead of ribbon. This is an especially good idea for gifts that need to be sent by mail, since bows usually get crushed.

➤ Make paper "ribbon" for bows out of strips from the same paper you're using for wrapping.

Bow made out of paper.

➤ Sometimes ribbon alone is enough. Wrap bundles of handmade candles in ribbon, yarn, or string.

Make a ribbon box to keep your ribbons organized. Use a sturdy shoe box and make slits or use grommets along the lengthwise sides. Make holes on either end and insert a ¼-inch dowel through the ribbon spools and box. Put a thumbtack on each dowel end to keep it from pulling through.

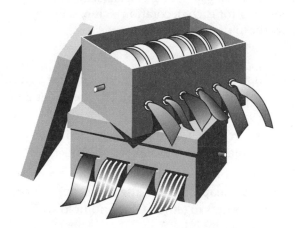

Make a box to keep your ribbons clean and organized.

Gifts Appropriately Tagged

A gift tag lets the giftee know your gift is meant especially for him or her. It can also add a whole other element to the package, both visually and verbally. It's the gift tag that personalizes the gift. In addition to the obvious "To" and "From," messages can be sent to lend even more meaning. Besides the informative or inspired tag, ornamental add-ons are mini gifts that start giving before the box or bag is even opened. Here are some ideas for both gift tags and add-ons:

➤ On a large Christmas tree light bulb, write "To" and "From" with a gold paint pen. Tie a strand of ribbon around the base of the bulb and attach to the main bow of your gift, letting it hang down.

➤ Make any one of the ornaments described in Chapter 22. This doesn't have to be for a Christmas gift if it's not the season. A heart-shaped ornament could decorate a Valentine's gift, for example.

➤ Live greens make a fragrant addition to holiday gifts. Holly, ivy, boxwood, or any sturdy greens work well if added to the gift shortly before giving. Try a live flower bouquet pulled through a paper doily and attached to a Mother's Day or Easter gift.

➤ Or make these pleated toppers that can double as ornaments for a Christmas or seasonal tree.

Project: Paper Accordion-Fold Decorations

Level: Easy

Age: 5 and up

Materials needed: Craft paper, origami paper, or gift wrap scraps, $^1/_4$-inch ribbon (approximate 6 inches long for each decoration), glue, scissors, a pencil, a ruler, spring-type clothespins

Directions:

1. Cut the paper into 6×9-inch rectangles. (Use a paper cutter if you have access to one.) Add glitter or other embellishments to the paper if you wish.

2. Working from one of the short ends, fold the paper accordion-style, using approximate $^1/_2$-inch folds, until it is completely folded.

3. Holding the paper closed in a completely folded condition, cut the ends on a diagonal or in a "V" shape. Fan out the facing corners of one side of the paper and bring corners together. Glue and hold with a clothespin.

4. Make a loop with the ribbon and glue to one of the remaining corners, then fan out the rest of the decoration so that the final corner meets it. Add extra glue if needed and secure with a clothespin.

5. You should now have a pleated circle with a loop. This decoration can be used as an ornament after it's removed from the gift.

A pleated paper bow can be made in the same way by tying a ribbon around the center and not gluing the corners. Just let the sides fan out and attach it to the package.

Pleated paper ornament and bow.

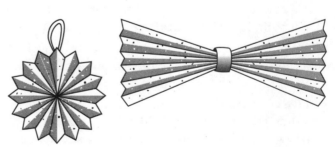

Totally Unexpected

And then there's the way of presenting a gift that's just so unique it's in a class all by itself. Children are especially inventive when asked to come up with these offbeat kinds of presentations. Just ask them! I've mentioned just a few to give you the idea.

➤ Use an abandoned (of course!) bird's nest to feature a small, delicate handmade gift, like beaded earrings or a tiny dollhouse miniature.

➤ Secure two oyster or scallop shells together with ribbon to hold a special smaller gift. Set it inside on cotton batting, straw, or cellophane "grass."

➤ Spread mylar or paper confetti inside the package.

➤ How about a piñata? You can purchase these unfilled at a party or paper store and put the gift inside. Be careful to warn the recipient that they may not want to bash it with a stick unless it's unbreakable!

The Least You Need to Know

➤ All kinds of containers can be used to hold a gift, many of which can be made from already-used household items or from scratch.

➤ Using fabric is an excellent way to wrap a gift, especially since the fabric can be reused by the receiver of the gift.

➤ Gift wrap can be made from newspaper, butcher's paper, brown paper, discarded maps, posters, and a host of other types of paper, and can be marbleized, printed on, or decorated in many different ways.

➤ There are many unique materials you can use to tie a gift, including raffia, ribbon, string, and yarn.

➤ Adding a gift tag or other decoration personalizes a gift and makes it that much more meaningful.

Show & Tell—
And Sell?

If you've reached this point, you've done a lot of crafting by now. Perhaps not everything covered in this book, but a few projects at least. Hopefully, you've established regular times with your child to create happily together, and, hopefully, he is happily creating on his own. But what to do with all those attempts, half-attempts, and finished beauties? How do you display them? Use them? Share them? Or even, sell them? That's what this chapter is all about.

Show It Off!

Other than displaying your child's artwork on the refrigerator, have you ever thought about providing a special place in your home to display her accomplishments and creations? What an ego boost to have her very own shelf in a prominent part of the house where everyone can see what she and you are proud of. Pack up some of your knickknacks and see if you can make a spot for each child (or family member, for that matter) to exhibit the things they've made. You might put the person's picture on their shelf as well.

Another way to show off crafts, depending on the size, is in one of those coffee tables with a glass-topped display case built in. Change the display monthly and share new craft projects with everyone who visits. This type of display-case coffee table would make a good furniture-making project for an adult.

If your child's favorite craft usually takes the form of something flat, make a place to hang things on the wall and rotate with new versions as they come along. A large clip-and-glass frame (the kind made of two pieces of glass pressed together and held by clips) can accommodate different-sized pieces.

Or how about a large bulletin board or a bulletin board border? Using 12-inch cork squares applied directly to the wall with an appropriate adhesive, create a border at about eye level around an entire room or along one wall. This would work well for a play or rec room. You can even band the cork border top and bottom with wallpaper trim. Now you have plenty of space to exhibit your child's latest works of art or anything else you'd like to show off.

Paper cutouts look beautiful on a window. Share them with the whole neighborhood. When my kids were little, they made some pictures, set up a table at the end of the driveway and made a big sign that said "Art Show." A few neighbors even stopped to look and one offered to buy a couple.

Why not have a neighborhood Arts and Crafts Show and Exchange? It could be held in someone's yard or garage and kids and adults could show what they do. We used to have a similar event where I worked. It was a Family Day and employees and their families brought in their hobbies to show. Consider this for your church or community organization.

Ask the staff at a local nursing home or hospital if they might like to borrow some colorful crafts to display at their facility. They may even want your child to come in and explain how the project was done. Combine bringing the crafts to display with a visit with some residents. Bake some cookies for the occasion.

Perhaps your child wants to preserve the memory of a project, but you don't have room to keep the project itself forever. Consider making a scrapbook. Take a picture of the project and incorporate it into a scrapbook, which becomes another craft project in itself. This can become a kind of portfolio and record you child's progress and changing interests.

If a lack of space is a consideration, how about scanning the picture (or having it scanned) into your computer and keeping picture files of projects? Take it a step further and put up a family Web site where you and your child can share crafting experiences and results with other families.

Bonding Experiences

A natural adjunct to crafting hobbies is photography. Get a quality camera and teach yourself and your child to take good pictures. Learn how to light crafts projects best and commit them to film. Explore different ways these photographs can be used, including manipulating them in your computer.

Hang It!

Look for ingenious ways to hang things. Using the same kind of hooks you would use to hang a houseplant, suspend a three-dimensional project from the ceiling. Again, a special corner could be reserved just for this in a room shared by the family.

The seasonal tree mentioned in Chapter 23 is a great way to display smaller items like beaded eggs, dough sculptures, or felt creatures. Just put a hanger on the item and suspend it from the branches. If seasonal themes are used, the objects can tie in nicely with the purpose of the tree—but it can be used to display things at any time.

Another way to display items is from a line (like a clothesline) using S hooks. This can be strung close to the wall if you are displaying smaller or flatter items, further away for bulkier ones.

Shadow boxes are useful to display three-dimensional objects. These can be made or bought. Compartmentalized shadow boxes, great for showing off smaller objects, are available from Northwood Products. A shadow box kit is available from Keepsake Frames, S&S Richards (Web site: http://www.yourhobby.com/keepsake.html). See Appendix A for ordering information.

Smaller lightweight objects can be made into a mobile. Origami crafts work well for this, as do small clay pieces or fabric shapes that have been stuffed and decorated or stiffened. Crocheted snowflakes that have been stiffened with starch can be hung for a wintry mobile. Mobiles are very adaptable.

Let's Play Interior Decorator

I always thought it would be cool for a kid to be able to decorate his room using his own crafting talents. Depending on your child's crafting interests, this could be an interesting project that could evolve over several months. He can pick a theme to tie it all together, such as Tropical, African, Country, Sports (or a particular sport), Dance, Garden, or anything else that appeals to him.

Scour magazines and books for ideas that could be adapted to your theme. Consider all the different aspects of the room, from ceilings and walls to floors, window treatments, and accessories. You and your child can change the entire room by refinishing old furniture using various painting techniques or decoupage. You can also build simple pieces of furniture from scratch, paint murals, sew accessories, and create mobiles or collages. Let your child design and create his own living space. This is something that would especially appeal to older children. There's a show on Home and Garden Television called *Awesome Interiors* that has some very simple and inexpensive ideas for decorating that could easily be adapted to a kid's room.

All the different crafts I've covered in this book will give you ideas for decorating and creating accessories. Paper projects could be framed for walls, or you could make a pierced paper lampshade together. Fabric techniques could be used to create bed coverings, window treatments, and pillow covers. Your metalwork projects could be used as embellishments for wooden furniture. Etched or stained glass could be used for windows or lighting fixtures. You could craft leather accessories. Poured molded plastic has an infinite number of possibilities for room decorations and desk accessories.

Stenciling techniques could be used on walls, ceilings, and furniture. A store-bought rug or pillows can be stenciled with fabric paint. Build boxes for storage, or cover existing boxes with creative fabrics and designs. Paint and decorate, use faux finishes (finishes that look like marble, stone, metal, wood, and so on but aren't), or cover surfaces with fabric or marbled papers that your child has made. These can then be covered with a coat of clear acrylic to help preserve them and make them easy to clean.

Try sponging or marbling both objects and surfaces. There are products on the market that give you all the tools, paints, and know-how in one package. Use needlework to decorate accessories or create them from scratch. Make frames or cover existing ones with fabric or decoupage. Use decorative painting techniques on furniture and accessories. Handmade baskets can also be used for decoration and storage. Make a wooden shelf or a rack with hooks to hang hats or jackets. Make a rag, needlepoint, or hooked rug for the room. Make a bed quilt together.

Add interesting details, like handcrafted pulls for the shades or drawers, a miniature room your child can set on a shelf or hang from the wall and change with the seasons, a small wreath on the door that changes with the holidays or seasons, even a miniature holiday tree.

Let your child's room be a virtual showcase for his talents and interests, even if it may look a little quirky sometimes. As long as he likes it, that's what counts. You may find that the more of himself he's allowed to put into his space, the better care he takes of it. It makes sense.

Wear It!

Some of your child's finished products can be easily adapted to wear; in fact, some of the projects you've done were probably intended for that purpose in the first place. But even if a project didn't start out as a piece of jewelry or clothing, it could end up there. Some things (a marbelized paper design, for example) can be made into fabric transfers by taking them to a T-shirt shop or print shop and having them ironed onto a sweatshirt, T-shirt, or tote. Or take a picture of the design and have a transfer made from that.

Leatherwork has all sorts of possibilities for everyday wear. A change purse, pocketbook, or wallet becomes a constant companion. A leather vest is easy to make and can be embellished in any number of ways, from painting to beadwork, stamping, carving, or lacing.

Use It!

One of the best ways to show someone you like what they've made for you is to use it. Whether it's wearing a piece of jewelry or using a quilted potholder to remove the roast from the oven, the maker is sure to enjoy seeing his creation put to use. When selecting crafts project to do with kids, try to pick things that are useful as well as decorative. A child can enjoy using the tote she made, wearing a hat or sneakers she decorated, or using a handmade bowl or vase.

Give It Away

Sometimes the fun is just in the creating. After your child has finished a project and is ready to move on, perhaps someone else might enjoy looking at or using what your child has made. Maybe your child would like to adopt a "grandma" or "grandpa" at a local nursing home and visit, bringing a homemade gift. Or she might like to visit a pediatric ward at the local hospital. Or a local charity might have some ideas. Look for opportunities for giving and sharing with others along with your child. You'll be glad you helped create this lifelong habit.

Crafts, Not Clutter

Sometimes crafting can pose a clutter problem. We have a tendency to want to keep everything we've made, even the not-so-good projects, just because we made them.

Parents may have to set limits on how much can be allowed to accumulate, and children should learn early that choices have to be made about what to keep and what to let go of. As we get better at something, we may want to keep the more shining examples of our work, although sometimes the first one is fun to keep for comparison. But we don't need to keep everything we do. Having a place to keep artwork and crafts projects is important for children, so see to it that there's a space in the closet, on a shelf, or in a container where your child can store his artwork and crafts projects. Then periodically reevaluate what's there and clean it out to make room for new things.

Kids' Crafts, Inc.

If your child really enjoys a particular craft and keeps creating new and better designs, he might want to consider selling some of what he makes. I believe it's up to parents to teach kids how to earn, manage, and spend money wisely, and here's a great opportunity to do that.

Using his allowance as initial capital, your child can start a small business and learn the various aspects of handling money and making a profit. Teaching your children entrepreneurial skills may be the best thing you can do for their future.

There are some great resources for teaching kids about money and helping kids earn and handle their own money. You might want to pick up a copy of *The Kid's Guide to Money: Earning It, Saving It, Spending It, Growing It, Sharing It* or *Better Than A Lemonade Stand: Small Business Ideas for Kids* by 15-year-old Daryl Bernstein (see Appendix A).

If your child really thinks he can turn his craft into cash, you'll both need to do some research, and, to ensure success, will need to keep some records and accounts. Here's a short checklist of things to do and ideas to ponder. This could be the beginning of an adventure that will affect the rest of your child's life!

Kid's Starting-Your-Own-Business Checklist

Ask yourself the following questions:

1. What items do you want to sell? Are there variations you can make to suit different tastes?

2. How long does it take to make each item and what does it cost for materials?

3. Will you need an inventory or will you make each item to order ? How will you deliver your products? What will this cost you?

4. Who are your customers? Who are your competitors? How does your product and workmanship compare to others being sold ?

5. How much should you charge for your product? What's the average price of products similar to yours? Can you make it and sell it for the same price or less than what's out there?

6. How will people know your product is available and how will they be able to buy it? What forms of money will you take—cash only? Checks? Trades?

7. Will you advertise? Go to craft shows? Approach shops to display and sell your items? Send out flyers?

8. How can you find out what people think of your product before you try to sell it? Are you willing to change your product to what people want? How well can you take critical comments? Can you learn from them?

9. Once you do sell your products, what will you do with the money? Do you need to have a separate bank account? How much money needs to be put back into your business? How much can you spend on other things? How much should you save?

10. How much time can you devote to your craft-making and business? Will your schoolwork or chores suffer? What about play? Is crafting still fun when it's a business?

Another interesting and informative preliminary activity is market research. Go on field trips together to crafts shops and shows and see if anyone is making anything similar. How is your product better? How is theirs better? What methods are they using to sell their product? Do they appear to be successful (are lots of people flocking to their booth and buying)? What can you learn?

> **Crafty Clues**
> One of the best ways to get a feel for selling and whether your child likes it or whether his product appeals to people is to do a craft show. It doesn't have to be a professional crafts show, either. He can do one for charity or a local church group. The money is donated to a good cause and both of you get invaluable information about your proposed venture.

Bonding Experiences

Have your child help you when you do your monthly bills. Show them how to balance a checkbook and reconcile a bank statement and explain why it's important. Show them some of the records you keep and explain why you keep them. Explain what a budget is and why it's important to have one. These are important life skills that parents often neglect to teach their kids, but ones that are extremely useful to have.

The Least You Need to Know

➤ Crafting is only half the fun. Sharing the results with others adds to the pleasure.

➤ Look around your house for ways to exhibit your child's creations. This fosters self-esteem and encourages further exploration into the world of crafts.

➤ Check out your community for ways to exhibit crafts and perhaps even sell them.

➤ Consider giving your crafts to local schools, hospitals, nursing homes, and charities.

5

A.   B.   C.

Resources

General Crafts

Catalogs

Dharma Trading Company
P.O. Box 150916
San Rafael, CA 94915
1-800-542-5227
Web site: www.dharmatrading.com
Textile crafts supplies and books.

Dick Blick Art Materials & Crafts Supplies
P.O. Box 1267
Galesburg, IL 61402
1-800-447-8192
Supplies, books, videos, kits, and tools. Good source for oriental papers and marbleizing
supplies. Bulk packages for larger groups, as well as individual sales.

Dover Publications
31 East Second Street
Mineola, NY 11501
1-516-294-7000
Publisher of excellent and inexpensive craft and design books, sticker books, art books
that you're free to copy from since their copyright has run out.

Heritage Handcrafts
P.O. Box 261176
Littleton, CO 80163-1176
1-303-683-0963
Solid brass embossing templates for creating raised paper designs, light boxes, stationery,
inks, acid-free album supplies, and scissors.

Herrschners
2800 Hoover Road
Stevens Point, WI 54492-0001
1-800-713-1239
Web site: www.herrschners.com
Needlework, crocheting, knitting, quilting, sewing, and general crafts supplies and kits.

Hobby Builders Supply
P.O. Box 921012
Norcross, GA 30092-7012
1-800-926-6464
Dollhouse and miniatures supplies.

Lark Books
P.O. Box 2580
Asheville, NC 28802-2580
1-800-284-3388
Web site: wwwlarkbooks.com
Books, kits, and supplies for just about any craft you can think of. They've also just acquired Folkwear vintage patterns.

Nasco Arts & Crafts

East:
901 Janesville Avenue
Fort Atkinson, WI 53538-0901
1-800-558-9595 or 1-920-563-2446

West:
4825 Stoddard Road
Modesto, CA 95356-9318
1-800-558-9595 or 1-209-545-1600

Web site: www.nascofa.com
Huge selection of every kind of art or craft supply you can imagine, plus lots of nifty teaching tools and equipment even a professional would love.

S&S Worldwide
P.O. Box 513
Colchester, CT
1-800-243-9232
Web site: www.snswwide.com
Crafts supplies.

Sax Arts & Crafts
P.O. Box 510710
New Berlin, WI 53151
1-800-323-0388
Art supplies, kits, puzzles, equipment, and artistic gifts.

Sunshine Discount Crafts
P.O. Box 301
Largo, FL 33779-0301
1-813-538-2878
Orders only: 1-800-729-2878
Web site: www.sunshinecrafts.com
Deep discount crafts supplies. Great for large groups.

Suzanne McNeill's Crafts Corner Catalog
Design Originals
2425 Cullen Street
Fort Worth, TX 76107
1-817-877-0067
How-to books from the queen of crafts. She also has a Scrapbooks and Photo Memory Albums catalog with lots of supplies for scrapbooking, plus a newsletter/catalog called Crafts & More.

Magazines

Arts & Crafts
700 E. State Street
Iola, WI 54900-0001
1-715-445-2214
A sumptuous crafts magazine with a view to the nostalgic.

Crafting Traditions
P.O. Box 5286
Harlan, IA 51593-0786
1-800-344-6913
Projects, patterns, recipes, and contests for the whole family.

Crafts
P.O. Box 56010
Boulder, CO 80323-6010
1-800-727-2387
This magazine has lots of projects each month, many of them adaptable to younger children and others challenging enough for an adult.

Crafts 'n Things
P.O. Box 5026
Des Plaines, IL 60017-5026
1-800-444-0441
Web site: www.clapper.com
Published 10 times a year by the same people who publish *Pack-O-Fun*, *Painting*, *The Cross Stitcher*, and *Bridal Crafts* magazines, this one offers ideas, how-to's, and tips.

Handcraft Illustrated
P.O. Box 7448
Red Oak, IA 51591-0448
1-800-526-8447
Quarterly magazine with a variety of crafts.

Kids at Home
Woman's Day Specials
30 Montgomery Street
Jersey City, NJ 07302
1-201-451-9420
A special-interest publication of *Woman's Day*, this magazine features activities for kids age 3 to 13.

Pack-O-Fun
P.O. Box 5034
Des Plaines, IL 60017-5034
1-800-444-0441
Projects for kids and families. Published six times a year.

Online Resources

Aunt Annie's Crafts Page
Web site: www.auntannie.com
Projects galore, with a project index to help you search for activities by holiday, difficulty, or materials. Instructions and patterns you can download to your printer.

Microsystems' Route 6-16
Web site: www.microsys.com/616/default.htm
Click on the Puzzles and Hobbies division for fun crafts and games from around the world.

The Exploratorium
Web site: www.exploratorium.edu
A San Francisco museum with interactive exhibits maintains this site with home experiments, lots of science information, and projects to do.

Organizations

Art & Creative Materials Institute, Inc.
100 Boylston Street 1050
Boston, MA 02116
1-617-426-6400
Fax: 1-617-426-6639
Email: *dfanning@aol.com*
Web site: www.creative-industries.com/acmi/index.html
Non-profit association of manufacturers of art, craft, and other creative materials. Safety certification program.

Society for Creative Anachronism
P.O. Box 360789
Milpitas, CA 95036-0789
1-800-789-7486
Web site: www.sca.org
Medieval recreation society with a strong interest in historical costume and handicrafts.

Software

Aunt Annie's Crafts is a Microsoft Windows program that serves as an electronic platform to run these electronic books: Paper Airplanes, Games to Make, Boxes and Bags, and Puppets Around the World. Order from the Aunt Annie Web site at www.auntannie.com.

Chapter 1: How Kids Learn About Crafts

Books

Awaken the Giant Within by Anthony Robbins, Fireside, 1991; ISBN 0671791540

Awakening Your Child's Natural Genius: Enhancing Curiosity, Creativity, and Learning Ability by Thomas Armstrong, J.P. Tarcher, 1991; ISBN 0874776082

Creative Companion: How to Free Your Creative Spirit by Sark, Celestial Arts, 1991; ISBN 0890876517

Creative Visualization by Shakti Gawain, New World Library, 1978; ISBN 0931432022

Dr. Sylvia Rimm's Smart Parenting: How to Parent So Children Will Learn by Sylvia Rimm, Crown, 1997; ISBN 060980121X

Drawing on the Artist Within: An Inspirational and Practical Guide to Increasing Your Creative Powers by Betty Edwards, Fireside, 1987; ISBN 067163514X

Drawing on the Right Side of the Brain by Betty Edwards, J.P. Tarcher, 1989; ISBN 0874775132

Living in the Light by Shakti Gawain, Whatever Publishing, Inc., 1986; ISBN 0931432146

Show Me: The Complete Guide to Storyboarding and Problem Solving by Harry I. Forsha, American Society for Quality, 1994; ISBN 0873892550

Simple Abundance by Sarah Ban Breathnach, Warner Books, Inc., 1995; ISBN 0446519138

The Artist's Way: A Spiritual Path to Higher Creativity by Julia Cameron, Putnam, 1992; ISBN 0874776945

The Brain Book by Peter Russell, E.P. Dutton, 1991; ISBN 0452267234

The Universal Traveler: A Soft-Systems Guide to Creativity, Problem-Solving and the Process of Reaching Goals by Don Koberg and Jim Bagnall, Crisp Publications, 1991; ISBN 1560520450

The Workshop Book by Scott Landis, Taunton Press, 1991; ISBN 0942391373

Think Out of the Box by Mike Vance and Diane Deacon, Career Press, 1995; ISBN 1564141861

Thinkertoys by Michael Michalko, Ten Speed Press, 1991; ISBN 0898154081

Unlimited Power by Anthony Robbins, Ballantine Books, 1986; ISBN 0449902803

Chapter 4: Safety First

Books

The Artist's Complete Health and Safety Guide by Monona Rossol, Allworth Press, 1994; ISBN 1880559188

Artist Beware by Michael McCann, The Lyons Press, 1993; ISBN 1558211756

Online Resources

CompuServe's Handicrafts Forum

Library 16: Technical/Safety

Here you'll find many excellent text files on crafts safety, from solvents to ventilation. Several are contributed by Dr. Michael McCann of the Center for Safety in the Arts (CSA).

Material Safety Data Sheet (MSDS) Search Page: http://research.nwfsc.noaa.gov/msds.html

Organizations

ACTS: Arts, Crafts, and Theater Safety
181 Thompson Street, 23
New York, NY 10012-2586
1-212-777-0062
Email: *ACTS@CaseWeb.Com*
Web site: www.caseweb.com/acts
Free art and theater hazards information by phone, mail, and email.

Center for Safety in the Arts
c/o New York Foundation for the Arts
155 Avenue of the Americas, 14th Floor
New York, NY 10013

Performing Arts Hazards Data Sheets, General Data Sheets, and Conservation Hazards Data Sheets available. Art Hazards Library. Art Hazards News, a regular publication, keeps subscribers up to date on new materials.

Chapter 5: How to Avoid Messes (and Clean them up Quick!)

Books

Don Aslett's Stainbuster's Bible: The Complete Guide to Stain Removal by Don Aslett, Plume, 1990; ISBN 0452263859

Chapter 6: Paper Power

Books

Best Ever Paper Airplanes by Norman Schmidt, Sterling, 1995; ISBN 1895569427

Chronology of the Origin and Progress of Paper and Paper-Making by Joel Munsell, Garland Publishing, 1980; ISBN 0824038789

How to Marbelize Paper: Step-By-Step Instructions for 12 Traditional Patterns by Gabriele Grunebaum, Dover, 1984; ISBN 048624655

Making Kites (Step-By-Step) by David Michael, Kingfisher Books, 1993; ISBN 1856979229

Memory Albums by Suzanne McNeill and Lani Stiles. To order this folder, ask for Design Originals folder #3172 (ISBN 1574210491) at your local crafts store or call Design Originals, 2425 Cullen Street, Fort Worth, TX 76107; 1-817-877-0067

Origami for Beginners: The Creative World of Paperfolding by Florence Temko, Charles E. Tuttle Co., 1991; ISBN 0804816883

Paper Airplanes by Nick Robinson, Chartwell Books, 1991; ISBN 1555217249

Paper Art: The Complete Guide to Papercraft Techniques by Diane Maurer-Mathison and Jennifer Philippoff, Watson-Guptill, 1997; ISBN 0823038408

Paper By Kids by Arnold Grummer, Dillon Press, 1980; ISBN 087518190

Paper Craft by North Light Books, 1993; ISBN 0891345418

Pulp and Paper Primer by David Saltman, Tappi Press, 1997; ISBN 0898524105

Rubber Stamp Album by Joni K. Miller, Workman, 1978; ISBN 0894800458

Scherenschnitte: Designs and Techniques for the Traditional Craft of Papercutting by Susanne Schlapfer-Geiser, Lark Books, 1997; ISBN 1887374183

Stampcraft: Dozens of Creative Ideas for Stamping on Cards, Clothing, Furniture, and More by Cari Haysom, Chilton, 1996; ISBN 0801988500

The Art & Craft of Papermaking: Step-By-Step Instructions for Creating Distinctive Handmade Paper by Sophie Dawson, Lark Books, 1997; ISBN 1887374248

The Art of Rubber Stamping: Easy as 1-2-3! by Michele Abel, Creative Press, 1995; ISBN 0963075608

The Color Printer Idea Book: 101 Cool Things You Can Make With Color Printers by Kay Hall, No Starch Press, 1998; ISBN 1886411204

Catalogs

Paper Models International
9910 S.W. Bonnie Braie Drive
Beaverton, OR 97005
1-503-646-4289
One of the largest mail-order sources for paper scale models in the U.S.

Online Resources

Dragonhome's Rubber Stamping Page: www.littlebit.com/rubber1.htm

Lots of links to rubber stamping Web pages, bulletin boards, suppliers, and stores all over the Web.

Software

KittyHawk Software, Inc.
P.O. Box 64189
Tucson, AZ 85728
1-800-388-9622
Web site: www.khs.com/khs/INDEX.HTM
Paper Animal Workshop software package for Windows and Macintosh lets you print out a full-color design and fold it using fully interactive 3-D folding instructions. Christmas Ornament Workshop, also for both Windows and Macintosh, teaches you how to make 12 full-color ornaments. Greatest Paper Airplanes (Windows/Macintosh) is a shareware demo program you can download from any one of several FTP sites, or you can order the complete version online or from the address above.

Tools, Supplies, and Equipment

Fascinating Folds
P.O. Box 10070
Glendale, AZ 85318
1-800-968-2418
Email: *sales@fascinating-folds.com*
Web site: www.fascinating-folds.com
Origami supplies.

Kim's Crane Origami Supplies and Crafts
3106 Hannah's Pond Lane
Herndon, VA 20171
1-703-758-0373
Email: *kcrane@kimscrane.com*
Web site: www.kimscrane.com
Origami papers, books, and videotapes.

Videos

"Planes for Brains"
Alexander Blace & Co., Inc.
170 Margin Street
Haverhill, MA 01832-5109
1-800-238-1279
How to create and fly 10 paper airplanes.

Chapter 7: Golden Threads: Crafts with Fiber and Fabric

Booklets

"One Hundred Embroidery Stitches," Coats & Clark's Book No. 150
"Learn How Book," Coats & Clark's Book No. 170-B
Order these from Coats & Clark.
P.O. Drawer 27067
Greenville, SC 29616
1-800-326-1610

Books

Crazy Quilt Odyssey: Adventures in Victorian Needlework by Judith Baker Montano, C & T Publishing, 1991; ISBN 0914881418

Crazy Quilt Stitches by Dorothy Bond; Dorothy Bond, 1981; ISBN 0960608605

New Lashings and Improvements to Old Favorites by Billy Malone, available from Woven Spirit Basketry, 635 N. Tamiami Trail, Nokomis, FL 34275, 1-800-697-6730

Quilts! Quilts! Quilts!: The Complete Guide to Quiltmaking by Diana McClun and Laura Nownes, Quilt Digest, 1997; ISBN 0844336173

The Art of Silk Ribbon Embroidery by Judith Baker Montano, C & T Publishing, 1993; ISBN 0914881558

The Crazy Quilt Handbook by Judith Baker Montano, C & T Publishing, 1991;ISBN 0914881051

The Quilter's Complete Guide by Marianne Fons and Liz Porter, Oxmoor House, 1993; ISBN 0848711521

Tie Dye, Back By Popular Demand by Virginia Gleser, Harmony (available from Dharma Trading Company; see listing for Dharma Trading Company in next section).

Catalogs

Clotilde
B3000
Louisiana, MO 63353-3000
1-800-772-2891
Notions and supplies for sewing, quilting, dolls, and other crafts.

Dharma Trading Company
P.O. Box 150916
San Rafael, CA 94915
1-800-542-5227
Web site: www.dharmatrading.com
Textile crafts supplies and books.

G Street Fabrics
12240 Wilkins Avenue
Rockville, MD 20852
1-800-333-9191
Threads, fabric, and everything else for sewing and quilting.

Nancy's Notions
333 Beichl Avenue
Beaver Dam, WI 53916-0683
1-800-833-0690
Sewing advisor: 1-800-595-6878
Web site: www.nancysnotions.com
Sewing and crafts supplies, video rental library.

The American Needlewoman
Box 6472
Fort Worth, TX 76115
1-817-293-1229
Needlecrafts supplies, kits, and accessories.

Organizations

American Sewing Guild
P.O. Box 8476
Medford, OR 97504-0476
1-503-772-4059

Software

CompuQuilt
2791F N. Texas Street
Suite 116
Fairfield, CA 94533
1-707-422-1529
Web site: www.compuquilt.com/quiltpro.htm
Quilt Pro quilting software.

Compucrafts
P.O. Box 6326
Lincoln Center, MA 01773
1-800-263-0045
Web site: www.compucrafts.com/
Stitch Crafts Gold for Windows and Stitch Craft for Mac.

Cochenille Design Studio
P.O. Box 4276
Encinitas, CA 92023-4276
1-619-259-1698
Web site: www.cochenille.comsp.htm
Stitch Painter for Macintosh, PC, and Amiga by Cochenille Design Studio for counted cross-stitch, plus add-on modules for other crafts such as beading, knitting, crocheting, and weaving.

Tools, Supplies, and Equipment

Evening Star Designs
69 Coolidge Avenue
Haverhill, MA 01832
1-508-372-3473
Web site: www.needlearts.com/evening_star/index.htm
Crazy quilt kits and supplies.

Videos

"Crazy Quilting" by Judith Baker Montano, VHS, International Video Network, 1997; ISBN 1571200134

"Embellishments" by Judith Baker Montano, VHS, International Video Network, 1997; ISBN 1571200363

"Silk Ribbon Embroidery" by Judith Baker Montano, VHS, International Video Network, 1997; ISBN 1571200142

"Tie-Dye Made Easy" by D. Feltus and D. Otten, VHS, Vv Publishing, 1994; ISBN 6303166598

Chapter 8: Bead It!

Books

Africa Adorned by Angela Fisher, Harry N. Abrams, 1984; ISBN 0810918234

Beaded Bracelets, Friendship Bracelets, and Crosses and *Friendship Chains, Seed and Bugle Beads*, both by Suzanne McNeill and available from your local crafts store or from Suzanne McNeill's Crafts Corner Catalog, Design Originals, 2425 Cullen Street, Fort Worth, TX 76107; 1-817-877-0067

Beaded Clothing Techniques by Therese Spears, Promenade Publishing, 1984; ISBN 0932255019

Complete Guide to Wire Work for Bead Jewelry by Kate Drew-Wilkinson, available from Nomad Press International, P.O. Box 1803, Bisbee, AZ; 1-520-432-7117

Embroidery With Beads by Angela Thompson, Lacis, 1992; ISBN 0916896382

Hairwrapping Techniques: Creative Jewelry for Hair by Darlene Roether, Roaring Forties Press, 1995; ISBN 0964417804

Pearl and Bead Stringing with Henrietta by Henrietta Virchik, Henrietta Designs, 1990; ISBN 0962713708

Peyote At Last!: A Peyote Beadwork Primer by Barbara L. Grainger. Available at your local bead store, or order direct from the author at: P.O. Box 5264, Oregon City, OR 97045.

The Best Little Beading Book by Wendy Simpson Conner, Interstellar Publishing Co., 1995; ISBN 0964595702

The History of Beads: From 30,000 B.C. to the Present, by Lois Sherr Dubin, Harry N. Abrams, 1995; ISBN 0810926172

Top Knots!: The Ultimate Bracelet and Hair-Wrapping Kit by Jennifer Dussling, Grosset & Dunlap, 1996; ISBN 0448411288

Catalogs

Bead Lovers' Catalog
Beadbox
P.O. Box 6035
Scottsdale, AZ 85261-6035
1-800-232-3269
Web site: www.beadlovers.com/index.html
Beads, findings, tools, and kits.

Fire Mountain Gems
28195 Redwood Highway
Cave Junction, OR 97523-9304
1-800-423-2319
Web site: www.firemtn.com
Jewelry making and beading supplies.

Griegers
2830 E. Foothill
Pasadena, CA 91107
1-800-423-4181
Jewelry making supplies and findings.

Shipwreck Beads
2727 Westmoor Court SW
Olympia, WA 98502
1-360-754-2323
Orders: 1-800-950-4232
Web site: www.shipwreck.com
Beads and findings.

Magazines

Bead & Button
21027 Crossroads Circle
P.O. Box 1612
Waukesha, WI 53187-1612
1-800-400-2482
Web site: www.beadandbutton.com
Excellent instruction and projects from novice to advanced.

Beadwork
Interweave Press
201 East Fourth Street
Loveland, CO 80537-5655
1-970-669-7672
Interweave Press Web site: www.interweave.com
Brand new and filled with projects.

Tools, Supplies, and Equipment

Henrietta's Beading Supply Co.
P.O. Box 260
Matawan, NJ 07747
1-800-325-3918
All the supplies you need for bead stringing, plus you can order Henrietta's book and video on the subject.

Chapter 9: Lessons in Leather

Books

How to Sew Leather, Suede, Fur by Phyllis W. Schwebke and Margaret B. Krohn, Macmillan Publishing, 1970; ISBN 0020119305

Leatherwork Manual by Al Stohlman, A. D. Patten and J. A. Wilson, Tandy Leather Company, 1969 (revised 1984); No ISBN

The Leatherworking Handbook: A Practical Illustrated Sourcebook of Techniques and Projects by Valerie Michael, Cassell Academic, 1995; ISBN 0304345113

Catalogs

Tandy Leather & Crafts
Advertising Dept.
P.O. Box 791
Fort Worth, TX 76101
1-800-555-3130
Web site: www.tandyleather.com

The Leather Factory
Advertising Dept.
Fort Worth, TX 76105-0429
1-800-433-3201
Web site: www.flash.net/~lfmidas2/

Magazines

The Leather Crafters and Saddlers Journal
331 Annette Court
Rhinelander, WI 54501-2902
1-715-362-5393
Considered THE leatherworkers magazine. Published six times a year.

Online Resources

International Internet Leathercrafter's Guild
Web site: www.peak.org/~iilg/
Links to leather crafters, suppliers, and lots of useful resources.

Chapter 10: Wondrous Wood

Books

A Beginners' Guide to the Dolls' House Hobby by Jean Nisbett, Sterling, 1997; ISBN 1861080379

Acrylic Decorative Painting Techniques: Discover the Secrets of Successful Decorative Painting by Sybil Edwards, North Light Books, 1997; ISBN 0891347836

Brush Sponge Stamp: A Creative Guide to Painting Beautiful Patterns on Everyday Surfaces by Paula Desimone and Pat Stewart, Rockport Publishing, 1998; ISBN 1564963535

Easy Carpentry Projects for Children by Jerome E. Leavitt, Dover Publications, 1986; ISBN 0486250571

Painted Ladies: San Francisco's Resplendent Victorians by Morley Baer, Elizabeth Pomada, and Michael Larsen, E.P. Dutton, 1986; ISBN 052548244X

Stencilling; How to Create Clever Paint Effects on Wood, Ceramics, Paper and Fabric by Kathy Fillion Ritchie, Henry Holt & Company, 1996; ISBN 0805042679

The Ultimate Dolls' House Book by Faith Eaton, Dorling-Kindersley, 1994; ISBN 1564586162

Woodworking for Kids by Kevin McGuire, Lark Books, 1994; ISBN 0806904305

Woodworking With Your Kids by Richard Starr, Taunton Press, 1990; ISBN 0942391616

Catalogs

Duckwork's Woodcrafts
7736 Ranchview Lane
Maple Grove, MN 55311-2100
1-800-420-5921
Web site: www.duckworks.com
Craft woods, kits, paints, books, and tools.

Northeastern Scale Models
99 Cross Street
Methuen, MA 01844
1-978-699-6019
Email: *nesm@tiasc.net*
Web site: nesm.com

Chapter 11: Heavy Metal

Books

A Beginner's Book of Tincraft by Lucy Sargent, ISBN 0396073549

Chasing by Marcia Lewis, ISBN 096442620x

Jewelry: Fundamentals of Metalsmithing by Tim McCreight, North Light Books, 1997; ISBN 1880140292

Making Wire Jewelry: 60 Easy Projects in Silver, Copper & Brass by Helen Clegg and Mary Larom, Lark Books, 1997; ISBN 157990002X

The Fine Art of the Tin Can: Techniques and Inspirations by Bobby Hansson, Lark Books, 1996; ISBN 1887374027

Tin Craft; A Work Book by Fern-Rae Abraham, Sunstone Press, 1994; ISBN 0865340986

Tinwork by Marion Elliot, Lorenz Books, 1996; ISBN 1859671438

Wire (Everyday Things) ed. by Suzanne Slesin, Abbeville Press, Inc., 1994; ISBN 1558597921

Wirework by Mary McGuire, Lorenz Books, 1996; ISBN 1859671489

Catalogs

Metalliferous, Inc.
34 W. 46th Street
New York, NY 10036-4114
1-212-944-0909
Metal beads and findings.

Tools, Supplies, and Equipment

Klenk Industries
20 Germay Industrial Park
Wilmington, DE 19804
1-302-652-0996
Aviation snips.

Chapter 12: Feats of Clay

Books

Creative Clay Jewelry: Extraordinary Colorful Fun: Designs to Make from Polymer Clay by Leslie Dirks, Lark Books, 1994; ISBN 0937274747

Mudworks: Creative Clay, Dough, And Modeling Experiences by Maryann Kohl, Bright Ring, 1992; ISBN 0935607021

The Art of Polymer Clay: Designs and Techniques for Making Jewelry, Pottery and Decorative Artwork by Donna Kato, Watson-Guptill, 1997; ISBN 0823002780

The Incredible Clay Book by Sherri Haab and Laura Torres, Klutz Press, 1994; ISBN 1878257730

The New Clay: Techniques and Approaches to Jewelry Making by Nan Roche, Flower Valley Press, 1992; ISBN 0962054348

Organizations

National Polymer Clay Guild
1350 Beverly Road
Suite 115-345
McLean, VA 22101
1-202-895-5212

Tools, Supplies, and Equipment

American Art Clay Co., Inc. (AMACO)
4717 West 16th Street
Indianapolis, IN 46222
1-800-374-1600
Web site: www.iquest.net/amaco/
Handcast cotton paper kits and Fimo polymer clay products.

Kemper Enterprises, Inc.
P.O. Box 696, 13595 12th Street
Chino, CA 91710
1-800-388-5367
CERNIT polymer clay products and Kemper tools.

Polyform Products, Inc.
1901 Estes Avenue
Elk Grove Village, IL 60007
1-847-427-0020
Sculpey polymer clay products and Pro-Mat Oven Bake.

Chapter 13: "I Have One Word For You, Son: Plastics!"

Books

Boondoggle: A Book of Lanyard & Lacing by the editors of Klutz Press, Klutz, 1994; ISBN 1878257722

Castin' Craft Idea Book by Casey Carlton, E.T.I., 1982 (For information, see "Tools, Supplies, and Equipment" below.)

Friendly Plastic Wear With Flair: 16 Jewelry Designs That Shine by Kimberly Garringer, Hot Off the Press, 1994; ISBN 1562312162

The Lanyard Book by Arlene Hamilton Stewart, Andrews and McMeel, 1994; ISBN 0836242238

Catalogs

Sunshine Discount Crafts
P.O. Box 301
Largo, FL 33779-0301
1-813-538-2878
Orders only: 1-800-729-2878
Web site: www.sunshinecrafts.com
Deep discount crafts supplies. Great for large groups.

Tools, Supplies, and Equipment

E.T.I.
P.O. Box 365
Fields Landing, CA 95537
1-707-443-9323
castin' craft brand products and books about resin casting.

Videos

Creative Pastimes in Video
P.O. Box 7
Walworth, WI 53184
1-800-327-5403
Distributors of "Styrofoam Wizardry," a video that demonstrates more than 20 projects that teach how to cut, shape, sculpt, cover, paint, and glue Styrofoam-brand plastic foam.

Chapter 14: Looking at Glass

Books

How to Work in Stained Glass by Anita Isenberg and Seymour Isenberg, Chilton Book Co., 1983; ISBN 0801973554

Making Glass Beads by Cindy Jenkins, Lark Books, 1997; ISBN 1887374167

Making Mosaics: Designs, Techniques and Projects by Leslie Dierks, Sterling Publications, 1998; ISBN 0806948728

More Than You Ever Wanted to Know About Glass Beadmaking by James Kervin, Glass Wear Studios, ISBN 0965145808

Stained Glass Primer Vol. 1: The Basic Skills by Peter Mollica, Mollica Stained Glass Press, 1987; ISBN 0960130667

Stained Glass Primer Vol. 2: Advanced Skills and Annotated Bibliography by Peter Mollica, Mollica Stained Glass Press, 1982; ISBN 0960130632

The Mosaic Book: Ideas, Projects and Techniques by Peggy Vance and Celia Goodrich-Clarke, Trafalgar Square, 1996; ISBN 1570760608

Catalogs

Delphi Stained Glass
3380 E. Jolly Road
Lansing, MI 48910
1-800-248-2048
Web site: www.delphiglass.com

Whittemore-Durgin Glass Co.
P.O. Box 2065
Hanover, MA 02334
1-800-262-1790
Web site: www.penrose.com/glass/

Videos

Vicki Payne stained glass videos
Web site: www.foryourhome.com

Chapter 15: Now You're Cookin! Crafts in the Kitchen

Books

Betty Crocker's Cooking With Kids by the Betty Crocker Editors, MacMillan General Reference, 1995; ISBN 002860363X

Kid's Cooking: A Very Slightly Messy Manual, Klutz Press, 1987; ISBN 0932592147

Play With Your Food by Joost Elffers, Stewart, Tabori & Chang, 1997; ISBN 1556706308

Super Formulas, Arts and Crafts: How to make more than 360 useful products that contain honey and beeswax by Elaine White, Valley Hills Press, 1993; ISBN 0963753975

Tassajara Bread Book by Edward Espe Brown, Shambhala Publications, 1995; ISBN 157062089X

The Candlemaker's Companion by Betty Oppenheimer, Storey Books, 1997; ISBN 088266944X

The Complete Candlemaker: Techniques, Projects, Inspirations by Norma Coney, Lark Books, 1997; ISBN 1887374507

The Natural Soap Book: Making Herbal and Vegetable-Based Soaps by Susan Cavitch, Storey Books, 1995; ISBN 088266889

The Scented Room by Barbara Milo Ohrback, Clarkson Potter, 1986; ISBN 051756081X

Chapter 16: Au Naturel: Crafts from the Outdoors

Books

Everlasting Design: Ideas and Techniques for Dried Flowers by Diana Penzner and Mary Forsell, Houghton Mifflin, 1988; ISBN 0395467284

Herbal Treasures: Inspiring Month-By-Month Projects For Gardening, Cooking, and Crafts by Phyllis V. Shaudys, Storey Books, 1990; ISBN 0882666185

How a Seed Grows by Helen Jordan, Harpercollins, 1992; ISBN 0064451070

Making Pot Pourri, Colognes, and Soaps: 102 Natural Recipes by David A. Webb, Tab Books, 1988; ISBN 0830629181

Nature Craft by North Light Books, 1993; ISBN 0891345426

Pressed Flower Work Station by Rita Warner, Price Stern Sloan, 1993; ISBN 0843136669

Terrarium by Scott Russell Sanders, Indiana University Press, 1996; ISBN 0253210216

Terrarium Habitats/Grades K-6 (teacher edition) by Kimi Hosoume and Jacqueline Barber, Gems, 1995; ISBN 0912511850

Catalogs

San Francisco Herb Co.
250 14th Street
San Francisco, CA 94103
1-800-227-4530
Web site: www.sfherb.com
Herbs, dried botanicals, and essential oils.

Tools, Supplies, and Equipment

Sunstone, Inc.
P.O. Box 788
Cooperstown, NY 13326
1-800-327-0306
Flower presses.

Nature's Pressed
P.O. Box 212
Orem, UT 84059
1-800-850-2499
Pre-dried, pressed flowers.

Chapter 17: Toyland: Handcrafted Toys for All Ages

Books

Easy-To-Make Articulated Wooden Toys: Patterns and Instructions for 18 Playthings That Move by Ed Sibbet, Dover Publications, 1984; ISBN 0486244113

I Can Make Puppets/So Easy to Make! by Mary Wallace, Owl Communications, 1994; ISBN 1895688248

The Big Book of Things to Make and Play With: Toys, Games, Puppets, Boyds Mill Press, 1994; ISBN 1563974738

Chapter 18: Mix and Beat Well: Music Making Crafts

Books

Kids Make Music! Clapping & Tapping from Bach to Rock! by Avery Hart, Paul Mantell, and Loretta Trezzo Braren, Williamson Publishing, 1993; ISBN 0913589691

Chapter 19: The Second Time Around: Crafts from Recyclables

Books

Tin Can Papermaking: Recycle for Earth and Art by Arnold Grummer, Greg Markim, 1993; ISBN 0938231015

Chapter 20: Love is the Answer: Crafts for Valentine's Day

Books

Tokens of Love by Roberta B. Etter, Abbeville Press, Inc., 1990; ISBN 1558591001

Chapter 21: Happy Haunting: A Handmade Halloween

Books

Child's Play: Quick and Easy Costumes by Leslie Hamilton, Crown Pub, 1995; ISBN 051788173X

Costumes for Plays and Playing by Gail E. Haley, Methuen, 1978; ISBN 0416305814

Halloween Costumes (Singer Sewing Reference Library), Cowles Creative Publishing, 1997; ISBN 0865733163

Men, Makeup, and Monsters: Hollywood's Masters of Illusion and Fx by Anthony Timpone, St. Martin's Press, 1996; ISBN 0312146787

Stage Makeup Step-By-Step: The Complete Guide to Basic Makeup, Planning and Designing Makeup, Adding and Reducing Age, Ethnic Makeup, Special Effects by Rosemarie Swinfield, Betterway Publications, 1995; ISBN 155870390X

Magazines

Better Homes and Gardens' Halloween Tricks & Treats
P.O. Box 9255
Des Moines, IA 50306-9255
1-800-572-9350
Look for this special issue each year on the newsstand or order from the information above. *Better Homes and Gardens* also publishes several other holiday issues magazines: *Collectible Country Ornaments, Christmas Woodcrafts, Holiday Ornaments,* and *Holiday Decorating* magazines.

Chapter 22: Christmas, Chanukah, and Kwanzaa: Celebrate with Crafts

Books

Celebrating Kwanzaa by Diane Holt-Goldsmith and Lawrence Migdale, Holiday House, 1994; ISBN 0823411303

Crafts for Hanukkah by Kathy Ross, Millbrook Press Trade, 1996; ISBN 0761300783

Crafts for Kwanzaa (Holiday Crafts for Kids series) by Kathy Ross, Millbrook Press Trade, 1994; ISBN 1562947400

The Children's Book of Kwanzaa: A Guide to Celebrating the Holiday by Delores Johnson, Aladdin Paperbacks, 1995; ISBN 0689815565

Online Resources

Kwanzaa Information Center
Web site: www.melnet.com/kwanzaa/

Chapter 23: Any Excuse to Celebrate!

Books

A Treasury of Flower Fairies by Cicely Mary Barker, the Penguin Group, 1991; ISBN 073237964

A World of Flower Fairies by Cicely Mary Barker, the Penguin Group, 1992; ISBN 0723240027

The Fourth of July Story by Alice Dalgliesh, Aladdin Paperbacks, 1995; ISBN 0689718764

The Secret Garden by Frances Hodgson Burnett, Harper Collins, 1998; ISBN 0060278536

Catalogs

Green Linnet/Xenophile Records
43 Beaver Brook Road
Danbury, CT 06810
1-800-468-6644
Web site: www.grnlinnet.com/index.html
Traditional Irish music for your collection.

Videos

Video4All
3291 S. Little Drive
Flagstaff, AZ 86001
Web site://Video4All.com
If you're looking for step-by-step instructions for traditional Irish dances, so you can make everyone green for St. Patrick's Day, this site has Colin Dunne's "Celtic Feet" and "Irish Dancing Made Easy."

Chapter 24: Wrap It Up!

Books

Gift Wrapping: Creative Ideas From Japan by Kunio Ekiguchi, Kodansha, 1987; ISBN 0870117688

Joyful Origami Boxes by Tomoko Fuse and Tamoko Fuse, Japan Publications, 1996; ISBN 0870409743

Making Your Own Decorative Boxes With Easy-To-Use Patterns by Karen Kjaeldgard-Larsen, Dover Publications, 1995; ISBN 048627814X

Marbling Techniques: How to Create Traditional and Contemporary Designs on Paper and Fabric by Wendy Addison Medeiros, Watson-Guptill, 1994; ISBN 823030059

Techniques for Marbleizing Paper by Gabriele Grunebaum, Dover Publications, 1995; ISBN 0486271560

The New Book of Boxes/A Stunning Collection of Elegant Gift Boxes by Kunio Ekiguchi, Kodansha, 1994; ISBN 4770017731

Chapter 25: Show & Tell—And Sell?

Books

Better Than A Lemonade Stand: Small Business Ideas for Kids by Daryl Bernstein, Beyond Words Publishing, 1992; ISBN 0941831752

Selling Your Crafts at Crafts Shows by Madelaine Gray, Storey Communications, 1996; ISBN 088266476X (order direct from the publisher at 1-800-441-5700 or from their Web site at www.storey.com)

The Kid's Guide to Money: Earning It, Saving It, Spending It, Growing It, Sharing It by Steve Otfinoski, Scholastic Trade, 1996; ISBN 0590538535

Tools, Supplies, and Equipment

Keepsake Frames, S&S Richards
Web site: www.yourhobby.com/keepsake.html
Shadow box kit.

Glossary

Appliqué—Ornamented by different material or a piece of the same type, sewn on or otherwise applied.

Batting—Cotton or wool fiber wadded in sheets used as a filling in quilts or bedcovers.

Boondoggle—A word coined by Robert H. Link, an American scoutmaster. It means a braided cord worn by Boy Scouts as a neckerchief slide, hat band, or ornament.

Came—A slender, grooved bar of lead used to hold together the pieces of glass in windows of latticework or stained glass.

Catalyst—A substance that causes or accelerates a chemical reaction without being permanently affected by the reaction.

Ceramics—The art of making objects of clay and similar materials treated by firing.

Chamois—Soft, pliable leather from any of various animal skins dressed with oil. It also refers to cotton cloth finished to simulate this leather.

Chasing—Indenting metal from the top side.

Couching—In paper making, the process of transferring a wet paper sheet from a mold onto something absorbent.

Crazy quilt—A patchwork quilt made of irregular patches combined with little or no regard to pattern.

Crimp bead—A small, metal bead used to end pieces strung on a tiger tail. Sometimes they're also used as spacers.

Deckle—An open frame that sits on top of the mold, used to make paper edges straight and flat after pulp is spread on the mold.

Embellish— The decorating of fabric. You can add beads, buttons, trims, sequins, embroidery, appliqué, and more to finished pieces.

Embossing—Raising metal from the reverse side by hammering or pressing it to form a design on the front side.

Finding—Anything in beading that is not a bead. This can include clasps, earring pieces, clamps, connectors, pin backs, separator bars, caps, and wire pins of various kinds.

Firing—The baking of pottery at a high temperature in a kiln to make it stronger and more durable.

Glaze—A glassy coating, melted onto a piece of clay during firing, adding strength and beauty to the clay while usually making it nonporous.

Glover's needle—A sharp-pointed three-sided needle used in hand-sewing thin leather. A *harness needle* is a blunt-pointed round needle used for hand-sewing thick leather. The round shape makes it slip easily through prepunched holes.

Greenware—An object produced by pouring runny clay (called slip) into a mold.

Grosgrain ribbon—A heavy, relatively stiff, corded ribbon made from rayon or silk. It can be purchased at craft or fabric stores.

Grout—A thin, coarse mortar used for filling masonry joints and spaces between tiles or pieces in a mosaic.

Kiln—The oven used to cook a pot after it has dried.

Lampwork—The art of making beads or other objects by forming molten glass that has been heated over a special lamp.

Lanyard—A small cord or rope for securing or suspending small objects, such as a whistle or key, around the neck, often woven of several flat strands of plastic, leather, or other material.

Leather knife—A special knife with either a round or an angled blade used especially for cutting leather, especially thick leather.

Leather shears—Large, heavy-duty scissors used for cutting.

Luminaria—Light sources that shine through paper bags.

Mold—In papermaking, this is a frame covered with mesh that can be nylon or metal screening. In ceramics, this is a hollow form used to create a particular shape.

Mosaic—A picture or decoration made of small pieces of inlaid stone, glass, and so on.

Origami—The Japanese art of paper folding to form flowers, animal figures, and other interesting shapes.

Paper—A sheet of interlaced fibers (usually cellulose fibers from plants, but sometimes rags or other fibrous materials are used) formed by making the fibers into a pulp and then causing them to felt or mat to form a solid surface.

Peyote—A type of bead weaving using the peyote stitch, which is a honeycomb network beadwork stitch worked spirallly to produce a beadwork tube.

Piercing—Making a hole through the metal, usually with an awl, nail, or other similarly sharp tool.

Planishing—Decorating metal by hammering it and overlapping rows of hammer spots to produce a faceted effect, which also hardens the piece.

Plaster casting—The art of creating objects by casting them in plaster. The plaster used is a gypsum product formulated especially for casting.

Polymer clay—A substance that is actually plastic, but since is acts, looks, and can be fired like clay, it's called "clay."

Potpourri—A mixture of dried flowers, herbs and spices, dried fruit peels or slices, enhanced by scented oils used to freshen a room, closet, or drawer. It is sometimes left dry in an open container, simmered in water, or sewn into sachets or other items.

Potter—A person who makes pottery by using a device called a potter's wheel.

Potter's Wheel—A rotating horizontal disk upon which clay is molded. The wheel can be manually or electrically operated.

Punching—Creating an impression on metal by striking a tool on one side and raising the metal on the other.

Pysanky—Highly decorated Easter eggs from the Ukraine.

Quilt—Stitching together two pieces of cloth and a soft interlining, usually in an ornamental pattern. The top layer may be made of small pieces of cut fabric sewn together in a design.

Quilt square—A design made from pieces of fabric sewn together to make a square.

Rasp—An instrument consisting of two sticks; one is notched and the other smooth. A sound is made by rubbing the sticks against each other.

Repoussé—A metalworking technique that uses the combined techniques of embossing and chasing.

Scrapbooking—The craft of putting photos and other mementoes into albums in creative and meaningful ways.

Stenciling—Producing a design using a thin sheet of plastic or other impervious material.

Stitching punch—A heavy metal tool that looks something like a fork with thick tines that when struck with a rawhide mallet punches a hole through leather for stitching. It is commonly available in either single-prong or four-prong type.

Stitching wheel—A wooden-handled tool with a metal shaft that holds a removable wheel with small dull points evenly spaced apart. Pressure is applied and it is rolled along the leather to create uniform impressions that can later be used as a guide for punching holes for stitching.

Strap cutter—A wooden tool made up of two ruled crossbars that slide through a handle. The bars house a replaceable blade at one end.

Terrarium—A glass case with earth in it, where plants and flowers can grow.

Thonging punch—An object similar to a stitching punch, except that the prongs are larger and it creates the larger holes needed for lacing leather.

Throwing—The technique potters use to shape the clay.

Thumb screw— This is on the handle of a strap cutter and is used to set the desired cutting width and the leather is pulled through the cutter.

Tie dyeing—Creating patterns on fabric by bunching and tying in certain areas and applying colored dyes.

Tiger tail—Wire, coming in differnent thicknesses, that's been covered with nylon cable.

Vertical slit—A method of adding more than one color area by weaving from opposite edges toward each other, meeting and then returning to the starting point.

Warp threads—In weaving, these are the threads that run vertically on which the weaving is worked.

Weft threads—In weaving, these are the threads that run horizontally over and under the warp.

Wire work—A way of connecting individual beads or groups of beads using wire bent into shape.

Index

Q-R

U-V

W-X-Y-Z